Whispers from Heaven...
Then she was gone

Karyl Rickard

Praise

Whispers from Heaven...Then she was gone is a beautiful tribute to an amazing young woman. People often focus on living long lives rather than meaningful ones. Renee made her life count. She filled her life with noble pursuits, special relationships, and pursuing God's will. While we cannot know why God chooses for some people's lives to seemingly end prematurely, we can be confident that our days are held firmly in His hands. You cannot choose how long you will live, but you can decide to live in such a way that there are many people who are sad to see you go. May Renee's life inspire you to live your life well. And, as Jonathan Swift advised: May you live all the days of your life.

- Richard Blackaby, President of Blackaby Ministries International, co-author. Experiencing God.

Renee was a letter, written on our hearts, known and read by everyone. She was 'a letter from Christ, written not with ink but with the Spirit of the living God on the tablets of human hearts' (2 Corinthians 3:2). That's why all those who knew her were so profoundly touched by her life.

- Ann Schwab, Registered Nurse and friend

This is a beautiful, beautiful testimony to the Lord's work in Renee's life. It takes the valleys and weaves them into a powerful testimony, a springboard for healing.

- Jen Leyes, friend of the family

In Christ, we are commanded to "rejoice with those who rejoice, and weep with those who weep" (Romans 12:15). I did both as I lived through these events with the Rickard family and now read this tender telling of Renee's story. My wife Linda found in it "a mother's heartfelt effort to make sense of an unthinkable loss." The account is steeped in Scripture, reflecting Karyl's daily dependence on the Word of God as her source of hope and strength. She also interviewed many of her daughter's teachers, pastors, mentors, and friends. The result is a volume that honors Renee, shows clearly the role faith and the local church played in her life, and demonstrates the caring, encouraging impact Renee had on those around her.

- James D. Craig, former pastor and friend of the family

On these pages, you will find stories of Renee, her laughter, adventure and a life lived to its fullest. Renee encouraged and inspired me to take challenges both in MMA and my personal life. I never felt judged, nothing but encouraged by extraordinary challenges. She had so much energy that it was contagious. The two of us brought life to the Academy. Because of Renee, and her inspiration, I am in college.

- Angie Speer, MMA friend

"I loved the book - the voice, emotion and authenticity. It definitely carries the energy of the Lord. The book is for anyone who needs more God in his or her life."

- best-selling author Tom Bird, and creator of the "Write a Book in a Weekend Retreat"

What a wonderful, life-giving book! Each chapter is a bite-size morsel of spiritual truth, shared through the "whispers from heaven" that undergirded Renee's life. This will nourish your soul.

- Debbie Abel, PhD, RDN, colleague,
Indiana University, and friend

The book captures Renee's enthusiasm for law enforcement. She was a solid, capable, professional and fair officer who got along with her peers and supervisors. Her performance of her duties reflected her moral compass.

- Aaron Mathewson, fellow Police Officer

Our days can be shortened just as Renee's were. The book showed the importance of intercessory prayers and, unbeknownst to her parents, how God answered them. Walking with the Lord as Renee did is the best gift we will ever have on this earth!

- Jane Jenkins, Bible Study Fellowship and friend

I loved reading the book and getting to know Renee. What fascinated me the most about Renee was that she remained the same from childhood through young adulthood. Her priorities in life were other people. She had a way of making people feel important and loved. She truly was an inspiring, incredible young woman!

- Dr. Scott Cooper, Chiropractor

This book is a testimony to the Hand of God. It is evident that the Holy Spirit guided Karyl's compilation of this book. It so clearly shows what a walk and relationship with the Lord is like - His Spirit in you.

- Louise Little, PhD, Emerita faculty, University of Delaware

Gene and Karyl Rickard have built a 35-year legacy of service and faith at Traders Point Christian Church. They introduced their children to Jesus and trusted Traders Point's Student Ministry to help connect their kids to Christ and to community. This book is a beautiful celebration of their daughter Renee, and TPCC is grateful to have played a small role in her extraordinary life.

- Aaron Brockett, Lead Pastor of Traders Point
Christian Church, Indianapolis, Indiana

ISBN: 978-1-64184-527-4 (Paperback)
ISBN: 978-1-64184-526-7 (Hardcover)
ISBN: 978-1-64184-528-1 (Ebook)

Library of Congress Control Number: 000000000

Published by Sojourn Publishing LLC, in the United States of America.

First printing edition 2020.

Contact: www.karylrickard.com

Contents

Dedication

To Renee, our daughter, who will always be a shining light!

To Gene, my beloved husband for fifty years, for his love,
his encouragement, his patience and his faithfulness,
without which this book would not have been written.

To Mark, our son, and his wonderful wife, Rorie, and our
grandchildren, Rachel and Peter, who all are twinkling
stars in the Lord's kingdom and bring us much joy.

And to the Lord who whispers from heaven,
is the Giver of all gifts and the Gift behind them all.

Foreword

How does one cope with the loss of a child? When the passages of life are out of order? Can one come to understand such tragedy? To accept such loss? To reach a place of peace? And possibly even joy? Can one still love? Can one learn to love even more?

These are questions every parent who has lost a child faces.

Karyl Rickard, a nationally renowned PhD pediatric nutritionist, is first and foremost a mother who lost her 28-year-old daughter suddenly and unexpectedly. This is in part Karyl's story of her ongoing journey of trying to understand. You will find an unshakeable faith here, trust in a loving Creator who is always present, who guides Karyl and her family through this perhaps most difficult of any challenge life can bring.

This book is a testament to Karyl and her family, but also a memoir of and for Renee. After Renee died, Karyl went back and met with countless relatives, friends, colleagues, mentors, and mentees – and gives us a rich and inspiring insight into Renee capturing her generous, vivacious, kind and humorous spirit. Karyl understands her daughter as an ordinary person – but with extraordinary gifts, which she shared humbly and continuously with others. Renee changed the nature of life for so many by simply being present – by being a constant in their lives, someone even children could turn to safely and share their deepest feelings, one who understood the importance of a tear or a laugh or a giggle, of a song, of a bird or turtle or puppy - who could help put life's challenges in perspective and embrace the joy or absurdity or import of moments we all share. One of her closest childhood friends gave Renee perhaps the greatest of compliments, saying…"Renee made me feel good about myself, exactly as I was without having to change, to look different, to have different interests. She loved me for who I was".

Karyl tackles all of the right questions, and describes her challenges in seeking answers - her own frailty in trying to understand, dealing with her own recurring doubts, and finally her ultimate trust in a loving God who embraces Renee, and is embraced by Renee. Karyl understands that if we believe in a Loving God, that somehow that Love has to be powerful enough to encompass the greatest joys and the greatest sorrows of our life passage. And this ultimately brings true peace and understanding to us, such that we can channel again that love for our Creator and for our Creation and all who dwell in it.

James A. Lemons, MD
Hugh McK. Landon Professor of Pediatrics, Emeritus
Indiana University School of Medicine, Indianapolis

Preface

O ur family loves the Lord and was called to fulfill ministries in our vocations, even while in college. During my undergraduate university years, I was introduced to a personal relationship with Jesus through InterVarsity, a Christian fellowship organization on college campuses. Reading the Bible daily, memorizing scripture, and praying fervently for everything became second nature. It was then that I became poignantly aware of whispers from heaven through the Holy Spirit.

God speaks to many people in the Bible in many ways, which I call "whispers from heaven."

- **He spoke through the _Word (Bible)_** in the book of Hebrews, recounting many prophets in the Old Testament who by faith followed the Lord (Hebrews 11:1-40) and to Peter at Pentecost (Acts 2:14-21) who referred to Joel in the Old Testament (Joel 2:28-32). In fact, the whole Bible is a progressive revelation of the Lord to His people.
- **He spoke through answered _prayer_** to Nehemiah who was allowed to go back to rebuild the Jerusalem wall (Nehemiah 1:4-11, 2:12); to Peter who escaped from prison (Acts 12:5-17); and to Paul and Silas. While they were praying, God sent an earthquake, prison doors flew open and Paul and Silas's prisoner chains came loose (Acts 16:23-34).
- **He spoke through _circumstances_** to King Darius who had Daniel thrown in the lion's den (Daniel 6:10-23) and to Paul on the road to Damascus (Acts 9:1-19).
- **He spoke through _people_,** such as Moses, who addressed the Israelites on Mt. Sinai (Exodus 19:3-6, 20:22-24);

Peter when speaking to the Sanhedrin (Acts 4:8-13); the Lord's prophets (Hebrews 1:1-2), for example Zechariah, who prophesized that Jesus would ride a donkey through Jerusalem (Zechariah 9:9) and Isaiah, who sends the Lord's message to good king Hezekiah (Isaiah 37:5-7, 14-20) or even an animal such as Balaam's donkey (Numbers 22:27-33).

- **He spoke through _dreams_ and _visions_,** that is, through _dreams_ to Joseph, betrothed to Mary (Mathew 1:20, 2:13, 2:19-20; 2:22) and to Joseph in the Old Testament who had a coat of many colors (Genesis 37:1-11); and through _visions_ such as to John who the Lord told to "write what you see" which became the book of Revelation (Revelation 1:19).

I have had a deep personal relationship with Jesus for many years. Sometimes, however, the Lord is silent, and I do not hear any whispers from heaven. During those times, I found I needed a fresh word from the Bible, pursued the Lord passionately who is the greatest pursuer of my heart and simply waited and TRUSTED God. It's not easy but it's always worth it. Sometimes, the Lord does not answer prayers, for whatever reason. He knows best.

I shared more than forty years of "Whispers from Heaven" in Renee's life (before, during, and after her passing to heaven), ones that redirected our lives and instilled purpose and meaning. This book is about experiencing God and finding new hope and trust in the Lord.

Some of you will read the book as you search for answers and meaning through the loss of a loved one. Perhaps you are in a place of despair and wonder how healing or something good can come from your loss. I hope this book will be of help to you, give you fresh eyes to see, and fresh hope to find ways to celebrate your loved one. God has not forgotten you and is, in fact, still with you.

Others will read the book with great interest in Renee's amazing, adventurous life filled to the brim. In many ways, she was an ordinary person. No particular fame, wealth, or authority. Yet, with the Lord's whispers, she lived an extraordinary life.

Regardless of the pain and suffering from the loss of your loved one, there is comfort and peace in walking with God. Eventually, strength and joy will come as you move through the grief journey, from mourning to joy. I am reminded that the Lord takes pleasure in those who honor Him, who trust in His constant love (Psalm 147:11)

May God bless and direct you as you read *"Whispers from Heaven...Then she was gone."*

Chapter 1

Cell Phone Rings –
"Renee Collapsed"

Call to Me and I will answer you, and I will
answer you and tell you great and unsearchable
things you do not know. (Jeremiah 33:3)
God is a Spirit who knows all things and
longs for us to call upon Him.
The closer we draw near to Him, the
more peace exists in our life.

It was a cloudy, cool Sunday. As I left for work early that chilly, overcast morning, I noticed that fall was coming to central Indiana. The many red and golden yellow leaves from the maple trees had not yet filled our yard. That morning, I was in my office at the Indiana University Medical Center, about twenty-five minutes away, working on an important presentation with Deb, my friend and colleague. I was trying to concentrate and to finish quickly. For some reason, I just couldn't focus. I wondered, "Maybe I am not able to focus and concentrate because I have not eaten." Indeed, that morning was quite unusual for several reasons: working on Sundays was highly unusual and I missed church; I was preparing for a medical procedure the next day that required no food for twenty-four hours. I had not eaten since the night before.

That September 19, 2010, at about 12:25 pm, I heard my cell phone ring. I could not get to it in time to answer because I was in Deb's office across the hall. At the last minute that morning, we changed the location of where Deb and I were planning to work without telling Gene, my husband of forty years. He was still asleep when I left. Without my cell phone, he would not have been able to reach me.

Gene's message, spoken in a rushed, concerned voice: "I need your help at home with Renee." I called Gene back; the line was busy.

Deb asked, "What did Gene want?"

"He asked me to come home and help with Renee."

Deb's response was a bit terse, "If you need to go home and take care of your husband and Renee, go." After all, she had gone to great lengths to get to the Medical Center. Boy, did I understand her reaction. We had a tiny window – that Sunday – to complete our work.

I was conflicted. Should I go home? Should I stay? I wanted to be in integrity with Deb and our students, but...my thoughts drifted. I just could not understand why Gene had left this message. This was so atypical of Gene.

Again, my cell phone rang. It was 12:35 pm – 10 minutes later on that soon-to-be dreadful day. Gene spoke in a husky, broken voice, "Renee collapsed. Her breathing is shallow."

"What, Gene? What did you say?" My thoughts raced. *Am I hearing Gene correctly?* In an anxious, urgent voice, Gene repeated, "Renee collapsed."

Renee was our vibrant, healthy, twenty-eight-year-old daughter who lived life full out. She had a zeal for adventure and a desire to discover the world. She was laid back but extraordinarily competent, knowing just what to do in stressful situations. Courage, adventure and perseverance were her middle names. Maybe some of her gumption came from both Gene and me. Definitely, she had more than enough to fill the shoes of a police officer.

She was quite responsible when it came to taking care of herself and others. She did this with a smile and she did this as a police officer as well. As an Indiana State Capitol Police Officer, she was committed to the safety of the Indiana legislators and the citizens of Indianapolis in the state buildings and the area of downtown Indianapolis.

"What happened?" I asked, still not comprehending what Gene was saying.

And then he went on to relay the incomprehensible. He seemed to pause forever before continuing, "I do not know."

"After early church service, I was working on my computer. Close to noon, I heard a loud thump. *That's odd*, I thought. I looked out the window and saw Renee's two puppies. It could not have been the dogs knocking something over. Within a minute, I went into the kitchen to see what the noise was, thinking, *Maybe something fell off the kitchen counter or maybe Renee dropped something or maybe Renee knocked a chair over.*"

Gene continued in a low, incredulously sad and fearful voice, "Renee was lying on her side, not moving on the kitchen floor near the top of the basement stairs." As Gene spoke, all I could think was, *Oh dear God. What happened? My daughter. My little girl.*

Gene was clearly and understandably in shock. This was evident by how he spoke and how he relayed things. It was like he was trying to protect me from the unimaginable, while trying to wrap his head around what was happening.

Gene continued, telling me, "I knelt down beside her and gently called her name – 'Renee. Renee. Renee.' She did *not* respond."

Gene took a breath before continuing, "I leaned over so I could see whether she was breathing. Her breathing was shallow. I called 911. Then I got the puppies inside and locked them in Renee's bedroom. I did not want them to bark at the EMTs or to chase the emergency vehicles," things they often did whenever strangers approached our home.

"The ambulance and the emergency medical personnel are here now. They came quickly, maybe within five minutes. A fire truck with a fireman came also. Then a police car with an officer came."

"What are they doing?" I asked.

"The paramedics are hooking up an IV line. They got a pulse, but it is faint. Her breathing is shallow. The ambulance will take her to St Vincent Hospital. Meet me there."

St. Vincent Hospital was the closest emergency room to our home.

By the grace of God, Gene was home from our summer cabin in the Colorado Rocky Mountains. He had just come home the night before. Gene, a tall, well-built man in his mid-sixties with dark brown, graying hair and brown eyes is a "Rock of Gibraltar" for our family. He is genuinely a nice guy. He has a well-developed analytical mind and a backbone as strong as an ox when it comes to his values – honesty and humility – and convictions. From the age of five, he worked beside his dad, helping with the farm chores and milking cows on the wheat and dairy farm. Although retired from Eli Lilly and Company (pharmaceuticals), he still consulted with startup companies that bring new drugs to market.

No time for more questions or explanations. Gene was always brief and to the point, nothing extra. He always analyzed with the data, not the emotions. As he relayed what was happening, he maintained his matter-of-fact way, but his voice betrayed his anxiety...his fear for Renee's life...his fear of the unknown.

Deb came into my office. "I heard you talking to Gene. What's wrong?"

"Gene said that Renee had collapsed and that the ambulance was taking her to St Vincent Hospital. I need to go."

Deb asked if I wanted her to drive me but I told her no. I just needed to get there as fast as possible.

My heart pounded. My thoughts raced as adrenalin poured into my bloodstream. I grabbed my cell phone, closed my computer and raced down a flight of stairs, two steps at a time, to the nearby parking garage. I was out of the garage in a flash, racing to the hospital. I was driving like a crazy person. I drove the fifteen miles to St. Vincent Hospital, usually a twenty-minute drive from my office, in record time. Gene had not yet arrived.

As I drove, questions kept coming to my mind. "What happened? Could our twenty-eight year old daughter, the epitome of health and fitness, just collapse? How could this be?"

I had spent the previous evening with Renee. We had had *sooo* much fun! She had thoroughly enjoyed the football games on TV. Her two Chihuahua puppies had snuggled all evening close to her, Lily on one side and Stokley on the other.

Unbeknownst to me, God was giving me this special evening, so full of wonderful memories of the last time Renee and I would spend together. She was relaxed, enjoying things she liked to do – coaching football players from her seat on the couch as to the plays they should be making, sharing her editorials with me during the commercials, playing with Lily and Stokley, as if she were playing with two little children. We were having fun. We shared in light-hearted conversation. It was an evening to remember. So unplanned. So unexpected. So perfect. Such a gift from God.

Time that evening went by too quickly. Suddenly, Renee reminded me, "Hurry, Mom, you will be late picking up Dad at the airport."

Oops. The time with Renee had flown quickly. I hurriedly left to pick up Gene, who came back from a short visit to our cabin in the Rocky Mountains.

Returning to my thoughts, the questions continued. *What would cause a collapse? Did Renee just faint? Perhaps something was out of whack with her electrolytes? She's never had heart issues. Did she choke on something?*

I was still wondering what could have happened? Then I did what I always do: I started talking to God. "Please, Lord. Help Renee be okay."

A little voice came into my mind. I don't know whether it was a voice or just a knowing, *Call Maria. Call Ann. Ask for prayers.*

I called Maria. No answer.

I tried Ann. She answered, praise God. "Please, Ann, pray. Renee collapsed. The ambulance is taking her to St Vincent Hospital. That's all I know."

I was blessed to have Ann, a retired nurse, as a friend. Ann was a master at listening and tapping into her intuition, divinely given, to know how to handle the most difficult situations. She had years of experience as a nurse in a hospital psych unit, a pain-management clinic and a mom and baby clinic. I met Ann years ago in our Nurture Group, one of the support groups within our church. She was a fellow prayer warrior.

Then I called Maria again. No answer. Bummer. Maria was another prayer warrior and friend who was a legend in her own right with her church and the greater Indianapolis Hispanic community. She was an expert bilingual interpreter and a saint with a heart of gold. I met Maria when our daughters were both playing soccer. Through twenty years of friendship and prayer time, she became a surrogate mother for Renee.

I just could not imagine what was going on. All I wanted was to be with Renee. To talk to her. My only daughter. My precious daughter...

I wanted to give her a hug.

I wanted to hear her voice.

I desperately needed to find out what was going on. I wanted to tell her one more time how much I loved her. I wanted to comfort her, to listen to her, to be there for her.

I arrived at the Emergency Entrance of St. Vincent Hospital, a well-known private hospital on the north side of Indianapolis. A large emergency sign directed me to the door. The few parking slots outside the Emergency entrance were filled so I quickly whipped into a nearby surface parking lot. I raced through the ER swinging doors and breathlessly went to the receptionist.

My mind was still racing through all the possibilities that could have happened.

"Where can I find my daughter? She just came in an ambulance."

A stout, stone-faced receptionist with long blonde hair and blue eyes was efficiently directing the patients. She said, "You need to check in with Admissions."

I was confused and was thinking, "What? I am not being admitted. It's my daughter that I want to see." I quickly told her, "My daughter is already here."

"Check in with admissions."

""You don't understand. I need to find my daughter."

"Just check in with admissions. She will help you."

All I can remember about the clerk with admissions was that she seemed as slow as molasses and did not seem to understand my urgency. She asked the usual questions: name, birthdate, address and insurance.

She did not understand my answers. I was talking too fast. She asked me to repeat over and over. All I could think was, *Please, please hurry, hurry, hurry. M'am, I just need to be with my daughter, Renee.*

It seemed like an eternity. In reality, it maybe was only five minutes. Finally, she pointed me to the ER door. The large doors swung open. A tall, slender, friendly ER nurse with shoulder length brown hair and brown eyes met me at the door.

"I am here to be with Renee, our daughter, who just came by ambulance."

She ushered me into a side room. This was NOT a good sign.

It seemed like I was walking in a dream, a world of great uncertainty. In the small waiting room in the ER area, I was flipping through my Bible, turning the pages quickly. My eyes rapidly scanned the pages, searching for the healing miracles in John, my favorite book of the Bible. I stopped to read the healing of the royal official's son; then, the healing of the paralytic by the pool of Bethesda; then, the healing of the man born blind; and lastly, the healing of Lazarus.

All I could say was, "Lord, I trust you. You are the Master Healer. Please heal Renee." Gently, a whisper came into in my being, "The Lord knows and sees all and knows what's best." Time stood still.

Gene, dressed in dark blue Polo pants and a blue cotton shirt, arrived. The worried expression on his face, his frazzled look and the sadness in his eyes expressed his concern. As we were sitting on the only two wooden chairs in the room, he reached for my hand and comforted me. With an intensity of spirit from the depths of our souls, we prayed, "Oh, Lord, we do not have a clue what is wrong. Please heal Renee."

We waited in silence, sensing the gravity of the situation. My head ached, probably from not eating since the night before. And I was thirsty.

I kept thinking, *What is taking so long? Why aren't they telling us what is going on with Renee?* If the room were larger, I would have paced back and forth. All I wanted to do was "be there" for Renee.

That somber day unfolded, just like watching a bad movie.

Finally, the same kind ER nurse came back to our room. In a concerned, but "matter of fact" voice, she said, "The doctors are working on Renee. You cannot go and see her."

I asked, "Is there anything you can tell us? Are you drawing blood? Are you doing anything else? Have you checked the electrolytes?" Both Gene and I had enough medical background to know some of the things we needed to know...to problem solve... to know what to look for and what to ask.

The nurse tactfully shifted the conversation saying, "I will keep you updated."

Gene and I prayed some more, BIG TIME, for God's grace and mercy. This was not looking good. "Lord, You are the 'Great I AM.' You know everything. You know what Renee needs. We trust You. Please provide. In advance, we thank You."

After a short time, the ER physician, a tall, brown-haired, slender man in his mid-thirties, came into the little waiting room. He was wearing a long white jacket over a white shirt and dark pants; a stethoscope was around his neck. In a quiet, low voice he said, "We were not able to stabilize your daughter. She didn't make it."

Suddenly, time stood still. The room was spinning. I was trying to wrap my head around the horrific words I thought I had heard. "She didn't make it."...I had to be mistaken. I had to have heard wrong.

I felt like lightning had pierced my heart. My mind went blank. It was like an out-of-body experience. I just watched from the ceiling. It seemed like Gene and I were going through the motions, emotionless. "What? How could this happen to a healthy young lady in great physical condition? Renee just completed a sprint triathlon (similar to a mini-triathlon) and half of a bicycle 'Ride Across Indiana.'" The doctor responded in a quiet, uncertain voice, "We do not know. The most common cause of death in healthy young adults this age is an embolism."

The news that Renee was gone was totally shocking: disbelief ... numbness ... shock. I had to remind myself to "breathe." The news that Renee was gone was not sinking in – it was unbelievably surreal. Shut down. I was shutting down. This was the "unthinkable," the worst nightmare. I was trying desperately to awaken to the reality of what happened. I felt paralyzed. My heart ached with a hole as large as a chasm in the Grand Canyon.

Breathe. My head hurt. My mind was reeling. My brain was not able to process or comprehend what was taking place, what we had just been told. All I could think was that this was not really happening. I forgot all about my hunger. "Renee, where are you? Don't leave us. This is not true. This can't be happening!"

Inside, I wanted to roll up into the tiniest ball possible...so small that I could not feel any emotion. On the outside, my mind was reeling. My brain was not able to process what was taking place, what we had just been told. Breathe. Incredulously, my next thought was, *Now what? What do we do next?*

Chapter 2

Good-bye – The Emergency Room

And over all these virtues put on love, which binds (people) all together in perfect unity.
(Colossians 3:14)
For where two or three are gathered in my name,
there am I with them. (Mathew 18:20)
Whispers from Heaven often come in the form of our family and friends around us. Unity of love is the most powerful representation of God speaking His love to us.

The rest of the afternoon in the Emergency Room with Renee had an eerie quietness. The mood was solemn, somber, with hushed and continuing prayers. Behind the scene, there was a beehive of activity with people quietly coming and going.

In a broken and husky voice, Gene told the sober-faced ER nurse, "We would like to see Renee." In a soft, tender voice, she explained, "We are cleaning her up. You can be with her when we are done." I was not sure what that meant. Maybe the nurses needed to clean Renee up after their attempts to stabilize her. I was back to watching everything from above.

We were in the little waiting room, numb. Gene and I held each other's hand tightly to comfort one another. We were silent.

Heads bowed. Just sitting motionless. No words. Deep, deep sadness engulfed my spirit, a darkness that sucked me into its depths. My dear, precious Renee…gone. How can that be? Why?

No more hugs. No more times to listen to her to whatever was on her mind – adventures, funny happenings, concerns. No more times to just be with her. No more times to tell her, "I love you."

While waiting for Renee, the caring ER nurse, God bless her soul, asked, "Do you have family you wish to call?" My mind came back down from the ceiling. *Oh…yes…we need to call our son, Mark who was in Michigan praying fervently for his sister, two years younger. Mark, with a logical, analytical mind was perfectly cast as a chemist. Like father, like son. He was trim and fit, mid-height with brown hair.*

We walked outside the hospital ER entrance to call Mark. This time, thankfully, Rorie, his thoughtful and caring wife, answered Mark's cell phone. She is the perfect life mate for Mark. Renee loved her. So do we. Mark usually did not carry his cell phone. "Just a minute," she said. "I'll get him."

Rorie would later say, "We threw everything into the car and left Michigan immediately." They brought Shiloh, their golden retriever mutt-mix dog. According to Rorie, who was driving, tears flowed down Mark's cheeks. They arrived early that evening, in five hours, a remarkably fast trip.

We also needed to call my older sister Mary Bess, who is a widow and lives alone here in Indy. I thought, *Maybe Deb, my dear friend, can pick up Mary Bess.* Deb was a red haired, middle-aged colleague who "moved mountains" at work. She seemed to have a direct connection to heaven. I was working with Deb when Gene's call came.

I called Deb. In a barely audible voice, I said, "Renee didn't make it."

Deb kept asking, "What?" in disbelief.

I repeated this at least three times. Finally, she comprehended what I was saying.

I continued, still hardly audible, "Is it possible for you to bring Mary Bess to the hospital?" Little did I realize the incredible burden of my request. Later, I would learn that Deb was supposed to have been off her feet that *entire week*, since she had just had foot surgery.

Thank you Lord, for sending people to help. Looking back, I recall that throughout the day, I found myself thanking God for so many things, including the people He had put in our paths that day to lighten our indescribable pain.

Mary Bess was recovering from major back surgery. She was at a point in her life where she could not be as independent as she was used to being. This was most difficult for my strong, independent, physician sister. This redheaded only sister of mine was short in stature but tall in her contributions to others. I knew she would want to get to the hospital as quickly as possible.

I called Maria again. Still no answer.

I called Ann. In a very low voice, choking with emotion, I told Ann, "Renee didn't make it."

Ann later told me, "The news took my breath away. I did not have any words for how I felt. I remember asking, 'May we come and be with you?'"

Finally, we were able to see Renee. The gentle, kind ER nurse ushered us into an examining room with Renee. The room was barren except for heart and respiratory monitors at the back, none hooked to Renee.

Renee was lying flat on a gurney, casually dressed in khaki pants and a white Polo shirt. Her face was white as a ghost, expressionless like a statue. How it pained me to see her this way.

Instinctively, I leaned over and kissed my precious daughter. I placed my kiss on her cheek. She was stone cold. I remember my lips feeling strange, as chills went through my body. This was not my Renee...our beautiful Renee who was always so warmhearted and alive. Renee was no longer there. Her body was, but her spirit was not. Suddenly, her death was real.

Gene and I just stood there. Lost in the moment, lost to the world. Motionless. Wordless. Gripping each other's hand.

The color drained from Gene's face. He looked down to the floor, lost in his own thoughts. As a strong introvert, that was the way he processed most things. He simply went inside his mind.

As for me, I was numb. I was still in the nightmare from which I could not awaken. Mindless. Not able to think or figure out what to do. Just be there…in body…but not in mind or spirit.

We were alone with Renee. Gene, and a gentle, kindhearted hospital chaplain and I were there. Earlier, the ER nurse had shared that either a nurse or chaplain had to be with us in the room when we were with Renee.

The chaplain asked if we would like to pray. Each of us took turns. We prayed in hushed, quiet voices, first the chaplain with a gentle spirit and voice, then Gene, and then I prayed. This time our prayers were different.

"Thank You, Lord, for Renee, for her precious life, one You entrusted to us. Lord, we do not understand. You have told us to trust You. You know more than we do. Renee is Yours. Welcome her into Your kingdom. She is Yours. Take good care of her. Please help her know that we love her dearly. Help us put one foot in front of the other, one step at a time and one day at a time. Help us know how to live without our precious, precious Renee."

I sensed the presence of angels filling the room. Maybe, even Renee was hovering over us. I do not know. But an unexplained *peace* came over me. It felt like I was on the ceiling, not literally but figuratively. Still not in my mind and body. In slow motion, the afternoon was proceeding.

But something happened. I felt a solemn quietness. *Is this the peace that transcends all understanding?* My mind just could not fathom all that was going on…and the peace in the midst of it.

Friends began to come almost immediately. The first to arrive were our dear friends, Barb B, Ann and her husband Rog, and Eileen and her husband Duane. They were ushered into the ER room with us. All are fellow prayer warriors. Their prayers moved mountains.

In hushed, solemn voices we each prayed. We were lifted above the circumstances. Unexplainable calm came over the room. The Lord's presence was there. It was a time when we felt that the Lord knew and saw what we were going through. He whispered his love and acceptance toward us. We had God's serenity in the eye of the storm. These friends were a treasure, more valuable than all the gold on the earth. Oh, how we needed those prayers.

A calm, kindhearted police chaplain came, introduced himself and solemnly shook our hands. Chaplain C was short, middle-aged and had very short dark hair graying around the temples. He wore black pants and a black shirt imprinted with the police insignia. The collar of his black shirt was the rounded collar of clergy.

Chaplain C said he knew Renee. Both worked in the Indiana State Capitol unit, Renee as an Indiana State Capitol Police Officer and he as the chaplain. As other friends joined us, he remained. He prayed with all the power of someone who is used to comforting families of police officers.

Friends kept coming, being ushered into the room with Renee, Gene, the chaplain and me.

Over the next four hours, thirty to forty of our closest friends, those in our Bible Studies and those in our Nurture Group, came and prayed with us. The mood was somber, the prayers quietly continuing. I had no idea how our dearest friends knew so soon about Renee.

Several police officers were in the hall near the nurses' station. My mind raced, asking myself, *Why are the police officers here? Is there a problem?* All but one were in their police uniform, solemnly standing.

I am thinking, *Renee...dead? And here are five police officers. I do not have a clue who they are, nor what's wrong.* I asked the police chaplain, "Why so many police officers?"

"They are here out of respect for Renee. Let me introduce you," he responded.

As tears flowed down my cheeks, I remembered the social graces my mother taught me.

"This is the head of the Indiana State Capitol Police." He was a tall, slim, middle-aged man with darker skin. I reached out and shook his hand, "Thank you for coming."

"This is the police officer in charge of Human Resources." She was off duty, in street clothes. She was shorter, in her forties and had long, slightly curly auburn hair. She shook my hand and said, "I am so sorry."

"This is Sergeant J, Renee's shift supervisor," a young, police officer with a short stature and buzzed hair. Tears were rolling down his cheeks.

"Oh, yes, I know you," I said as I shook his hand. Renee had introduced me to him earlier that year.

"This is the Director of Public Relations (PR) for the Indiana State Troopers." He was a tall, slender officer with light brown hair; he was holding his wide brimmed police hat in his hand.

Later, when in a small private ER waiting room, the PR Director asked Gene, "In your words, please tell me what happened to Renee. The police officers throughout the state will want to know."

Gene recounted the details briefly. We were drained. No energy. No emotions. No ability to think. No ability to problem-solve. Present in body but absent in spirit. Gene seemed to be doing better than I was.

The fifth was a young metropolitan police officer, short, trim and fit with dark hair cut very short. He responded to the 911 call and came to our house with the medics and ambulance. Evidently, when someone collapses and is unconscious, a police officer comes also.

He recognized Renee's Indiana State Capitol Police Officer's jacket hanging over a chair in the kitchen and sent a message on the police radio, "Off-duty officer down. She is being transported to St Vincent Hospital." Word came through the police radio, about 10 minutes later, "She did not make it."

That was why the police officers knew and came so quickly.

It was surreal: five police officers, the hospital chaplain, the police chaplain, all our friends and my sister in the ER. In my experience, there were way too many people in the ER area. I asked the hospital chaplain, "What about all these people in the ER? Are there too many?"

The gentle, benevolent chaplain said, "I'll tell the nurses that these are your family."

This was unbelievably generous. I was overwhelmed with gratitude. My spirit was *soooo* humbled.

Thankfully, that afternoon no other patients came into the ER. Definitely, that was a sign of God's providence. Praise the Lord for the chaplain, the sensitive and compassionate ER staff and our dear friends who began the long grief journey with us.

Eventually, Reverend Jim, a pastor and long-time family friend, came. He had a worried and solemn look on his face as he hugged us. He is tall, solidly built with graying brown hair and is in his mid-fifties. He knew Renee well.

We, with our friends, were ushered upstairs to a larger room, while Renee was "prepared for viewing." Now that seemed weird, since everyone already was with us in the ER. Evidently, the designated viewing room was upstairs; the staff had graciously allowed us to be with Renee in the ER. According to the ER nurse, "We cannot move Renee to the viewing room upstairs until the pathologist comes."

Finally, a young small woman with short brown hair – an assistant to the pathologist – came. She was abrupt in manner and down to business. Just the facts. She quizzed us extensively about Renee's lifestyle.

Our response, "She was healthy and in top shape physically. No, she is not taking any medications or drugs. No, she has never taken any illegal drugs." The state pathologist's report some weeks later confirmed "no drugs."

Upstairs, we all circled around Renee and held hands. Reverend Jim led a prayer for Renee, for our family and for the Lord's mercy and grace in our journey ahead. Oh, how we needed that.

I was there in body, but my spirit and mind were elsewhere. Why was I able to do "just what was needed" – greet, hug and graciously thank all those who came? These were our dearest friends, our "family in the Lord" and Renee's "police family." They put aside everything they were doing to come and be with us. They came. They stayed.

The moments of this day reminded me of one of Renee's most precious characteristics – her willingness to walk the journey with her friends when they really needed it. The love and support of our friends reminded me of my daughter.

Again, it was like a dream, like this could not be happening. Nothing made sense. So many friends and my sister in the ER, the police arriving soon after Renee passed, the ER allowing "our family" to continue to be with us. And then there was a special viewing of Renee with our pastor.

As if I were watching a movie, I began to see God answering many of the prayers of those who were there. I knew Jesus was with me protecting my heart and mind with an inner peace beyond my understanding. This gave me the courage *to go on.*

Later, I would learn from four of my closest friends their perspective of what took place on that fateful day. Their recounting helped me to better understand some things.

The love of fellow believers in Christ was palpably present… in action, in real time. In those moments, I realized that we are here on earth to help each other and to walk with each other in times when words are not needed. This is God's love in action.

Indeed, the Emergency Room was filled with angels…and answered prayers…many, many that were going up to our Lord. Prayers…fervent prayers…throughout the whole afternoon.

Chapter 3

The Lord Shows Up in Many Ways

In all your ways submit to Him, and He
will make your paths straight.
(Proverbs 3:6)
The Lord comforts us through His whispers by our circumstances,
events and decisions throughout our lives. When we seek Him,
we can obtain a glimpse of His majestic
plan for our lives unfolding.

Looking back, we saw the Lord's hand, we sensed His whispers and we witnessed His miracles on that fateful Sunday. This was clearly seen the day when God called Renee home. It was also obvious the day before and it continues to be evident years later.

Miracles of timing and "God-incidences" occurred that only could have happened with the Lord's hand in the bigger picture of life. As I walk this journey, I know I do not walk it alone. God *is* with me as are so many good friends.

The following are incredible examples of how the Lord showed up for us.

The Saturday before Renee's passing, I attended a Beth Moore Simulcast to about 500 churches on the topic of "The Desires of Your Heart (Psalm 37)." Beth Moore is a nationally recognized evangelist and women's leader who teaches women how to "love and live on God's Word." At the very end of the six-hour televised session, Beth Moore shared a story about a dream she had. Beth Moore said, "I could see every single person in the front row of this large auditorium in Chicago, just like what I see now (for the televised program that day)." Beth Moore was not nervous so she knew the performance was not about her. Rather, she dreamed that she saw Beth Chapman with her four-year-old daughter in shining lights beside her, speaking to a large crowd. Beth Chapman had just completed writing a book about the tragic loss of their daughter. She is the wife of Grammy and Dove Award-winning recording artist Steven Curtis Chapman.

With some nervousness, Beth Moore said she finally called Beth Chapman, "Happy Birthday, Beth. I think the Lord is calling you to a new ministry. I had a dream. I saw you speaking to a large audience with your daughter at your side. Beth Chapman started sobbing. She and her husband had just gone to their church altar and asked the Lord, 'What do you want us to do next in our ministry?'"

As I left the symposium that afternoon, I looked at Jane, one of my dear friends from Bible Study Fellowship (BSF) who went with me, "That was a strange way to end the symposium." She agreed. Jane, a treasurer for BSF for many years, was a petite powerhouse with beautiful silver hair. In my heart, I know this was the Lord's way of showing ME that he uses dreams for communicating.

The Lord never gives up. My work plans changed at the last minute on that Sunday, thanks to misplacing my cell phone at home. I could not find the cell phone anywhere. Finally, I heard it ring downstairs in the workroom. The phone had been in my hand; I had laid it down when I fed the cats. The cell phone rang six times from Deb. I thought, "Now, that's funny. I just talked to Deb."

So, I called her back, "My phone must not be working," she said, "I didn't call you."

At that last minute, just before leaving to go to Deb's home, we changed plans. Deb said, "Let's meet at the office (twenty-five minutes away) instead of my home (one hour away)." Deb, a red-haired "earth angel," is a wise, kind, and inspirational colleague and friend who loves the Lord.

God must have directed her to change our plans. Gene did not know where I was, since we had changed plans at the last minute. Thankfully, I had my cell phone and I was closer to the hospital. Gene reached me with the words, "Renee collapsed. I called 911. She still is breathing, very shallowly."

Jacqueline, Renee's best friend since second grade, was in Indianapolis for a Colts football game. Jacqueline and Renee were inseparable, adventurous, and enjoyed life with great laughter and commitment to each other. Miraculously, Jacqueline had her law books, ones needed for her studies at Notre Dame. So, she was able to stay in Indianapolis until after the funeral. This was a Godsend and huge blessing. Jacqueline helped call all Renee's friends and gave the eulogy at the funeral.

Gene arrived from Tincup, Colorado late Saturday night, the night before Renee collapsed. He gave Renee a big hug before bedtime. Thankfully, Gene was with Renee when she collapsed on Sunday and present for the coming week. I could not imagine walking through that week and journey without Gene, my "rock of Gibraltar."

The Lord showed up the next morning, after Renee's passing. We went to bed very, very late (1:00 a.m.) on the evening of Renee's passing. Tears flooded down my cheeks all night long. I did not sleep a wink. At 4:00 a.m., I arose, walked outside in our wooded neighborhood and talked to God. A million thoughts and concerns were rolling around in my numb mind. As I blurted out everything to the Lord, my tears began to slow down.

"Lord, I don't even know how to pray. We are clueless about a cemetery, funeral home, how to do this, what to say in an obituary, what needs to be done when, who to call or what to do with the Honor service. Please, my precious Lord, be with us and direct us."

As I was walking and talking to God, a still, small voice came into my mind: "Call Maggie." At first, I thought I heard wrong. The voice or thought came again. "Call Maggie." My response,

"Lord, we hardly know her and Renee doesn't know her at all. Why?" No answer.

Early in that day, I mentioned the message to "Call Maggie" to Rorie and Mark. They did not know her and they were too busy to call her. Mark was working with Gene on what seemed like a million details, searching for access to Renee's computer and photos of Renee. Later, I got lost in the packed moments of that first day and forgot the Lord's message.

As the tears flowed uncontrollably down my cheeks the next night, again around 4:00 a.m. I arose, went outside, walked and talked with the Lord. "Completely numb, in shock and yet humbly, I come to you, my Lord. Thank you for so many answered prayers yesterday. I know you are with us, my precious Lord. Just help us get through the rest of the week, one day at a time."

Again, a thought returned – the kind that is not readily dismissed came to me. I am not sure whether it was a voice or a clear "knowing:" "Call Maggie." I asked, "Why Maggie, my Lord, I only know her a little?" No answer. Maggie was a daughter-in-law of a very dear colleague and friend of mine, Granny Mary, now in heaven. After talking some more with the Lord and then praying with Deb, a dear friend, I felt compelled in my heart to make the call.

I returned to the kitchen and called Maggie. She answered the phone, was pleased to hear from me and said, "On Sunday night, I had a dream that was *soooo* real I awakened. All day yesterday, I puzzled over its meaning." Sunday was the day of Renee's passing.

"I dreamed that a huge sea turtle was swimming away from me in a huge sea with large waves. I kept trying to catch it, but could not catch it. The turtle kept swimming away. Then, I awakened."

"Maggie. I know what this means." You see, for Granny Mary and I, the turtle was the secret symbol of play. Granny Mary was such a close person in my life, it felt like she was a mother to me. She was the Director of Child Life Services at Riley Hospital for Children in Indianapolis. As a Master Teacher, she worked with me to create fun and effective fitness and nutrition activities for young children. We used the "Play Approach to Learning" derived from Piaget's learning model. Piaget was the first psychologist to make a systematic study of the cognitive development of children and their play. He considered play to be their "work."

In 1995, during the time when we were writing the curriculum, a poisonous spider bit Granny Mary. She became very, very ill and went into a coma. I prayed to the Lord, "Please heal Granny Mary. She is yours and very important to her family, our family, the children at Riley Hospital and all that we are doing together. Without Granny Mary, I will not be able to finish the 'active play, healthy eating' curriculum for young children. Oh, Lord, help me see you and your hand in this and be able to smile, like when we are developing the play curriculum."

A turtle came to mind. Not an ordinary turtle. No, a turtle that always wins. I called it our Granny Mary Turtle. Interestingly, Granny Mary said, after she recovered, "I too had a vision of a turtle when in the coma." I never shared the turtle story with anyone except Granny Mary.

Our Granny Mary Turtle always wins. It skates with roller skates. It flies with angel wings. It turns over and floats on its back really, really fast down a swift river. It is a safe haven for those who want to read inside its shell. It is just plain creative, fun, and playful!

Renee, too, loved to laugh, be creative, and have fun. Her friends said (at the visitation and subsequent celebrations), "The one thing I will always remember about Renee is laughing and having fun with Renee." Amazing, really amazing, since Renee was pretty laid back, made things happen and at the same time, seemed to be "care free." The "laid back" picture was deceptive since she, in a flash, could do what was needed, e.g., get packed in a half-hour for long trips or carry on conversations while working on the computer.

"Maggie, this is prophetic, a perfect metaphor for what just happened with Renee. She went into the arms of Jesus in heaven. Granny Mary was there to welcome her and play!" At that moment, a vision of Granny Mary and Renee appeared in my mind. They were laughing and playing, true to both of their natures. I was awed and stunned. This was the Lord's way of letting ME know that Renee IS IN HEAVEN. She is well and having great fun with Granny Mary, a dear saint and friend.

My dear Granny Mary in heaven is playing with Renee. I would love to be doing that with them! Maybe someday.

Chapter 4

Here I am –
Everything Prayed
for and More

Before I formed you in the womb I knew you,
before you were born I set you apart;
I appointed you as a prophet. (Jeremiah 1:5, NLT)
During two years while I was jogging, I prayed to the Lord
for a little girl and He answered. God had a purpose and
plan for Renee, as a voice for Him, in her own way.

RENEE, BIGGER THAN LIFE, came into our lives on May 26, 1982. We have never been the same since then. With Renee, we began an incredible journey, rather the adventure of our lifetime. Renee embodies the best in a young lady whose life was cut short. Renee lived life fully, yet humbly, with adventure and an ability to see the humor in life.

It is the Lord's light through Renee that has healed, brought hope in the Lord and definitely a new perspective on heaven. This book is about Renee touching our lives, widening our horizons and ultimately having the precious opportunity to see the Lord mold and shape our lives through her journey. She brought richness, a tapestry in our lives that lives on forever. We celebrate her life!

When Mark, Renee's older brother, came into our family, we were thrilled! At birth, he was delivered with his fist on his chin, pondering the world. Indeed, he is a scholar and reader to this day.

Every crisp early morning, with the dawn awakening to green, red or no leaves on the trees and the sun popping over the horizon, I jogged and prayed for a little girl, one who was healthy and fun, smart and active physically. In this time with the Lord, Renee's name came and even her middle name, Allene, my mother's first name. Renee Allene Rickard sounded like the name of a shining star. She was, in her own way!

After several years of prayers for a little girl, Renee was born. She came fully alert with gently waving dark brown curls and blue eyes alert, not missing anything. No problem for her breastfeeding. She had a warm, quiet way about her. Even as an infant, she made things happen.

Little did we know the adventure we were about to begin with Renee. She was an "out of the box" little girl who was strong-willed and persistent. Yes, Renee was persistent; it seemed like persistence at the 99th percentile. I thought Mark was strong-willed, but soon revised that to "He really knows what he wants." Indeed, Renee was divinely made with some extra endearing strengths; an ability to bring harmony, laughter and love in the midst.

Chapter 5

Growing Up – Those Early Molding Years

But as for you, be strong and do not give
up, for your work will be rewarded.
(2 Chronicles 15:7)
God whispers to us through our children even when
they have strong, persistent, and loving personalities,
ones that show up in a variety of unique ways.
God's creations are all unique!

E ven as an infant, Renee made things happen. She wanted to be breastfed, every two to three hours, with a quiet but persistent way. At four months of age when I attended a meeting in California for two days, Gene fed her breast milk from a bottle. That was very successful! So successful that, when I returned, Renee clearly did not want any more of the breastfeeding. Interestingly, she readily began a feeding schedule every four hours and jumped from the 25th to the 50th percentile weight for height. She knew what she needed.

At six months of age, I invited a Physical Therapist (PT) colleague at Indiana University who specialized in infant development to come and see how Renee was doing. She showed her how to pull up on the side of a couch. Renee persisted in learning to pull up the whole time the PT was with her. The PT predicted,

"Renee is very high in persistence, a trait found at birth. This will be a characteristic of hers the rest of her life." By the end of the day, Renee could pull up by herself, well ahead of usual development. Indeed, tenacity and perseverance were hallmark characteristics of Renee.

Renee eagerly began eating mashed and finely cut table foods at around five months of age; then at six months, she got a serious ear infection and needed oral antibiotics. But Renee flat-out refused them. She spit the antibiotics out every time. Unfortunately, her strong will and unwillingness to take the antibiotic medicine resulted in another round of antibiotics (twenty days total). By then, she refused all foods that had the consistency of baby foods.

Much to my concern and chagrin, she would not even eat mashed potatoes or anything mashed. She wanted whole green beans and other foods just like ours. What were we to do? Renee persisted. So, Renee began eating the foods we ate! That was easier than having an issue every time Renee ate solids. As a Pediatric Dietitian/Nutritionist, I was concerned that she would develop a negative attitude toward eating.

Many instances of her strong will and persistent personality became evident during her toddler and preschool years. For example, she was unwilling to wear her seat belt until finally, we just pulled over to the side of the road and waited until she buckled it back up.

At two years of age, she decided that she was not wearing dresses any more. Thankfully, we have an adorable picture of her as a two-year-old in a red velvet dress with Gene's parents. She also refused to wear a winter coat to preschool, even though it was freezing outside. Both Gene and I allowed her to choose when she was ready to wear her coat and learn the consequences of not wearing a coat in freezing weather. We sent the coat along with her. A huge lesson for us was learning to allow Renee to discover consequences!

Renee always wanted to do what Mark was doing. Except taking care of dolls. When Renee was one year old, Mark, three years old, gave Renee his doll and stuffed lion. They were of no interest to him, much to Renee's delight. She already had a bed heaped full of stuffed animals. Her favorites were an albino tiger and her two dolls, the one from Mark and hers. They went to bed with her.

We found a fabulous Preschool Cooperative Program with wonderful, licensed teachers. Mark and Renee participated in all the preschool classes from three through five years of age. This was a gift! They learned everything they needed to know by the time they were in kindergarten.

Some of the things Renee learned in preschool were similar to those listed in Fulghum's book, *All I Really Need to Know I Learned in Kindergarten* (1988): "Share everything, play fair, put things back where you found them, clean up your own mess, wash your hands before you eat, flush, and live a 'balanced life' – learn some, drink some, draw some, paint some and when you go into the world, watch for traffic, hold hands, stick together and 'wonder' how a little seed in a Styrofoam container becomes a plant." (Robert Fulghum, Villard Books, New York, NY 1988).

The best part was that I, too, was tutored regarding expectations of children at each age and ways to facilitate interactive, learning behavior. It was a delight to participate in Mark's and Renee's classrooms as the teacher's assistant every three weeks. Each of the children uniquely had their own personalities and growth patterns. It gave me such hope and joy to see them develop their interactive, social, problem-solving and motor skills.

When Renee was two years old, she visited Mark's four-year-old class and loved it. She quickly and easily made a colored salt picture and a wonderful potato print picture. After that, Renee was ready to go to school with Mark. Renee's favorite teacher (in her three-year-old class) welcomed her every day with a smile. Renee loved school, the craft activities and especially, playing with her friends. Interestingly, with her craft activities and artwork, she added a huge amount of detail and always had very interesting, fun colors. For example a fish drawn in the first grade was pink-orange, with beautiful psychedelic colors.

Renee was most comfortable when playing with someone she knew. So, we often arranged play times outside of preschool. The richness of the preschool learning and social activities established a quiet confidence in Renee that transcended into later school years and young adulthood. She was so blessed to be in the pre-school cooperative system.

Since I worked part-time (very part-time!) and I wanted both Mark and Renee to develop friends with others in the preschool, we car-pooled almost every day of the week. Friends and car-pooling turned out to be a gift, especially significant in Renee's adjustment to preschool. When Renee was playing with other children she knew, she seemed secure and adjusted. Interestingly, that may have been because she grew up – literally from birth – with a brother, one whom she adored and with whom she often played.

Renee readily and easily played with boys, especially Mark, who loved building with blocks. I mean, BIG blocks, building forts, castles, and bomb shelters. His days would be filled with Legos, Lego machines, playing with trucks (big trucks!), construction equipment and best of all, watching the REAL thing – huge construction equipment building real buildings. Yes. Renee became quite creative in building BIG things with Mark.

When Renee was three, she and Mark began weekly gymnastic classes for preschoolers. This increased her awareness of her body, coordination and motor skills as well as her sense of confidence. As the years passed, we realized that Renee was extraordinarily gifted with hand-eye and large motor coordination. Honestly, though, what she liked most was playing with friends.

During Renee's fourth year of life, we moved to a wooded area bordered by a creek and a large forested ravine, one like a natural wild-life preserve. This seemed like a dream home for our family. I now had woods; and Gene had plenty of space for a work-room. Thanks to our generous neighbor, Gene also had a plot for his garden. Best of all, Renee and Mark had an ample amount of play space in the woods and creek and a place to play free from city concerns.

Anything outside was of great interest, especially playing in the sand near the creek (half foot or so deep) at the back of our house. They busily made sand castles, dug ditches, poured water into the ditches and caught water bugs along the creek. Even in the winter, they thoroughly enjoyed sledding down our back hill and playing on the frozen ice on the creek.

A friend and colleague, Judy, was a very real part of the first five years of Mark's and Renee's lives. She loved children and her life's career dream was to work with infants and children. For years, she was the dietitian for newborns in intensive care and later pursued work with vulnerable children in Romania and Africa.

Judy recalled, "I remember the day Renee was born. While you were on your way to the hospital that evening, I came over and cared for Mark, asleep that night. I don't even know if he knew I was there." Renee popped into this world quickly late that night, no lost time!

"When Renee was about three years old, we were sitting on the steps outside of the front door of your home. Renee said, 'You know, everyone thinks I am a boy and they think I am wearing Mark's clothes. But I am not. When he has a red top and blue bottoms, I have a blue top and red bottoms. And, I am really a girl underneath.' I will never forget that!

"Another time, I remember helping Renee at Mary Bess's wedding. I was in charge of Renee because you were in the wedding."

Mary Bess, my sister, lived in Chicago at the time. Renee, four years old, was the flower girl and Mark, six years old, was the ring-bearer. We found a darling peach dress with ruffles for Renee. The only problem was that she was not at all excited about wearing a dress.

Judy continued, "We had to bribe Renee to get her to wear the dress. She wore shorts underneath (oh, well). Then, there was the problem with curling her hair. With some coaxing, we were able to make just a few curls (with a curling iron) on the top of her head. She looked like a precious doll!

"Renee carefully dropped the pink petals all the way to the front of the church with Mary Bess and Chris, her 'to be' husband. When she got to the front, she sat down on the top step up to the altar, put her hand under her chin and turned and watched Chris and Mary Bess, with the sweetest look of fascination."

In the midst, as the Matron of Honor, I was praying, "Dear Lord, please help Renee be respectful and don't let Renee do anything weird."

According to Judy, "after the ceremony, she was done with the dress and more interested in climbing under the pews."

Renee came to love Chris, a former college football player with the University of Denver. He was actively involved in real estate and at one time he was the President of the Realtors Board in Chicago. Chris was 6'2" and just as large with his sense of humor and the twinkle in his eyes. He was amazingly adept at finding the funny side of life, with a light-hearted, caring spirit. He was the perfect husband for Mary Bess, busy with her medical practice. The same humor endeared Renee to Chris. In a birthday card sent to Chris, Renee called Chris "my favorite uncle!"

In the interview with Judy, I reminded her that she gave both Mark and Renee underwater goggles and large fins for their feet when swimming. They loved swimming in the pool at Judy's apartment complex and especially swimming with the different colored "noodles."

"I gave them rides like the human dolphins. Renee really liked it! Yep!" said Judy.

"I remember the special Easter eggs that we colored almost every year. We took onion skins, cut them into fine pieces, put the eggs into a soft cotton rag, covered the eggs with the onion skins and tied the rag with a string. After the eggs were boiled, we opened the rags. The hard-cooked eggs looked like stained glass windows, the color of onion skins, yellowish or red. My father taught us how to do this!"

Chapter 6

A New Grandmother

*Do not be anxious about anything, but in every situation, by
prayer and petition, with thanksgiving, present your requests to
God. And the peace of God, which transcends all understanding,
will guard your hearts and your minds in Christ Jesus.
(Philippians 4:6-7)
Whispers from Heaven come in answered prayers,
especially when they affect major decisions in our lives.*

When Renee was five years old, Ruth, a dear "grand-mother," part-time baby sitter and eventual house sitter came into our lives with great joy. She instantly endeared herself to both Mark and Renee. This was no small feat since Renee, at five years of age, had "fired" an earlier baby sitter after several weeks.

We were astounded when the baby sitter told us that she was not coming any more. I asked, "Why?" She said, "Renee fired me." To this day, we have no idea where Renee learned this language and concept. It certainly was not our table-talk and conversation! Interestingly, from a young age through her last days, Renee accurately observed and some times commented upon what she saw, i.e., called an ace an ace. This was one of her most amazing verbal and observational skills, to 'call an ace an ace' with such candor and in a way that was not offensive. When asked why, Renee's response was, "She was driving around with us running errands." We had no idea that the baby-sitter was doing this.

I knew that I would not be able to go back to work, even part-time, if I did not have a babysitter whom I could absolutely trust, one who loved the Lord and had a walking, living faith in Jesus. We prayed for someone who would become a "grandmother" for our family and someone whom we could bless.

"Oh, Lord, what now? Am I to continue working? What am I to do about the grant responsibilities? How am I ever going to continue working without someone I can absolutely trust with our children – someone like a grandmother who dearly loves and cares for Mark and Renee as her own and loves you too?"

After searching every resource and asking friends and neighbors if they knew anyone who would be interested in working very part-time, I finally said to the Lord, "If I am unable to find someone who will come into our home, I will take that as a message from you that I am to quit work."

Finally, on New Year's Day, I remembered one last person to call – a mother of one of Renee's preschool friends. In fact, I thought of her earlier but assumed that she would not be of much help. She said, "My husband, Barry, and I just ran into Ruth, the "nanny" of more than twenty years for his family. Both were thrilled to see each other. She just retired from the Indiana University Medical Center. You might ask her."

God's timing is amazing. It seemed like a miracle that Ruth was available. This was a long shot, but we agreed to meet. And she said, "Let's see how it goes with your children."

I worked part-time for ten years, two or three days a week. She was willing to assist with some of the wash and housework, too. But the children were always her first priority.

She said, "I really enjoy Renee." Best of all, Renee loved her immediately. She was positive, cheerful, and encouraging.

Through Ruth's encouragement and inspiration, her son Allan became a medical doctor. Her husband, also retired, drove her back and forth to our home until his untimely stroke and death.

Following her husband's death, I prayed with Ruth twice daily during the ride to and from her home (thirty five minutes each way). This precious prayer time was a gift. We shared our concerns and I listened to years of Ruth's spiritual and practical wisdom. God knew. Even though others considered this too far to transport Ruth, God had other plans. She loved, supported, and encouraged us. She loved Mark and Renee as her own children. Ruth was in their lives until they left for college, first grade through high school for Mark, preschool through high school for Renee.

Mark and Renee were thrilled to see Ruth, even after they went off to college and began careers as young adults. During the last visit at Thanksgiving – when Ruth was ninety years old – we realized that Ruth had a great need for cabinets and a remodeled kitchen. She had no money, no resources nor family who could help with this. She shared, "I am praying for a new kitchen." As we left Ruth's home, the three of us – Mark, Rorie and I – prayed for Ruth, "Lord, Ruth is YOUR faithful servant. She has been for many years. Please listen to her and meet her need for cabinets and a remodeled kitchen."

Amazingly, God answered these prayers. Mark and Rorie significantly contributed to Rick H's Inner City ministry in Renee's honor, without our knowledge. Rick H, an inner-city pastor, used these resources to remodel Ruth's kitchen and assist several inner-city youth gain construction and remodeling skills. The young men loved Ruth and her wisdom. She told them, "Live right, love the Lord and serve him."

Ruth was petite and feminine, well dressed and "put together," with a warm generous heart and the youngest ninety-year-old! One of her favorite prayers was, "Lord, let me live from day-to-day in such an unforgettable way, my prayers shall be for others, that I may live like thee!"

She was a living, walking testimony to the goodness of the Lord in her life, a legend in her time. She was a founding member of a Baptist church that began in her living room. By the time of her passing, the church had grown to 300 members. She was trustworthy, dependable, very generous, and caring. Her cheerful, positive personality brought the Lord's light into the lives of others. In the eulogy for her funeral services, I humbly and gratefully shared the gift of her presence in our family.

One of Ruth's favorite sayings was, "You can tell the character of a person by the way they treat their animals." Indeed, if this is true, Renee was at the top of the *character* list. She treated her animals like royalty!

Excerpts Read at Ruth Murrell's funeral, January 31, 2014

Ruth has been an integral and beloved part of our family for the past twenty-six years. She took precious care of our children part-time from the time they began school. I will read a part of a Mother's Day note that I gave Ruth five years ago. I am so glad I had the chance to tell her these things.

Happy Mother's Day, May 11, 2008

My dear Ruth, you have been a
'grandmother,' 'friend' and an 'angel' for our family.......
since Mark was six years old and Renee four
years old (about twenty years☺).
God is so awesome!
When we ask God for help, for the
perfect person for our children,
he sent you☺☺☺
Your influence in shaping Mark and Renee's character
was positive and powerful.
You listened... guided... laughed... played and,
brought God's presence into their lives.
You helped Mark and Renee be
responsible...be compassionate...
be truthful and treat others with respect.
You showed them God's character through your
kindness and TLC (Tender Loving Care).
You extended TLC to 'all living creatures'
including our three cats---Million Dollar
Princess, Mufasa and Scar ☺☺☺
There are so many memories that you shared with us,
as Mark and Renee grew through the years.
You loved Mark and helped him know
he was loved and special too...
As he went straight through his journey
from elementary school through graduate school....
You knew him so well and,
he holds you as one of the dearest souls in his life.
You loved Renee and guided her when she needed someone
who would listen...laugh...and have fun with her---
over the mountains and thru the valleys,
from kindergarten through high school and beyond.

Thank you for walking this precious journey with our family.
You have many stars in your crown for your care
of Mark and Renee and for your care of Gene and me.
You have been a Sister in the Lord…. a role model …
confidante…and, person of prayer, one
guided daily by the Holy Spirit.
This was the true treasure
…. having our faith strengthened daily through
your witness…. your walk…your prayers…
and, answered prayers!
God is soooo good☺ Praise the Lord!!!
Love, The Rickards---Gene, Karyl, Mark and Renee

Even though this was written five years ago, the same holds true had I written it today. I know Ruth is in heaven celebrating with Renee, who preceded her in death.

Chapter 7

Fifth Birthday Request – Dog, Cat, Racehorse, or Motorcycle

Therefore, I tell you, whatever you ask for in prayer,
believe that you have received it,
and it will be yours.
(Mark 11:24).
God's whispers from heaven can come through a five-year-
old child, who makes unusual requests. Then, watching
over the years – God answers those special desires!

For Renee's fifth birthday she said, "I want a dog, cat, race-horse, or motorcycle." Dogs and cats were out of the picture because of Mark's allergies. Mark was "deathly" allergic to cats. When around cats, he had several severe asthmatic attacks, ones that required emergency care.

Racehorse and motorcycle, *at five years of age?* Where in the world did Renee come up with these requests? I will never know how she knew about racehorses. The motorcycle request probably came from seeing a neighbor ride a motorcycle. A racehorse and motorcycle were *not* options. Little did I know that her birthday requests would continue throughout her lifetime and that she would eventually make every one of them a reality.

Chapter 8

Next Best Thing to a Racehorse

And He took the children in his arms,
placed His hands on them and blessed them.
(Mark 10:16).
When we come to the Lord in prayer,
He whispers solutions and answers to perplexing dilemmas.

The best option for a birthday gift seemed to be horse lessons. With Mark's allergies, the other options – a dog or cat – were not possible. We took Renee to a horse farm on the north side of Indianapolis that gave lessons and ran a summer camp. The owner said, "I only accept six-year-olds. But since Renee wants to ride so much, I will see how she does."

Sure enough, Renee rode with confidence and ease on a large horse, one who responded positively to her commands. Renee's legs only came half way down the horse, more than twice her height. Her horse-riding lessons began. Renee was thrilled!

The next summer, when Renee was six, she enrolled in a horse camp, six hours a day, five days a week for two weeks. She rode many different horses, groomed the horses and cleaned the stalls. She loved caring for the horses.

One day when I came to pick her up, I noticed she was grooming a very large horse, even picking up his back hoof to clean.

Wow. That was something we were *not* allowed to do on the ranch. Horses can kick and kill in a flash.

I asked the instructor, "Is that safe?"

She replied, "Renee is amazing. She is superb with the horses. Out of all my years of teaching, she is the only one of more than one hundred of my students who has such sensitivity and ability to work with all of the horses. She calms the horses." Renee's calming, charismatic personality continued throughout young adulthood.

At the end of the camp, she rode with the other older children in an organized riding show for the parents. Renee was only six then, and continued horse lessons through sixth grade, routinely jumping with horses.

Chapter 9

Adopted by Duber

In that day you will no longer ask me
anything. Very truly I tell you,
my Father will give you whatever you ask in my name.
Until now you have not asked for anything in my name.
Ask and you will receive, and your joy will
be complete. (John 16:23-24)
Watching Renee's joy through a neighbor's dog
brought tears as I saw the love of God for my child.

There was magic in the air, great excitement as we moved into our new home on the northwest side of Indianapolis. The leaves were turning beautiful colors — orange, yellow, red — some beginning to turn brown. It was just beautiful. We moved into a quiet suburban neighborhood backed by a large ravine and woods. Our home was in a cul-de-sac so it was safe from busy, thoroughfare traffic. Renee and Mark, four and six years old, could play in the woods to their hearts' content.

As we moved into our home, suddenly a gang of dogs appeared, fighting and snarling in our yard. This continued for several months, in spite of prayers for protection and deliverance from danger for Mark and Renee. Finally, I suggested, "Let's call the Dog Pound."

Gene's response, "I don't think that's the best way to begin with our neighbors."

One of our neighbors, the one who lived next door, was outside. So, I asked, "Do you know any of the dogs who congregate in our yard?"

"I know only one of the dogs – Duber – the gray and black husky, Malamute dog. He's a pretty good dog."

Shortly after that on a cold wintery day, Mark and Renee were playing down at the creek. When Mark was crossing the frozen creek, it cracked. One of his feet went into the water. As he pulled his foot from the ice, his boot came off. Duber snatched the boot and ran off with it, back to his home two houses down the block.

As a "concerned" mother, I grudgingly went to the neighbors, knocked on the door, introduced myself and asked, "Do you by any chance have our son's boot? Duber ran off with it."

Then, I mentioned the snarling, growling dog pack that was in our yard almost every day.

The neighbor's reaction, "I don't think they are any of our neighbors' dogs. Just use buck shot." My response, "I don't think so...."

The next day, I noticed that no dogs, not even Duber, were around. Several days later, Renee came in the house with Duber's collar and dog tag. *Groan.* Back to the neighbors with Duber's dog collar.

I mentioned to Duber's owner, "I have not seen the dogs the last few days, not even Duber."

He said, "Yes, we kept Duber inside. I used buckshot on the others."

He went on to say, regarding my concerns about Duber jumping for sticks and barking at tricycle wheels, "Just say 'No.'"

Amazingly, Duber *did* stop instantly with a 'No!'

Worse than barking in our yard, Duber started jogging with me, way behind at first, then closer. That was scary. The last thing I wanted on my watch was the neighbor's dog hit by a car. Amazingly, Duber heeled every time a car came and then wandered all over.

One rainy day when Gene and I ran three miles, with Duber heeling behind us, "out of nowhere" two BIG dogs attacked Duber. They were not with anyone and not on a leash. Much to my surprise, I became vicious, snarling and yelling at the big dogs. One bit Duber on the back. Duber was shaking and hurt, too much to run back with us. I stayed by the roadside with Duber while Gene ran home for the car. All I could do was comfort and love Duber as the rain continued.

We loaded up Duber and brought him to his owners. Duber did not want to get out of the car. The owners suggested that he might be embarrassed. We wondered if he just had become our dog, outside of our home of course.

"We're so sorry this happened. We'll be happy to take him to the veterinarian."

"No," they said, "we will." He recovered quickly, thankfully.

We realized at that moment, that "Duber is now a part of our family and certainly Renee's." She adored him. Suddenly, the pile of stuffed animals on her bed was not so important to her. Duber was the perfect solution – a beautiful, smart dog that Renee loved.

Duber had become our dog, even though we only gave him a few dog treats during the day and sent him home at night for his daily rations.

I finally knew, "This dog is our answer to Renee's prayers for a dog and Renee dearly loves him." God has such a good sense of humor. We prayed for wisdom to know what to do regarding the pack of dogs and Renee's request for a dog. Indeed, God answered both our prayers.

One day I said to Gene, "We need to clean this dog up with some great smelling dog shampoo. He smells awful."

Gene, with a crooked grin, said, "Duber has won you over!"

Duber loved those baths, outside of course. My reaction, "Three cheers! Now he smells great and he is sooooo happy having those baths."

Duber ferociously guarded Renee and loved playing with her. No stick throwing, though. Yes. Duber played soccer. Duber ran with the ball between his legs. Quite deftly! Renee laughed as she practiced her soccer skills, only sometimes getting the ball from Duber. Duber was soooo happy!

As Duber got older (ten years old), we noticed he was slowing down. It was harder and harder for him to go jogging with us.

One day the phone rang. It was Sonja, Duber's owner. "Duber has a tumor and his spleen was removed. He is recovering at the Veterinarian's Hospital but we can't get him to eat. Will Renee care for him and see if she can get him to eat?"

So, against all my former house rules, I let Duber into our home on the front door rug. Renee offered food and water. Sure enough, he began to eat and slowly recovered with her tender loving care.

Duber must have known how concerned I was about having dogs in our home. He had never been in the house before because of Mark's severe allergies. Amazingly, Duber just lay on the rug and allowed Renee to love him and feed him. He lived another year, still adored and cared for by Renee.

Renee definitely had a calming spirit, a special one that connected with all kinds of animals -- and people, too.

Chapter 10

A Sick Kitten Rescued

LORD my God, I called to You for help,
and You healed me. (Psalm 30:2)
The precious faith and love of a child brings
healing whispers from heaven.

I n the barn of our neighbor's riding stable, Renee caught a little kitten. Amazing. This kitten was wild. Indeed, a feral kitten, fiercely wild (afraid) and probably never handled by humans. In Renee's arms, the kitten purred like a running motor, calm and content to stay in her arms. Renee carried the kitten to our home, several blocks from the riding stable. She insisted on keeping her in the garage. The house was not an option because Mark had severe asthma, diagnosed when we moved to our new home.

Mark was deathly allergic, especially to cats. In fact, Mark received medication for severe asthma from the time he was six years old. When Renee rescued the kitten, Mark was fourteen years old. So, that was eight years of careful and in some ways, heroic treatment to manage the symptoms without Mark missing school. Renee knew our concerns about Mark. She promised, "I will only keep the kitten in the garage."

Renee fed the kitten milk. Whoops. Not a good idea. The kitten had severe diarrhea and looked pathetic, i.e., severely malnourished. Yes. The kitten had fleas, too. But when she was in

Renee's arms, she purred contentedly. No one else could catch the kitten in the garage.

Finally, I said to Gene and Renee, "We have to take her to the veterinarian; she will not make it otherwise." Sure enough, the kitten had fleas, mites, and parasites and was severely malnourished. The veterinarian informed Renee, "The flea treatment, medical treatment and required vaccinations will be $250."

My reaction, "Is this kitten worth that much? If you want a kitten, Renee, you will need to provide for it. Surely, we can find a healthy kitten."

The veterinarian said, "Yes. We can find a healthy kitten."

Suddenly, it occurred to me that "healthy" may not be the only issue. What if another kitten had a bad personality? So, I asked the veterinarian, "So, what kind of a personality does this kitten have?"

"Well, it's pretty good"

My question was, "How good? At the 99th percentile?"

NO. Renee did not want another kitten. She wanted this one.

"How are you going to pay for this?"

"I will use my allowance – $4 per week."

"That means you will be paying for this kitten's medical treatment for over a year, Renee."

"That's OK, Mom. That's what I want."

So, we went back home with the kitten. By then, I called her 'Million Dollar Princess.' Renee named her "Wind Star."

Guess who helped Renee hold the wild kitten while she gave her the sulfa drugs for the tapeworms. Yes. Yours truly. And guess who was the only one who could call "Million Dollar Princess" and rescue her from the woods outdoors. Yes. Yours truly, probably because I held her, soothed and calmed her while Renee gave her the sulfa drugs.

The kitten was rescued in the dead of winter, four degrees below zero. Renee still cared for her in our garage. She fed her fancy, very expensive cat food for re-nourishing her. The diarrhea stopped. After three days, someone inadvertently left the back door to the garage open just a crack. "Million Dollar Princess" found the cracked door and was gone.

Renee was devastated. She sobbed, "Will you help me find her?"

We went door-to-door asking our neighbors, "Have you seen a skinny black kitten?"

Nope. No one had seen a black kitten. No surprise, since the kitten was a wild one. We were not sure if "Million Dollar Princess" knew where our home was, either. Renee was bummed, ready to give up after the kitten was gone three days.

"The only thing I know to do is pray, Renee. Let's pray fervently."

"Lord, please bring this kitten back to the garage. In this freezing cold weather, do not let anything happen to Million Dollar Princess.'"

"Renee, let's leave the garage door up some tonight and turn the light on inside the garage so the kitten will know where to come." About 3:00 am the next morning, I awakened and went to the garage. There was "Million Dollar Princess" shivering; her back leg was severely hurt.

Gene, Renee's dad, grew up on a dairy farm where cats and dogs lived outside. He said, "Just let nature take its course."

For Renee, that was not an option.

I thought, *Are you kidding? We already spent $250 on this kitten.*

We went back to the veterinarian. He said, "A large dog bit the kitten seriously on the back and hurt her back leg. It will heal by itself as long as there is no infection."

Bummer. We started another antibiotic, Penicillin, to prevent infections. Thankfully, surgery was not needed. Now, I was holding "Million Dollar Princess" as Renee administered both the antibiotic and sulfa drugs.

This was one of the coldest winters in Indiana with many days at or below zero. Renee begged, "Please let me bring the kitten downstairs to the warm workroom."

Yes. By then, I too, loved this dear little kitten, freezing in the garage. So the kitten went down to the workroom. Unbeknown to us, "Million Dollar Princess" also slept with Renee at night.

Renee had asked Mark, "Can I bring the kitten upstairs? I promise to only let the kitten into my bedroom."

Mark agreed, "Yes, you may, as long as the kitten is never in my room."

By then, Mark was swimming year round to expand his lung capacity and decrease the issues related to breathing capacity and his asthma. The next spring, he had a routine visit scheduled with a pulmonologist at Riley Hospital for Children.

Mark, without the doctor's permission, stopped his inhalers and some of his asthma medication. Before a lung-function test, the MD, in a kind but firm way, scolded Mark. God works in mysterious and wonderful ways. Mark's lung function was 120% of the others his age, without any medication.

The MD shook his hand and said, "You were right, you do not need these medications now."

Mark left with a sloppy grin on his face, like the cat that ate the canary! Renee was thrilled. She could keep the cat in her room and in other select areas of the house. But not in Mark's room.

The cat story continued. God kept working with me, expanding my boundaries. The next spring, we estimated the kitten to be eight months old. This was just a guess. While visiting friends in England, Renee called with sad news, "Duber died." She went on to say, "I think Wind Star is pregnant."

When I got home, I called the veterinarian, who said, "That's probably a pseudo-pregnancy."

No way, I thought. *I have seen pregnant animals before – all those cows, sheep and cats – when I was growing up on the ranch.*

Sure enough, Million Dollar Princess was pregnant. One afternoon in May, on Renee's birthday, Renee called me at work, "Wind Star is having kittens."

"Where are they?"

"On your bed"

"Oh, no. Are they on a towel? Hurry and get a large bath towel."

Four kittens were born on Renee's 12th birthday; one was a gray striped kitten, one a white kitten, one a black kitten and one that looked like a Siamese kitten.

These kittens brought great love and joy into our home. They were kept downstairs in the family room and office areas in a special box. Renee adored these kittens. They soon were playing and having lots of fun chasing little balls with bells inside, a fish on a pole and other "whirly-twirly" birds.

Barbara W, our neighbor who was our "cat-sitter," said, "I have never seen such loving kittens, each with their own unique personality."

Mufasa, the Siamese king, was a larger cat who watched everything we did; he could open drawers. He was my favorite. Scar was the daredevil who was extremely athletic and could leap onto and walk atop the banister without falling down the stairs. The female kitten was a sweet, white furry ball. At eight weeks of age, all the kittens were ready to be given away. Renee gave one, the gray-striped kitten, to our neighbor friends and the sweet little female kitten to another friend in a wheelchair.

Renee gave these away without any conversation with us. When I was jogging with Gene, I asked him, "Why did Renee give them away without even discussing it with us?" I was crying. Simba, the white female kitten, was my favorite.

"The third kitten – Scar – is to go to our friend's son. We arranged that with his mom."

Renee's response, "No, I am keeping both of them. How would you feel if I told you that you had to give away Mark or me?"

"You and Mark are not the same as these kittens, Renee."

Renee made her point, though, especially remembering how disappointed I was when she gave away Simba. We kept two of the kittens, Mufasa and Scar. Actually, having two kittens ended up being a gift. They played together, slept together, and were true and fast buddies. The Million Dollar Princess still was a part of Renee's family, too.

Three cats – that was a menagerie beyond my farthest imagination. When we lived on the ranch, my mother had a long hard-

and-fast rule that we were not to bring any animals, cats or dogs, into the house. They belonged outside. Renee successfully pleaded her case; our family was transformed forever. Thankfully, Mark did not have any asthma attacks. He was declared cleared of his severe asthma.

Now that was God's incredible care. Mark's lungs expanded so much that he did not have any more severe asthma attacks. Indeed, God does have a great sense of humor. The Lord turns the dark cloud – cats in our home – into a silver lining for Renee. The cats were her "therapy" when she was discouraged or upset.

The cat story goes on. Renee left for the Air Force Academy. *Oops.* The cats were left behind in my care. They were an established part of our family. Mark was off to college, too, not that Mark ever cared for them. The cats were the last residue of our children; we were not empty nesters yet!

Much to my sadness, Mufasa passed away when he was about twelve years old. Scar died at nineteen years of age and Million Dollar Princess at twenty years, with diagnoses of asthma, kidney disease, hyper-parathyroid disease and arthritis. She still purred like a motor when I held and petted her, though.

Renee did a great job of developing loving, gentle personalities in all of the cats, a blessing. When Million Dollar Princess passed on, Scar loved 100% of the attention, brushing and petting. He was a handsome, suave guy with a positive personality. According to the veterinarian, nineteen or twenty years of age is incredibly old for a cat.

Chapter 11

Younger School Years – Friendships Blossom and Character 'in the Lord' Begins

Perfume and incense bring joy to the heart,
and the pleasantness of a friend springs from
their heartfelt advice. (Proverbs 27:9)
Renee became a Christian and was baptized
during this time of her life.
Looking back, I am thankful that God brought neighbors
and friends who were instrumental in influencing Renee
in her character development and her Christian faith.

When we moved to our home in Northwest Indy, the children of our neighbors were older, in high school or college. Our new home was the perfect place for Mark and Renee to play and grow in a beautiful, secure woods (tall maple, oak, ash, and walnut trees) with a shallow creek for stomping in the water and sandbanks for building castles. Little did we realize there were no other similar-aged children in our neighborhood. We knew that developing friendships with other children was an important part of Mark and Renee's development, so we searched high and low for other families with children of similar age – not only our immediate neighborhood but also surrounding ones. The only thing we knew to do was to begin praying for friends who were Mark and Renee's ages.

Neighborhood Friends

An incredible answer to these prayers came when Rick and Cathy H's family built and moved into a house across the street from ours. This was manna from heaven. We grew to love their family – Rick and Cathy H – and their two sons, Scott and Gabe, similar in age to Mark and Renee.

God answered another prayer, as well, through this family. We were fervently seeking God's wisdom and direction in finding a church in the neighborhood (Pike Township), one with a vibrant children's and youth ministry.

Rick H was the Youth Pastor for Trader's Point Christian Church (TPCC), a church that was only five minutes away from our neighborhood. He invited us to visit, and we became members of this thriving, Spirit-filled church and volunteered to assist in the children's Sunday school, the 4's and then the 5's. Renee's reluctance to attend Sunday school soon disappeared as we assisted and she became friends with others in the program. Our children were blessed with life-changing youth ministries (Bible Bowl, Youth Ministry, D Bible Study team).

At TPCC, Rick H baptized Renee (10 years old) and Mark (12 years old) with their profession of faith in Jesus. Importantly, their faith became a personal relationship with the Lord. TPCC believes in the inherent truth of the Bible and the importance of teaching not only the Word (Bible) but also the practical application of its "truths."

A third blessing was that Cathy H, the mother of Scott and Gabe, agreed to assist in after-school care for Mark and Renee several afternoons a week, if needed. We always wanted to be certain our children were welcomed after school by a loving, safe adult – Ruth, Cathy H or myself. In an interview with Cathy H, she shared this:

"All four of the children were about the same age. Scott was six months younger than Mark; Renee a year and half younger than Scott and Gabe a year younger than Renee.

"All of them played together. There was not any need for discipline for your kids. Whatever they did, they worked it out. They were good kids but active, very active. I remember Renee was more the stoic one, not a drama queen or cry-baby. Whatever the guys dished out, she took. Playing football, she was there. I remember her being the one in charge, 'You go here, I will do this.'"

Indeed, Mark and Renee were thrilled to play with Scott and Gabe. They played baseball "until the cows came home," and when they got older, they played tag football. Yes, Renee was considered one of the "guys." They needed her to even the teams, although Renee would have loved to have friends in our neighborhood who were girls.

Rick H shared, "Once a month, Renee and Mark, my sons and two boys from another family played with several guys from the inner-city ministry named Cheese and Pooh. They usually played baseball or football."

Evidently, one evening the kids began playing tackle football, even though they were supposed to be playing tag football. Rick H said, "I saw Renee take down a really large guy from the inner city. He was totally taken by surprise."

Renee saw the inclusiveness and nonjudgmental attitude of Rick H's inner-city ministry modeled. Perhaps that's why Renee was so inclusive and nonjudgmental with other youth, regardless of their economic and racial status. It was through the baseball and football games with Mark and the other guys, Scott and Gabe and their friends, that she really learned how to be with the guys.

Even though she played with the guys, she was a nurturer and would not, on her life, let them know. "Nurturing" was not a cool thing.

Soccer and Friends

When Renee was five years old, she began soccer on a "mixed girl and boy" Pike soccer team, coached by Beth W, our neighbor. One evening when she babysat Renee, she said "Come and join our soccer team for five-year-olds. I'm the coach." In all honesty, I was only lukewarm about the idea of Renee beginning soccer (or any competitive sport) when she was only five years old. Renee, however, was eager to learn to play soccer so we agreed to have her play that fall. Little did we know that this would begin a journey through her K-12 school years that would open other doors.

Interestingly, we rarely did evening activities that needed babysitters. Soccer must have been a "whisper from heaven." From the get-go, Renee loved playing soccer. Even, if she and the other five-year-old children looked like bees swarming after the ball, Renee became totally 'hooked' on soccer after that fall season. No surprise! Their team won all six games and was champion for that age group.

Beth W, a physically fit young lady with dark brown hair and a great sense of humor, was a wonderful coach for these five-year-olds. If a child did not listen to her instructions, she had him or her sit on the sidelines until he or she was ready to listen. She herself was a starter for the Pike High School soccer team so she really understood the game.

Soccer came with other *huge* bonuses. Jacqueline, who became Renee's best friend, and she played on the same soccer team when Renee was in the first grade. It was on the soccer field where I met Jacqueline's mother, Maria.

Amazingly, both Jacqueline and Renee entered the Extended Learning (EL) Program (Gifted and Talented Program) for Pike Township that fall. When we realized this, Maria and I began a weekly prayer time for our girls. Oh, how we prayed and prayed and prayed about everything – learning, friendships, activities, and teachers. This was the beginning of a precious, God-given friendship for both Renee and I with Jacqueline and Maria. Eventually, Maria's family considered Renee a surrogate daughter. What a gift! When they were together, they laughed, sang old-time songs with the radio and generally had a good time.

Other Activities and Friends:

Swimming

Swimming began a major activity in Renee and Mark's younger lives. Renee and Mark entered the summer swimming program at Westchester Swimming Pool.

Eventually, both Mark and Renee joined the Indianapolis swim team. Renee had tough and challenging competition in her age groups. This was a bonus for her as she loved a challenge. Most of the swimmers in the summer and year-round program were girls in the elementary age groups. The early challenges paid off, though. By the time she entered middle school, she was competitively swimming for the Guion Swimming team and did well!

Water Parks

The water parks were another activity that captured their imagination and skills in swimming. They loved going to a water park on the north side of Indianapolis, especially since they went with their friends, Marlene – Renee's age; and Luke – Mark's age. The tall, tall – yes, very tall – water slides were the favorite for all of them. Renee and Mark loved to swim; they were like fish!

At Renee's younger age, I was reluctant to let her go to the top of the slide, *some forty feet high*, without going up with her. Gulp. And yes, I was afraid of heights. A mother will do a lot for her children! I went up with Renee.

Renee had neither fears nor concerns. She easily and readily put her water mat on the slide and down she went, curving and turning, finally sailing out beyond the end of the slide onto the water.

The thrill was incredible! The big inner tubes that went round and round on another slide were less thrilling but fun as well.

Renee and Mark and their friends had such fun those evenings. The children were totally exhausted by the time we left.

Twirling

An out-of-the-box activity for Renee was learning to twirl a baton. When Renee was in the 5th grade, Marlene heard that I taught twirling lessons while in high school and my early college years.

She beseeched me, "Please, will you teach me to twirl?"

With some reluctance, I agreed, "I will give you and Renee a series of six lessons with two conditions: you practice daily and then after the final lesson, you perform a duet twirling routine for a nursing home."

Marlene loved the lessons and practiced every day. I never saw Renee practice. She was lukewarm about the whole idea. At every lesson, though, Renee was quite able to do everything I taught.

Both were really excited about their darling (my version!) twirling outfits – royal blue sparkly, shining fabric for shorts and vest over short sleeve white blouse. Royal blue fringe lined the edge of the vest and the shorts.

At the nursing home, both performed in unison a relatively difficult twirling routine flawlessly. I was so pleased and proud of them. That was when I knew that Renee was extraordinarily coordinated in hand-eye and motor movement. I will never know how she learned the routine without practicing!

God does have a great sense of humor. Indeed, God uses everything, even those twirling lessons. At the Air Force Academy, that experience allowed her to become the chosen (by the rest of the flag team) team leader for the band's flag team.

Marlene posted on Renee's Memorial Tribute page: "My childhood will forever be entwined with Renee's and I will keep many memories of our times together close to my heart."

Chapter 12

Elementary School Years

I will instruct you and teach you in the way you should go;
I will counsel you with my loving eye on you. (Psalm 32:8)
Renee's elementary teachers and school friends during
these foundational years influenced learning and the
development of healthy lifestyle habits – physical
activity, curiosity, creativity, and critical thinking.

R enee's first day of school was exciting and long coming! She readily got on the school bus and had no need to wave good-bye. For the previous two years, she watched Mark go to school and always wanted to go with him.

First Grade

In the first grade, Renee loved going to school and especially assisting her first-grade teacher. On one occasion, the first graders had a toy exchange to learn some basics about math. Renee was the bank teller. She loved helping others and controlling the "bank." This may have been a predictor of what was to come later, a position as Bank Teller and assistant who closed the Charter Bank in the evenings.

Second and Third Grade

Ms. Julie G, Renee's second-grade teacher and Mrs. Karen A, Renee's third-grade teacher, were willing to share their memories of Renee in the following interview. Ms. Julie G and Mrs. Karen A were gifted teachers for the Extended Learning (EL) program. The EL program was called the gifted and talented program (top three percent of each grade level) until Renee was in the fifth grade. Oh, so many times what happens in the second and third grades affects children for the rest of their lives.

Karyl: "I have a sense that what Renee had in the second and third grades with you two was very special. Perhaps, this will be an inspiration to others."

Mrs. Karen A: "The second and third graders had a very enriched early environment and then when they got into the fourth grade, they had more and more reading and learning activities. The EL became very intense. They were expected to have more creativity, individual thoughtfulness and ownership in their writing, scientific thinking and other homework."

Karyl: "What were some memories of Renee in your classes?"

Ms. Julie G: "Renee's class in the second grade was a very special class with only ten children, a rare happening. The relationships that the children developed with each other and with the teacher were extraordinary. Renee was a very bright young lady, very eager to please. She was a little perfectionistic, meticulous with some things. She was outgoing if she knew you or got to know you, but would be reserved if she didn't know you. She had really close bonds, at recess especially, with Jacqueline, Jeff, and Andy. That's when they played soccer.

"For the Cinderella play, Renee was one of the ugly stepsisters. The mother of Andy, Mrs. Barb M, assisted in organizing and finding costumes for the Cinderella play. Renee was to wear a long ball gown and heels. Just getting her to be willing to wear them (a pink bathrobe and heels) was very challenging (*laughter*). We had to twist some arms on that because she wasn't really interested in dressing up! Seeing her walk in the heels was very comical, especially watching her walk, with much frustration, on the side of the heels. She did not miss a word with her lines, even though she rolled her eyes at Julie. *(laughter)*."

Karyl: "No, Renee was not into wearing dresses and certainly not heels! *(laughter)*." When she was dressed up, a pillow was added to her rear. It was hysterically funny to see her come on stage barely able to walk with the heels, holding up her rear pillow. Both Gene and I laughed our heads off and thoroughly enjoyed that introduction of Renee to theatre!

Ms. Julie G: "Then, when we did our Thanksgiving feast, Renee was very comfortable with cooking. It was obvious that you had worked with her. She was a "little pro" at doing things in the kitchen."

Karyl: "Tell me a little more about the Thanksgiving feast."

Ms. Julie G. "We made 'No Peek' Stew. The children cut up and added the potatoes, carrots and meat to the stew. Renee had her little apron. She was like a 'Sous-Chef' compared to the other kids. She enjoyed every bit of it. Prior to eating, we had a little program when each child shared different things about Indians or pilgrims, information found with some research.

"Renee was fascinated with science experiments. One time, we went out and found a caterpillar – the eggs, and watched it turn into a chrysalis. Then, it became a Monarch butterfly that we released. It was a big change to see the caterpillar eat its weight every day.

"Another memory I have of Renee was when she came back with the high school and did a Veterans Day Program. Renee played *Taps*. She was wearing all black. The lights were dimmed when she was playing the *Taps* solo with her trumpet. It was very powerful. Breathtaking. Amazing. It brought tears to our eyes; we had to work very hard not to cry. All the adults were surprised. The really neat thing was that each child would stand up and say, 'I am so and so, I had such and such as a teacher in the second grade at College Park.' This built relationships with the kids."

Karyl: "What were some of your memories of Renee in the 3rd grade?"

Mrs. Karen A: "We had eighteen in our third-grade class, six from the second-grade extended learning class. One of the things that I remember about Renee was that she was really smart but she also was very quiet in third grade. She and Jacqueline were such good friends – they would lean on each other a little. Marlene was another part of their friendship."

Ms. Julie G: "Renee was really close with Jeff and Andy, too. When they left their home school and friends to be in this program, they had a whole new group of kids. So, they started from scratch and developed bonds of friendship."

Mrs. Karen A: "I really remember Renee's friendships. It wasn't that she was not open to other kids; it was just that she was very comfortable with those who were with her in the second grade."

"We did two major projects in the third grade – the 'Wax Museum' and the 'Medieval Times.' For the Wax Museum project, each child selected one person they wanted to become. They did lots of research, made a timeline and wrote their own speech, three to five minutes in length. They gathered together a costume representing their character. Then, we invited the second-grade students and the parents to the museum (in the gymnasium) where each child told their character's story. They could be anyone they were interested in, regardless of their ethnicity. Renee was Ronald Reagan, perhaps because he was in charge (40th president, 1981 – 1989)! Andy was John Adams, 2nd president (1797-1801); Jacqueline was Thomas Jefferson, 3rd president (1801 – 1809); Jeff was George H. W. Bush, the 41st president (1989 – 1993) and Marlene was Florence Nightingale, founder of modern nursing (1820 – 1910). Most of the kids totally loved this project.

"The other major project was a Medieval Times project where each student took a part in society at that time. They drew a name to become a character, such as king, queen, jester, fife and drummer, or cook. The children had to research each role, interpret it through dress and develop a play to show what they were doing and who they were."

"Renee was a cook, with an apron and huge pot for cooking. The children prepared food (baked chicken, soup, tortillas), eaten with no utensils. The king and queen and their court ate fancy food. Those who were not part of the upper echelon had to sit on the floor and eat, not much of the good food – just scraps. They hated that! Oh, my gosh! I almost had a mutiny on my hands because they were so upset. What a great learning experience for the children! So, the two together – Wax Museum and Medieval Times – were good activities for learning to speak."

Ms. Julie G: "One thing I remember about Renee: She was so compassionate with all her peers. If someone was having a rough day or something bad happened or if things were not looking chipper for the other one, Renee would gravitate to those children to try to make things better. Michael, a classmate in second and third grades, had a strong personality. She would help him fit in and be valued. She just always did.

"She was a leader in the second grade. Renee did have a natural knack for getting things accomplished and getting everybody on the same boat, on the same page, in a nice way. Sometimes in the second grade, the children have not developed their leadership skills and it is more 'my way' or they would pout or cry."

Mrs. Karen A: "I do remember Michael. Renee was able to calm him, which was hard to do and help him be accepted in the group. When we took I-STEP (Indiana Statewide Testing for Educational Progress) tests, all the children's desks were facing the wall to prevent cheating. He could not sit still – he would stand up, sit down, put his leg over the desk, make noises. I remember at one point, we stopped and I said, 'Michael do you think there is something we can all do to help you?' Renee suggested, 'Put him in the middle of the room.' Seriously, that was what we did and he did not bother anyone since the others were all facing the wall.

"Another time, while in our classroom, Laura found out from her mom, 'We have some bad news. Scotty (Laura's dog) died.' Laura became hysterical and wouldn't quit crying. It went on and on. Finally, she calmed down and came back into the class. I said,

'Well, we have kind of a sad thing. Laura's dog died (Laura was crying).'

"Renee went over and patted her on the back and said, 'Oh, I am so sorry.' She was the only kid who would even go near Laura because the others thought she had lost it. Renee was willing to go and try to make it better. I think that Renee really helped Laura get through the rest of the day.

"I remember times when we were doing 'reading.' Renee would share her book with Marlene to be included in a higher group even though she was not in the group. I thought that was really very nice."

Ms. Julie G: "Renee was always an excellent reader and she was phenomenal at expression and inflection. When she read aloud, she drew everyone in. All the children were excellent readers but not all had expression, inflection, or fluency."

Karyl: "Say a little about your teaching philosophy."

Ms. Julie G: "You knew what you needed to accomplish, curriculum and standards wise, then I gave the children the freedom to work together cooperatively in groups. They took you far beyond where you probably would have taken them to begin with but they got to do it their way. This was great!

"You did not just have to go from point A to point B. We might go from A to F to Z and all round, but we got there and more. It was a phenomenal experience for a teacher, once in a lifetime, really."

Mrs. Karen A: "Yes it was. They were a good group of kids. I really believed that the kids could send us where we needed to go. Back then, it was a teachable moment and discussion where a child was passionate. We would go with that. Now you can't do that. And, those kids were so bright."

Karyl: "So you gave them experiences where they could own them, thrive in them and shine!"

Mrs. Karen A: "Sometimes the transition to the 4th grade is difficult. I have always said to my classes, 'The 4th grade EL is intense. It's not all fun and games.'

"One of the things that I thought Renee was really good at was her writing. She and I did a lot of writing when she came home with me."

Karyl: "Renee was frustrated because her writing was not the way Mrs. Kris M, her 4th grade EL teacher, wanted. So, we sought you out as a tutor. Later in Renee's life, she was coaching some eight- to ten-year-olds, and said, 'If you are not doing so well, it's OK to get tutoring. I did' (Mrs. Karen A: *Nice, nice.)*"

Mrs. Karen A: "When we first started, I remember she was kind of upset about it because she thought she did not need it. Well, she didn't need it. But we needed to work on her attitude about how she would get there. I think things were easy for her in second and third grades. Then, she went to fourth grade where it was not structured in the same way as the second and third grades.

"So one of the things you and I did was come up with a plan that would help her. She could earn points as an incentive to help her do her homework."

Ms. Julie G: "Renee loved incentives. They didn't even have to be big incentives!"

Mrs. Karen A: "Well, *one incentive was a BIG one.* We wrote down all the short-term things she would like to do and then one really big activity. She wanted to ride the train to Chicago, go to a baseball game and to the Renaissance Festival. She had to earn 1000 points to do that. I remember she said, 'I know some of these things my mom or dad won't want to do.' I said, 'Well you don't know. Let's ask. Heck, let's put it down and if they don't want to do these things, we will find something else.'"

Ms. Julie G: "Renee was big on incentives. In physical education, the children had Presidential Fitness Goals. Renee was really into that. She tried to be the one to set the mark for the whole grade level that year, whether it was push-ups, pull-ups or sit-ups. She was on a mission. Every time we went to Physical Education, we talked about what they needed to do to meet the goals. She was there and then some!"

Mrs. Karen A: "Didn't they have to crawl up ropes? I remember Renee crawled way up to the top. Not only got up there, but way up there, quick."

Ms. Julie G: "Jeff would look up in amazement and say, 'What? A girl doing that?' She would put them to shame sometimes!"

Karyl: "Renee didn't really want to write – that's what I remember."

Ms. Julie G: "Getting Renee to write initially was hard but when she finished, it was excellent. It took her a while to kind of percolate, to get her thoughts down. She had to think about it and then she started writing. It was a longer process for her but it was really wonderful when she finished."

Mrs. Karen A: "That was one of the things that we worked on for the fourth grade. Put those ideas down and then put them in the order she wanted. In the third grade, lots of times we talked about the topic we were going to write about. But in the fourth grade, it was more independently coming up with the content. She needed some help to get there, but really improved.

"Once Renee started the writing process, feeling like she really got into it, it was a lot easier. I remember she wrote a big blurb about your trip to Chicago and how much fun she had!

"Another thing I remember about Renee was her sense of humor. She would bring that out in her writing. She had an excellent voice in her writing. She pulled you right in!"

Ms. Julie G: "Renee had a great sense of humor but it was a dry sense of humor. You had to catch on to it!"

Karyl: "So, with Renee's writing, what you really did was help Renee think through what she was going to write, get it organized, then write it."

Mrs. Karen A: "Right."

Ms. Julie G. "Mrs. Kris M, Renee's 4th grade teacher, wanted me to share with you that not only was Renee articulate, she was articulate from the word go and could express herself very well. She also remembers that she was passionate about everything she did."

Renee's BIG incentive for writing – a trip to Chicago

Renee earned an incredibly fun trip to Chicago when working with Mrs. Karen A and her writing. Our family (Mark, Renee and I) with Luke and Marlene's family (including Andrea, their mother) went to Chicago for the day on Amtrak, the first train ride for all the children. Very exciting for them!

First, we went to the Chicago White Sox baseball game at Comiskey Park on the south side of Chicago. Then, we ate at the Water Tower building on Michigan Avenue, second floor dining area that had food bars with a great variety of food.

Early evening, we went to suburban Chicago to the Medieval Times Dinner Theatre. We mastered riding the Chicago Train Authority 'EL' train service to and from the ballpark to downtown Chicago and then the Metro train to Schaumburg, IL for the dinner theater. It was an adventure riding the 'EL' and the Metro trains. Very different from Indy!

The Medieval Times Dinner Theatre advertises, "Inside the stone walls of our 11th century-style castles, Medieval Spain will come to life before your eyes." Indeed, Medieval Spain did come alive. The Medieval Times dinner theatre is based upon authentic medieval history and the true story of a noble family in the 11th century. We saw an electrifying show featuring heroic knights on spirited horses displaying astounding athletic feats and thrilling swordplay.

Each section of the huge stadium had guests joining in the revelry of fun, each section cheering for one of the heroic knights and his magnificent stallion in authentic jousting matches and dangerous sword fights. The knights donned ironclad armor and wielded the most advanced weaponry of the Middle Ages to duel each other. They called upon their training, bravery, and gallant steeds to win the tournament. The guests cheered wildly for the knight assigned to their side of the arena.

During the jousting, we, as the 'noble guests,' ate 1600s style with our fingers (no utensils) and feasted on garlic bread, roasted chicken, sweet buttered corn, herb-basted potatoes, the pastry of the Castle and drank tomato bisque soup from the bowl.

Then, we visited the spectacular array of medieval weaponry and the Museum of Torture that displayed reproductions of torture instruments used in the middle ages. Ugh. The torture gadgets used in the 1100s were gruesome. Inhumane. The children were fascinated. Not my favorite.

We took the Metro train back to the Amtrak station and returned home very late that evening. That was quite a packed, fun day with lots of new adventures.

Fifth Grade

When Renee graduated from the fifth grade at Guion Creek Middle School, she was the only girl who wore jeans and a tie-dyed shirt. On the way to graduation, she told us, "My teacher told the girls to wear nice dresses. I told her, 'I do not have any dresses.'" Groan. It was too late to do anything about a dress.

Renee, with her jeans and tie-dyed shirt, received several awards and a special award, the Counselor's Award, for good sportsmanship. The counselor said, "Several times, I observed all the children playing on the playground. Renee played tag football with the guys. She included everyone and encouraged them all to play together."

Teamwork and encouragement of others turned out to be a long-term trademark of Renee. At the funeral visitation sharing time, her many friends shared how Renee included everyone, encouraged and inspired them be their best. Yes, and to have fun in the midst – LOTS of fun!

Interestingly, Mrs. R, the teacher of the teachers for preschool cooperatives, observed the same characteristic when Renee was in kindergarten. She shared, "I visited Renee's kindergarten. Renee was playing a board game with three others, encouraging each to follow the rules and take turns. She was facilitating a really respectful and fun game." This was the ultimate compliment from a seasoned preschool teacher. Thank you, Mrs. R.

Chapter 13

Middle School Years

I instruct you in the way of wisdom and
lead you along straight paths.
When you walk, your steps will not be hampered;
when you run, you will not stumble.
(Proverbs 4:11-12)
It was God's whispers in problem-solving
that kept Renee from stumbling.

During the sixth grade, Renee was in the Extended Learning (EL) Program, and attended Lincoln Middle School. The next year, going into seventh grade, all of the EL program students were switched to Guion Creek Middle School. Some of Renee's friends planned to continue at Lincoln Middle School, so Renee wanted to go there. This was a major crossroads for Renee. If she left the EL program, she would not be able to re-enter in high school.

Renee announced, "I will run away if I have to go to Guion Creek Middle School."

Whoa. That was beyond anything we knew how to handle. So our family went to a family counselor. Mark's reaction, "I don't know why I have to go. It's not my problem."

We all went, Renee with Scar, her 'tame enough' cat, comforter, and emotional therapist. There we created what turned out to be stellar problem-solving, thanks to the counselor. He suggested that we find some solution that honors Renee's wishes and allows her to make an honest choice.

We asked the principal of Guion Creek Middle School, "Is it possible for you to arrange an introductory tour for the children in the EL program who potentially are coming to Guion Creek Middle School next year? It would be wonderful if you can introduce their potential teachers, the music program, athletic activities and anything else you think will be exciting."

After the visit to Guion Creek Middle School, there were no more conversations about running away. Some of the kids were sold on going to Guion Creek Middle School. Whew! It turned out that Renee really liked the music program and the assistant principal who was very personable. Renee was playing trumpet and joined the Junior High jazz ensemble!

As Renee was growing, we wanted her to learn to share and be a cheerful giver. Since Lilly Foundation Inc. matched donations to schools in Indiana, we asked Renee if she would like to acknowledge a teacher with a contribution. We shared our desires with the principal: "Renee would like to honor Mr. David P for his program." The principal was taken aback and said, "We have never had anything like this."

On the loud speaker, the principal requested, "Renee, will you please come to my office." Then, he requested that Mr. David P come to his office. Mr. David P had not a clue about what was to transpire. Renee was able to say, "Mr. David P, we would like you to have this for the music department." He was dumb-founded, at a loss for words and all he could say was 'thank you.' The fun part was seeing Renee sooooo happy! With that funding, Mr. David P purchased sheet music for the jazz ensemble.

One of Renee's really good friends, Joy, went to Guion with the EL program. After she returned from three years in the Peace Corp in Ghana where she taught art in a deaf and blind school, she shared with me some of her memories of Renee. According to Joy, a soft-spoken, kind and rather shy young lady, "I was an outsider in the 6th grade when I joined the EL program at Lincoln. Renee was really good friends with Jacqueline, Marlene, Jeff, and Andy who had all grown up together in the same program and knew each other very well."

Karyl: "When did you meet Renee and what were some of your memories of her?"

Joy: "I met Renee in the sixth grade at Lincoln when all the elementary schools were combined into that middle school, but really got to know Renee well when the EL program moved to Guion Middle School. Melissa and Marlene also went to Guion.

"I remember we just had fun! We were a small group of kids who had a lot of our classes together. Our teachers were pretty laid back and we got to know them a little more personally. It made learning fun for us.

"In the eighth grade, Renee, Melissa and I did the yearbook. I remember taking pictures of some events, doing some layouts and just hanging out with Renee. The thing I remember the most was the three of us taking the late bus home, the only ones on the north side of town. We sat all the way in the back and sometimes sat backwards on the seat. We would lean way back on the seat and really thought we were cool!" *(Laughter)*

Karyl: "Interesting. Renee just did things, lots of different things!"

Joy: "Yeh, on a whim, she just would sign up for stuff and have a blast with it *(laughter)*. She never was afraid to try something new. She just dove in!

"Oh, in the 8th grade, we took a trip to Washington, D.C. Mr. Cody S, the social studies teacher and Mrs. Melanie R, the math teacher and swimming coach, arranged the trip. Mr. Cody S was a really good teacher, nice too. It's a combination of not just being nice but making you learn.

"It was an overnight trip to get there. Renee, Melissa and I sat at the back of the bus and did our makeup. The two main things I remember most were going to the Vietnam Memorial Wall and the Holocaust Museum. A lot of the details escape me because it was so long ago. We also went to Williamsburg where Renee and I had a picture taken with us in the stockades in the jail.

"Renee was on the swim team in junior high. I don't know how she did it; she was so busy. Melissa was on the swim team, too. Everything Renee did, she did well."

Karyl: "When we went to the swim meets, we sat on the side-lines and waited for what seemed like hours. Then, Renee would swim thirty seconds in the fifty-yard crawl. Again, we waited for Renee to swim in the medleys, another few minutes! So there was lots of waiting. But Renee loved the swimming."

Karyl: "What do you remember most about Renee?"

Joy: "Renee had tons of friends. She was just so accepting of everyone. Everyone kind of flocked to her and she connected with people really easily. That's probably part of how I got to know Renee because I was very shy as a kid, especially in middle school. You know, everyone is kind of awkward and uncomfortable at that age.

"Renee loved Spanish and her teacher, Mrs. Linda C. Spanish in the 7th grade was her first language class."

In an interview with Mrs. Linda C, she described Renee: "I saw Renee as a very bright young lady who could be easily bored. In the classroom, she was quiet. If I asked her a question, she would respond. She had a good work ethic and applied what she knew."

Amazingly, Renee continued with Spanish throughout high school. The summer of her junior year of high school, she went to Spain with an Indiana University Honors Program. While in Spain, she was allowed to speak only Spanish for ten weeks. Maria, Jacqueline's mother, who was fluent in Spanish said, "Renee's diction and linguistic skills are excellent." Renee's Spanish came in handy later in her life when she was a police officer.

In my conversation with Mr. (Reverend Jim) and Mrs. Linda C, I mentioned that what people remembered most about Renee was that she made them laugh, sometimes hysterically. According to Reverend Jim, "That's because she understood irony and plays on words. Renee would notice irony and comment on it in a way that people found infectious. She was quietly influential with a depth and authenticity. Her humor was more British in that sense, understated and ironic, rather than slapstick and overstated."

Chapter 14

High School Years – Activities that Challenged and Enriched

The Lord your God has blessed you in all the work of your hands.
He has watched over your journey through this vast wilderness.
These forty years the Lord your God has been with you,
and you have not lacked anything. (Deuteronomy 2:7)
Renee grew during her high school years.
After I listened to the stories of those who knew her,
I knew what God meant by this scripture.
I began to realize how much God watched
over Renee here on earth.
I could trust Him with her destiny in eternal life.

Renee's high school years were filled to the brim with activities, more than I could imagine possible. That's why this chapter is filled to the brim! She simply signed up most of the time without any unnecessary (in her mind) conversations with us and proceeded. Amazingly, she always seemed to make time for everything and still keep up with her schoolwork.

Musical Activities

She was one of the first trumpets in the highest-level band and the first trumpet for the symphony orchestra at Pike High School. Pike High School had one of the best music programs in Indiana, with five bands and five symphony orchestras. In summers, Renee participated in band camps and the State Fair band competitions with the Pike Marching Band. As though this was not enough, her senior year, she was a trumpet player in the pit orchestra for the show choir.

In an interview with Mr. Ed S, the Pike symphony teacher and Mr. John M, the Pike band teacher, I learned more about Renee's life in the high school music world and about their philosophy of teaching.

Mr. John M: "Two words describe what I do with the band and individuals: ownership and passion. We tried to instill the ideas that 'this is a '*we*' not '*me*' telling you what to do.' Let's have the ownership – preparation and caring. That's critical.

"You have to practice and bring your best game to a rehearsal. One time, John B., band director at Indiana State University, told the Pike band, 'The purpose of going to rehearsal is to learn the roles of the other instruments. In other words, when you are playing in a band, you need to know, 'Do the clarinets have the most important line now? Maybe, as a trumpet player, I am background.' For that to work, everybody needs to bring their best preparation to the rehearsal.

"Passion is important. I love looking at little kids' eyes. In a rehearsal, I like to look at eyes because I can tell if somebody is *really* with me, *kind of* with me, or *not* with me at all. Renee watched like a hawk. I might be in a description or be using an analogy to convey what our purpose was with this particular passage. When scanning for eyes, Renee's eyes were right on me. I'll never forget her look because it had that brightness to it. She was taking this in and weighing what was being said and making it hers. When I was describing a phrase or how we might articulate something, she was one of the people I could count on that would be there – what we just talked about.

"So, passion and ownership for a musician and for somebody in life is important in whatever they do. I always tell all the students, 'I hope you play for the rest of your life! But if you don't, I want you to be the best at what you are doing because of your preparation along the way.'"

Mr. Ed S: "Renee was first trumpet for the symphony. I had her because Mr. John M would send over the best. Orchestra was voluntary. It wasn't a class. They came over once a week during class and one evening a week."

Mr. John M: "Yes, the kids were volunteering but I did not have to twist arms. Renee and the other students that went over to orchestra were getting huge edification as players in another ensemble. I didn't have to say 'come on.' Instead I said, 'I would like you, you, and you, as better players, to have the opportunity to do the symphony with Mr. Ed S.' They valued the opportunity."

Mr. Ed S: "The other advantage when the best trumpet players came over was that those left could not hide behind the leaders. 'Oh, oh, I better practice my part. She's not going to be there Tuesday.' As a band director that was good for the rest of his sections. Another advantage to the winds coming over voluntarily: 'It's sort of like being a grandparent, I could have fun with them, and I didn't have to give them a grade. It's like giving the kids back to the parent – Mr. John M.'"

Mr. John M: "We had the meat and potatoes in the wind band and the symphonic band."

Mr. Ed S: "I had Renee for two years in the symphony. Renee was in the top symphony and we went to state. We made a CD with all the kids' names on the CD, including Renee."

Karyl: "Was Renee first chair? She never talked about it."

Mr. Ed S: "Oh, yes, she was our first chair for trumpets."

Mr. John M: "She was a hero for us."

Mr. Ed S: "When Renee was a senior in high school with the Pike Red Symphony (the top symphony), they played the *Duke Ellington Medley* (from *Sophisticated Ladies*) by Duke Ellington and *Symphonic Reflections* by Andrew Lloyd Webber. Those are popular music, but to play *American Salute* by Morton Gould and

Night on Bald Mountain by Modest Mussorgsky is BIG TIME. These are major-league songs. If the Indianapolis Symphony were playing these songs, they would use the same sheet music as we used."

Karyl: "At the Indiana State School Music Association, the Pike Symphony Red (top concert orchestra) received a Superior Rating in Group 1. Best of all, the Pike Symphony Red qualified as one of the top eight orchestras in the State, the fourth time in the last five years. Wow! It was wonderful to have this caliber of opportunity with the symphony and wind bands! Well done, Mr. Ed S and Mr. John M."

Mr. John M: "All the music that we were playing with the wind band ensembles especially for finals or contest was that which would be played by upper-level collegiate groups or by professional caliber groups like the Dallas Wind Symphony.

"The other band activities year round kept the kids there for each other. Marching band, pep band, and the pit orchestra; all were voluntary. The kids were there for each other not because of a threat but because of a want and desire. Renee participated in summer marching band camp at St Joseph's College in Rensselaer, Indiana, about 90 miles northwest of Indianapolis. I required attendance at the band camp for those who participated in the state fair competition for marching bands. We were all there for each other. When you are together 24 hours a day, ownership and bonding occur. We worked hard. We played hard. Renee did both well!!!

"Renee played in the pit orchestra for the musical, *Secret Garden*. I chose the wind players who played in the pit orchestra. In the pit orchestra for this musical, there were only two trumpets, each with their own part."

The *Secret Garden* musical is based on a novel (1911) written by Frances Hodgson Burnett. Pulitzer Prize winner Marsha Norman wrote the musical's script and lyrics, with music by Lucy Simon. The musical first was played on Broadway in 1991. The setting for the story was in the early 20th century. Mary Lennox, a young English girl born and raised in the British Raj, loses her parents to a cholera outbreak in India. She is sent to live with relatives whom she had never met, in Yorkshire, England. Her uncle, hermit Archibald Craven, lives in a secluded manor. Since her Aunt Lily's death, Mary's uncle pushed away surviving loved ones leaving his bedridden son, Colin, alone. Mary discovers Aunt Lily's hidden garden overgrown with vines; she is determined to restore its beauty. Her own personality blossoms as she and a young gardener bring new life to this neglected garden, as well as to her sickly cousin and uncle.

Karyl: "So, Renee really was on her own."

Mr. Ed S: "Oh, yes. That was true in orchestra, too. There is only one on a part. The second trumpet player has something different."

Mr. John M: "In the orchestra, it's your baby. Unlike the band where you might have three people playing the first part."

Karyl: "Renee's second grade teacher said, 'Renee played *Taps* on Memorial Day at College Park. They lowered the lights when *Taps* was being played and tears came to our eyes. The adults were touched deeply.' So, I just wanted to be sure that was true."

Mr. John M: "Yes, that was true. She was one of my choices."

Karyl: "I remember one football game, 'I was amazed (shocked) when I saw Renee and you playing the Star Spangled Banner. Renee didn't mention that she was going to do that."

Mr. John M: "As I remember, it was inclement weather and I asked for volunteers."

Mr. Ed S: "You think it is an easy thing to play *Taps*. However, when there is pressure on, it is so easy to miss a note."

Mr. John M: "That's a passion and ownership thing. If you are playing *Taps* or the Star Spangled banner, it's just YOU."

Karyl: "Well, it was you (Mr. John M) and she…."

Mr. Ed S: "Still, what a great thing. If you miss a note, everybody knows it and it's so easy to do."

Mr. John M: "The truth is, with she and I playing, if she missed a note, you still would have heard it!"

Karyl: "What was your remembrance of her?"

Mr. Ed S: "Always solid and reliable. It's similar in sports and music. You do things over and over until they are right. You might do a musical passage a dozen times so you can almost do it in your sleep. Renee was always up for that with no complaints like, 'Oh, we've already done it three times.'"

Mr. John M: "That's part of the ownership thing. Passion is not enough. It's absolutely necessary but what are you willing to do to prepare *(own it!)?*"

Mr. Ed S: "Don't forget that Renee always looked like she was having fun!!!"

Karyl: "Well, she *did* have fun!!!"

Mr. John M: "Yes, that's part of her eyes."

Mr. Ed S: "That makes it fine, too, like if she ever did make a mistake, she was like, 'I'll get it next time.' Not that she did make a mistake, but when you have that kind of an attitude, it's not all cut-and-dry, super-serious."

Mr. John M: "You knew Renee was having a good time; that's also infectious to the rest of the group in a very positive way."

Boundary Waters Canoe Area Wilderness Trip in Minnesota

Mr. Ed S: "Renee liked challenges. She did. She went to the Boundary Waters Canoe Area (BWCA) Wilderness in Northern Minnesota with us. That was a challenge for the girls!

"The canoe trips were all my wife's idea. Several summers in a row, my wife arranged for thirty of her eighth-grade girls to go on a BWCA camping expedition in northern Minnesota. My students heard about it (I talked about it). So, one year, a bunch of my students wanted to go. We rode up to the BWCA on the bus with the eighth graders and then divided into our own group of nine including myself.

"The first night at the base camp, the Boundary Waters outfitters showed videos about the trip and how to treat the forest. They also showed us how to carry canoes. The first day, we paddled across the lake and then carried the canoes maybe two rods, or a quarter of a mile, to the next river and went back to get the backpacks. Then, we did the next river. That continued until we found a camping spot."

"Usually, the girls would go two or three to a canoe. A lot of times you are going through a lot of mud or up hills. The hardest thing would be carrying a sixty-pound back pack *and* the canoe. They didn't have to. They went back for their backpacks. They all had a wonderful time. They bonded well.

"After Renee's senior year, the girls asked to go back again. So, since my wife was done with Boundary Trips by then, we rented a van and seven of us did a second trip. Renee went back a second time.

"I would start the fire at 6:00 a.m. and at 7:00 a.m. I would awaken everyone. Then, as the girls were taking down their tents, I fixed breakfast. We had to be on the water by 8:00 a.m. It was a great experience."

Karyl: "What a team experience!"

Mr. Ed S: "Renee was a star…."

Karyl: "Meaning?"

Mr. Ed S: "Renee volunteered to carry one of the three canoes by herself over rough terrain to the next river. She was the *only one* who successfully portaged a canoe on her own. Sometimes, other girls would just pick up a couple of paddles and say, 'I am going to carry these.'"

"The girls cooked too. To the freeze-dried food from the out-fitter's base, you add water from the lake, mix it, warm it and presto…. it's lasagna! At home, you would just look at it and won-der, 'What is that?' But when you are out there, you are so hungry you don't care. By the fourth day lunch, when you are making a cheese sandwich and the cheese falls on the ground. You just pick it up and eat it….*no ten-second rules!*"

Karyl: "Did you have fun?"

Mr. Ed S: "I loved it! It was beautiful country. Those were fun summer adventures."

At the funeral visitation, Mr. Ed S. gave us the journal the girls wrote in each night while at the Boundary Waters. It was a very special gift that gave us great insight into the fun these girls had. Clearly, Renee and the other girls laughed a lot and had lots of fun in spite of tipping over canoes, getting wet, exploring islands.

The journal from the 1999 Boundary Waters trip documented the challenging five days. Each of the girls under pseudo names wrote in a daily journal. Renee used the nickname "Snapmouth."

"At the end of the first day, Snapmouth posted, 'I've never been canoeing before but I like it. The lakes are gorgeous and peaceful. The only rotten things about this trip so far are the bugs. The horseflies and mosquitoes are getting on my nerves! I'm not tired, even though we're supposed to be.'"

Some other journal posts gave an idea of the unique and awesome experiences these girls had:

"The first day is filled with 'Bugs, Bugs, Bugs,' mosquitos and horseflies" (Joy, Snapmouth, Tinkle). After miles of walking and portaging, even on the first days, several girls got blisters and "all of us drank lake water. Ewww!!! It tastes fine, but I can just imagine what's in it" (Cyclops, day one).

"No doubt the bugs are a real pain and they probably will continue. Today was fun, though! It was so fun and challenging at the same time. I probably lost five or so pounds today ... those portages make you so tired" (Tinkle, day one).

"I can't believe how great this trip has been so far. In just the first day, I am already learning important things like teamwork, patience, and the true meaning of hard work. I love being out here in this secluded beautiful place. There are some things, however, that don't please me too much. The mosquitos and horseflies await fresh blood coming out of the tents. That stinks!" (Nippy, day one).

"I am extremely worn out from today but I guess that means that we worked real hard. We canoed an estimated thirteen miles and had eight portages. The weather has been very nice but we all got a little bit too much sun. My face is so burned that I can't move it. It hurts to laugh or smile" (Tinkle, day two).

"Today, Erin and I went and visited three or four islands we discovered and named. I picked blueberry-type things (I think they were blueberries). The pictographs along the walls were interesting. The bugs weren't as bad today, but I still don't like them. More than anything else, though, I think I have gotten closer to everyone." (Snapmouth, day two).

"Today was an easy day but I had a pack on my back and tipped over into the water. All of my stuff (personal stuff) got wet and I got a nasty bruise." (Snapmouth, day three).

"When we got to our campsite, Erin, Jessi, Mary, Alice, Ashley J and I went exploring on an island that we called 'Ivy Island.' Everyone thought they got poison ivy but they didn't. Erin, Jessi and I stayed and got firewood while everyone else left. I love it here because there are almost no bugs!" (Snapmouth, day three).

"Mary gave me a back massage. Life is good now! I tried to sleep in the six-man tent but everyone kept sitting on me. I got smushed. Oh, well, things are going pretty good and I'm content." (Snapmouth, day three).

"I spent all day clowning with Mary and Erin! It was awesome! Mary and I canoed together a lot and we just couldn't stop laughing. Mary fell in the water twice. I tripped about a million times. I was in a canoe with Joy in a big long river full of beaver dams. Mary, Kristen, and Alice were almost across (over) one, when they tipped over. I don't think that I've laughed that hard in a long time. I was rollin'!!" (Snapmouth, day four).

"Joy and I did pretty well, actually. Later, we got to the last two lakes and they took forever! The wind was against us the entire way. I was not a happy camper! Finally, after a decade had passed by, we reached our campsite." (Snapmouth, day four).

"Then, we pulled the canoe up on land, put away our paddles and life jackets and got ready to rest. Oh – but guess what!! The wind was soooo darn strong that it picked up one of the canoes and threw it in the lake! We were shocked!" (Snapmouth, day four).

"After a couple of moments, we ran for life jackets, paddles and the other canoe. Erin took that time to try to swim after the canoe but Mr. Ed S called her back. Then, Erin, Mr. Ed S and I jumped in a canoe and proceeded to tip it over! We sat there splashing and laughing until we finally struggled out of the water. Mr. Ed S and I jumped back into the canoe (cautiously, this time) while Erin ran along the coast to the canoe" (Snapmouth, day four).

"When we finally paddled over to the canoe, we grabbed onto it and tried to drag it behind the other canoe. It didn't work. We were heading for the middle of the lake. So we paddled back to shore. Then we got out and decided to walk the canoes back to shore. Erin joined us and helped us drag them back to shore. We left the canoes in the woods so they wouldn't blow away. As it got dark, we all went in the big tent and bonded. It was a great week" (Snapmouth, day four).

"Today, we (Erin, Renee, Nippy, Mr. Ed S) got up and watched the sunrise. It was incredible! We broke camp and started off two hours later. We had two portages, one easy and one an endless river" (Snapmouth, day five).

"Today was a memorable one because it was our last day. Mr. Ed S woke Erin, Renee, and I up early so we could watch the sunrise. It was absolutely beautiful. The mist on the water had turned a light shade of pink as the sun's golden rays sliced through morning. I went back to the tent feeling that I experienced what few people experience. After three portages, ten, one hundred forty, and thirty rods, we arrived at the pickup destination. We were greeted with pops, a bus, and radio. We finally reached our cabin place and unloaded. I don't ever remember a shower feeling so good! The same with dry clothes" (Nippy, day five).

"Our wonderful teacher Mr. Ed S is a marvelous teacher and canoe guide. He was so patient with us this entire time and would always help us whether our canoe was tipping over or if we had a splinter. I want to thank him for this once-in-a-lifetime experience that I will never forget" (Tinkle, day five).

Thank you, Mr. Ed S, for sharing these very special memories of an incredibly wonderful week in the Boundary Waters made possible by you and your wife. God is good, all the time. And you are part of that goodness.

Mr. Ed S posted the following tribute on the Memorial site.

"We are all diminished without Renee with us; many of us were enriched by her too brief time with us. Ordinarily, a former teacher may reminisce about how Renee was a star trumpet player in a wonderful symphony at school, but Renee was far from ordinary.

"I have a large photo album in front of me with many pages of pictures of Renee and seven of her Pike sophomore classmates from the 1999 trip to the Minnesota Boundary Waters. There are pictures of her carrying a canoe, paddling across a lake, portaging across trails and beaver dams and generally loving nature. More importantly, there are many pictures of Renee with her friends which show their love for her and hers for them."

Extended Learning (EL) Classes

Renee was willing to do the work for all the Extended Learning classes and even completed nine Advance Placement college courses by the end of her senior year. Thankfully, she was with others who were up for the challenge of extra enrichment projects and debates or discussions at a deeper level.

Mrs. Mary Beth D, Renee's English teacher, posted on the Memorial tribute page, "I loved what Renee added to my English class many years ago at Pike High School. She had such a dry sense of humor and pleasant disposition. She was one of the finest writers in her graduating class."

Renee loved Mrs. Donna C's debate class where the youth learned debate strategies. They debated such topics as: "Which is better – a pen or a pencil?" and "Which is better – an elevator or escalator?" In fact, the following year, during a study hall, Renee volunteered to assist Mrs. Donna C in her debate class. Indeed, Renee mastered the language of debate and persuasion. We were not sure if this was for better or for worse, for us! I always thought she would have been a great lawyer. It seemed like she always had something to say and usually had the final word.

The interview with Mrs. Donna C was fascinating:

"Renee was an extremely happy young lady. Her mode of operation was 'Nothing bothers me, everything is great.' I am not always sure that it was. Different kiddos have different ways of reacting to the turmoil of the teenage years.

"Her mode of operation was 'I'm tougher than this. I know what I want to do.' She was determined to join the Air Force and be able to do the pull-ups necessary to get into the Academy. I can see her fighting for right over evil. She demonstrated this in her debate class.

"I taught many of the extended learning classes, both English and debate. In the EL program, the kids are finding their way, inquisitive, exposed to learning from an early age. The kids were sponges for knowledge although they did not have too much savvy in the world. That's why I spent more time explaining the innuendos in some of the literature like Shakespeare's.

"The way I taught depended upon the classes. It was not unusual to give the students an assignment to create an interpretation of the literature. They were asked, 'Do you have a different conclusion?' I gave the students a choice of videoing, writing, or creating music for the story. Not all the students did the same thing. A group of students could do a video and then change the ending. Some liked working with the camera, some being the boss *(there were lots of those!),* some acting. Most students in the EL program loathe group work. They don't want to listen to others or do what others suggest. They hated it!

"I do remember the video from the assignment related to Romeo and Juliet, one that Renee and her group completed (included Jacqueline and Joy). Their video was hysterical! They had such fun creating, improvising, and laughing. They loved doing it.

"In debate, my goal was for the kids to go into the real world with an ability to explore why they thought the way they did. They needed to get out of their own skin – neighborhood, race, country – to decide who was right or wrong thoughtfully."

"In English class, my goal was for the children to gain the skills to discern, analyze, and express themselves in a thoughtful manner. In literature, they learned how people see situations and express themselves, sometimes in the vernacular, not the best English but effective. When they read the literature, they were asked to reflect on 'How did you feel? Where were you stretched?

What did you learn from reading this?' So, Renee had the opportunity to analyze situations and find the language she needed to communicate effectively, to use what worked best. I was very fortunate to have her as a student."

The EL program with many competent and bright students may have been why Renee's life was marked by an endearing humbleness and ability to laugh at herself. Interestingly, Renee's ability to positively communicate with others became a hallmark characteristic of her 'customer service' when she worked at Arby's in high school, later at the bank, and as a downtown capitol police officer.

Soccer

Soccer dominated Renee's time and activities in high school. As a freshman, she made the first team and thereafter, she was "addicted." Renee's hand-eye coordination was remarkable and her love of running and love of team play with the other girls made soccer a perfect sport for her. Interestingly, her avid interest in soccer from five years old through high school became important in gaining acceptance to the Air Force Academy (AFA) in Colorado Springs.

During the spring of her senior year, she also played on a travel recreational team, the Indy Burn Team. The Indy Burn Team won the league. It seemed surreal as she finished her soccer career in high school.

Renee played indoor soccer with Kelly and Mandy. Their team was called the Fish and they each had a T-shirt with a fish in the center of the front.

Ron, the indoor soccer coach, shared a memory of Renee: "I was coaching one game and Renee kept running forward, wanting to play forward. I finally took her out of the game."

She asked, "Why did you take me out of the game?" I said, "Because you weren't listening." She said, "I want to go back in."

"No. When you can play defense where I have you, you can go back in." She didn't like that idea very well. She kept coming up, asking, "Can I go in?" "Can I go in?"

"Can you play where you are supposed to play?"

"Well...."

"Then, go sit down. Until you can do what you are asked to do, you are going to sit over there on the bench." She finally decided she could play where she was told to play.

Kelly played soccer with the Pike High School soccer team, and knew Renee well as a fellow soccer player. In an interview with her, she shared these insights:

"Renee was amazing. She had the biggest heart though she didn't always have the best foot skills. She wasn't necessarily the fastest, but you better believe she had the biggest heart of anybody on the team. Rick R, the coach, knew that about her. He would push her and challenge her because he knew that she had it in her. She would outrun all of us because she wanted to be sure she never lost her spot on the team.

"It was easy to lose your spot on the team because the freshmen coming in were always so good. Rick R would be very quick to pull you off the field if you weren't pulling your weight. Renee never talked back or got sassy with the coach like some of the girls did. She would just keep quiet and try that much harder.

"She did it. She kept her spot all four years on varsity. A lot of other girls didn't. It wasn't always because she was the most talented but it was because she had the biggest heart and the mindset to be on the team. She put forth the most effort; she wanted to be on that field more than anyone else. Yes, she was a champion."

Karyl: "Renee really loved soccer."

Kelly: "Yes, she did. Her head was always in the game at every practice. We would be over chatting about something; she was focused on that drill. You had better believe she would run you down for that ball. She wouldn't joke about it. She was always putting forth her best effort. So, she shined in soccer especially at Pike. The whole team respected her for that."

"The Pike High School soccer team was sectional champs in 2000, Renee's junior year. That was pretty cool especially because Pike was in a good division, playing some pretty big schools."

Working at Arby's

During the summer following her sophomore year in high school, Renee began working at an Arby's restaurant about two miles from our home on the northwest side of Indianapolis. She was eager to earn gas money so she could share a ride to high school with Mark. This was Mark's deal, "If you want to ride with me, you need to split the gas costs."

Lunch rush hours were Renee's favorite times to work. Renee loved the "bustling" activity. She was at her best in the midst of activity and even crises – efficient, organized and unflappable. She quietly organized everyone and the workflow, so much so that Arby's asked her to consider being an Assistant Manager.

Interestingly, the six simple principles taught to the Arby Team Members in their training program became a part of Renee's work ethic for the remainder of her life. These principles – dream big, work hard, get it done, play fair, have fun, and make a difference – were foundational for many of her young adult activities. They were integrated into her as a cadet at the AFA, co-manager of the Academy Prep School football team, manager of the AFA girls recreational softball team, bank teller, and police officer.

Friends in High School

Joy, a friend throughout most of junior high and high school, played a violin in the symphony. Both she and Renee went on the Boundary Waters Canoe Area Wilderness trip (northern Minnesota). As was already shared, this trip was steeped in fun, fun, fun and laughter.

In the Boundary Waters journal, Joy posted at the end of the first day: "Bugs, Bugs, Bugs! That plus sunscreen is an awful combination. Ouch! The scenery is beautiful! So peaceful. That uphill and downhill portage was awful! I thought I wouldn't survive. The next one was fun – the wood swamp thing. Tomorrow is going to be a long day."

On her third day, Joy posted: "Today was an easy day. We had a portage that was two rods. It was great! We saw Mrs. Ed S's group and they thought they saw a white-tailed giraffe. It was hilarious. I took a long nap! It felt sooo good! Dinner was good. The bugs were pretty bad."

On Joy's fourth day, she posted: "Today was a tough day. The wind was impossible. At one portage, I tried to get out of my canoe and another one was coming. I went over.

"It was really funny but I think I bruised my butt. When I got to the other side of the portage, I tried to hold a canoe in place and I slipped on my butt again. Then at lunch I was freezing because of the wind and I fell over a log. Again."

"We had to fight the wind the whole way home after canoeing through the beaver dams and watching Mary, Alice, and Kristin tip their canoe. When we finally got to the campsite, we pulled the canoes up and then one blew away! Mr. Ed S, Renee, and Erin went to chase it and they tripped! It was so funny. I took a short nap and felt good."

On the last day, Joy posted: "We broke camp after breakfast. Then, we had a short portage followed by an impossible one. It was 140 rods uphill and down. We all walked it three times. Luckily, I didn't have to carry a canoe. We had another short portage. Then we were back where we started last week. The van picked us up. Coke has never tasted so weird and good. We took showers (ahh!) and reloaded the bus. Everyone was signing pillowcases for each other. We are all sad that this trip is ending."

Renee was in her element with her friends. Laughter, fun, and adventure marked her many relationships. Joy shared many pictures and memories of Renee with her friends (Jacqueline, Melissa, Jenny M, Jessica H, Alicia, Courtney, Khadija, Daisy) hanging out together including Joy's 16th and 18th birthday parties and Jacqueline's 16th birthday party. Surprisingly, Renee went to four years of spring prom, mostly with friends. In her prom pictures, Renee was all dressed up and her hair was done.

According to Joy, "Renee always thought you enjoyed getting her dressed up for prom! She always looked gorgeous. She had fun, too. She told me all about it. I never cared to go myself. It is not common to go to prom all four years. Normally, Renee wore a soccer shirt and jeans."

On the back of one of the prom pictures given to Joy, Renee wrote: "Joy, Hey how's it going? I'm good. I had an awesome time at the prom. You should go next year! You have to make sure that you always are carefree and stress free. Almost impossible, I think, but life will be much more fun. We'll help each other out. Later, Renee"

According to Joy, "That summarizes what I thought of Renee, her perspective on life – always relaxed and having fun. Don't worry about the nitty gritty, just have fun!"

Chapter 15

Youth Ministry Activities

*May the God of hope fill you with all joy
and peace as you trust in him,
so that you may overflow with hope by the power
of the Holy Spirit. (Romans 15:13)
We were blessed to have a vibrant and active
youth ministry at our church.
As I visited with the youth leaders, I came
to fully realize that they shared
the richness of the Lord's jewels – Word,
wisdom, and principles for living.*

Don, a slender, soft-spoken pastor, was the lead youth pastor when Renee was in the junior and senior high youth ministries. He spoke quickly and succinctly while giving a compelling case for the relevance and excellence of the youth ministry activities.

Karyl: "First, share with me your responsibilities."

Don: "My responsibilities here at Traders Point Christian Church (TPCC) were threefold: (1) oversee the junior and senior high ministry; (2) help kids understand who Jesus Christ is and why; and (3) then help the kids grow in their relationship with Christ.

"Our ministry was very relational because we felt that relationships of people of faith can help. You need to know but you also need to see that one's walk with God is real. In other words, what we are asked to do in the Spirit, like overcoming flesh and overcoming temptation, needs to be seen. It can't be just discussed.

"One can read and study about the Holy Spirit but it needs to be what I call, 'fleshed out' with people to discover: Is this really true? Why is this better? Why does God challenge us this way when my flesh wants to do the opposite?

"Our youth needed encouragement through significant discussions. So, we broke down our ministry into smaller groups, like Brenda's D team group (seven girls in high school). Then the youth could have the types of relationships that allowed them to discuss and be encouraged to walk in the faith as opposed to walking in the 'flesh.' When I say 'flesh,' I mean walking in willing sin and the ways of the world.

"Brenda was a group leader for the girls. We did the groups on a gender basis because we felt that would allow the youth to be the most open, accountable, and authentic. The leader helped the girls understand the reasoning behind what God says.

"The Sunday-evening youth ministry was one aspect of my job. Another aspect was trying to get the students places to land that would make them uncomfortable. Renee participated in several of these activities. We wanted to challenge the youth to see the world differently and allow them to start practicing what they were learning.

"So, when Jesus says, 'It's better to serve the least of these,' the youth are being challenged to do that. In this part of the world – Pike and Zionsville High Schools – they are being challenged with worldly things. You can have material things but it doesn't mean that life is better with them.

"The youth, when physically serving the poor on a pretty regular basis or on a one-time basis, see 'Wow, these people without material blessings seem to experience peace and contentment more than the youth and I who have so much more.'

"I believe that as a follower of Christ, we have to stretch ourselves. In our U.S. culture, we do not know what poverty is. It is hard for us to understand that 90 percent of the world lives in poverty. We think everyone lives like us with clean bathrooms, running water, and food in our fridge. The statistics show that we are the 10 percent.

"So, in our student ministry, we take someone like Renee when she was sixteen and teach them how to walk with God, why to walk with God, how to worship God, how to love Him and how to help others see Him.

"At times, we had to get them out of the Zionsville and Pike areas. A short-term mission is an incredible way to see God work differently."

Mexico Mission Trip

Don continued to share about the mission trips. "So, Renee went with us on a Mexico mission trip, south of Tijuana. This was not a third-world country but it was the closest we could get for the cheapest price and still 'do good.' She got the satisfaction of helping people who were living in a shack with dirt floor. She was able to participate in building a concrete 11 x 22 house similar in size to a garage. But, for those who lived in the shack, this new house had two windows, a door, security, a shingled roof and was dry during the rainy season because they had a concrete slab instead of dirt.

"For example, when we arrived in Mexico, one of the houses was made from four garage doors nailed together with a tarp covering the top. When we were there, we never saw the husband because he was at work. We only saw the mom and two kids trying to survive."

"Renee worked with a team of high-school students. A team consisted of eighteen to twenty students with four or five adults, about twenty-five in total. They mixed, poured, and laid concrete by hand. They framed the house, framed the roof and did a stucco wall. Stucco walls worked better than dry wall because they were cooler. It was almost like a concrete mix over chicken wire.

"Renee dealt with a number of challenges each day. She camped on a rock quarry type, almost like a desert with forty (the smallest group) to seventy students. The youth were divided into three teams; Renee worked with one team for four days to build a house. She fixed her own breakfast, lunch, and dinner and slept in a tent. We had two gallons of water for showers – total for everyone."

"An eye opener for almost all our kids in Mexico was what we call 'the bathroom experience:'"

"'Hey Don, I have to go to the bathroom. Where is it?'"

"'It's right there …' It's usually a shack with hundreds of flies and really smelled bad. Usually, we would say, 'Take two pieces of toilet paper, stick them up your nose and go to the bathroom.'"

"If you talked to other kids that had gone, they said, 'Oh, yeah, I remember the banos' or they would say, 'After that, my body shut down and I did not go for a couple of days.'"

"I think, if Renee were here to tell you, she would say, 'That was humbling.'"

Don continued the story: "Each evening, we would sit down and debrief. 'What was your picture of the day? What did you see? What are you going to take from this?'"

"Usually, most of the kids at the end really appreciated the trip. They reflected and became more aware of those in need, the vulnerable. It was tough – you slept on rocks, but it was a refreshing, simple lifestyle – you lived out of a suitcase in a tent.

"We went to the homes and saw the families. Those who knew Spanish were able to cross the language barrier. They saw that the children were happy. The mom was incredibly thankful, grateful and at peace.

"For me, this was a huge teaching lesson when struggling with scripture that says, 'we will always have the poor among us' and sometimes the poor are better off than the rich. When you are poor and have to depend on God daily, that's actually a good place to be. But when you are affluent and 'busy,' you may not think of God nor take time to seek Him.

"The challenge that we have is 'no matter whether we are rich or poor, we have the ability to be content and happy.'

"One of the best things we did for our student ministry was get them out of the context they live in. Short-term missions provided that they would come back to their place of living fifty-one weeks of the year but for a week we were able to show them something different. Hopefully, it moved them later in life to see....”

Brooklyn Mission Trip

Don: “Our trip to Brooklyn was probably the hardest trip. It was the smallest trip – thirteen kids and five adults. I've taken up to 300 on a trip. It was tough because it was in an area totally different in context even though it was in the city. When you go from 100,000 in a county to 100,000 in a block, it's just a different dynamic. We were overconfident that we could reach and help these kids.

“Wow, this is urban, these kids are tough.”

In an interview with Ron and Marty, two of the adult sponsors, they vividly described the activities of that week.

Marty: “We went to work with the Brooklyn Boot Camp Metro Ministries in the church shuttle bus. Before we began our mission in Brooklyn, we went through a team building ropes course – high ropes. Then, we went to a house in Brooklyn in a Puerto Rican neighborhood.”

Ron: “As I was walking down the street, I noticed that some of the people were roasting something on a spit – some animal, probably a pig. It smelled good but I didn't eat it!

“We stayed in an old house across the street from a crack house. We slept in the basement next to a room that had cases and cases of candy. We were told, ‘If you see something on the pipes that looks like a fuzzy slipper, it's probably not a slipper and it's going to move. It's a rat!’

“Yes, there were rats on the pipes at night while we were sleeping there. They were huge, as big as a cat – gargantuan, the biggest I have ever seen. They had a tail ten to twelve inches long.”

Marty: “The ministry theme for the year was ‘Heroes of the Bible.’ On weekdays, the ministry went to the different neighborhoods and opened a panel truck that had costumes and sets for whatever theme they were doing that week.

"They had big speakers and sang songs, then gave the story of the Bible hero. After the main theme, they would play games or have little activities. The children sat on tarps; the girls sat on one tarp and the boys on the other. If one of the children misbehaved, they had to get off the tarp. If you weren't on the tarp at the end of the program, you did not get candy.

"The other thing we did was pass out flyers in the projects to invite the kids to the program on Saturday morning. That was in the gymnasium in that area. They would do the same program as during the weekdays, but a longer version of it. It was very strictly disciplined."

Ron: "There were probably a thousand children in that gym. Amazing."

"We went to the projects in these big tall high rises but you had to kick away the needles and the crack stuff. Someone from the ministry went with our kids to pass out flyers that invited them to the Saturday program.

"On Saturday, the buses would come. Kids came running out of these apartments. The five-year-old would be dragging a three-year-old with them. They rode the buses to the gym; then, the buses brought the kids back and dropped them off. The parents knew they would get their kids back.

"Then, we went to Times Square Church and on top of the Twin Towers. We weren't there a full week, but we did a lot!"

Spring Break/Retreat in Florida

Don: "Renee went with us for a weeklong retreat to Florida during Spring Break. Those goals were different. Our Spring Break trip was much like the weekly girls' discipleship with the High School D (Discipleship) team. These were the goals: (1) feed them spiritually; (2) refocus and spend concentrated time in God's Word; and (3) worship discussing the things of God."

"Normally, the kids do not get this extra discussion time in the rhythm of school and family. They may have only four hours once a week on Sunday night compared to the other hundreds of hours they are doing things. Here was the schedule during the spring break retreat:

- Wake up around 9:00 a.m., personal devotional in the morning;
- Before lunch, for forty-five minutes, concentrated teaching on a certain topic, just for girls, for guys, for juniors or for seniors;
- After lunch, 12:45 to 1:45 p.m., additional discussion time;
- Free time 2:00 to 5:00 p.m. – on the beach where they played volleyball or could go to the pool. We were 100 yards from the ocean;
- After dinner, worship time 7:00 to 9:00 p.m. We would worship, teach, then do something interactive that would prove the point of the teaching;
- Fun time from 9:00 to 11:00 or 11:30 p.m., we would do fun stuff such as rented go-cart places so the kids could enjoy just BEING there!
- Midnight, lights out in their dorms, girls with their sponsors and guys with their sponsors.

"The whole goal was to have the kids immersed in an encouraging place to wrestle with what we were learning, build some spiritual disciplines and provide a place where they could discuss and be encouraged to walk with Christ."

Sunday Evenings

"Sunday evenings first were geared around relationships. What I tried to do was give Renee an adult relationship where she could be mentored or discipled, if she wanted. The key was 'if she wanted.' That's when they will grow. We did not force the youth to be in small groups (participate in the D teams). We encouraged them because there are certain things we know. They will grow in their walk with Christ if:

- someone is reading the Word on a regular basis,
- they are moved to study the Word on their own,

- they talk with God and meet with others.

"It's not that hard. It's just that we have to put it into practice.

"So, we provided a place where – if Renee wanted to come – which she did and if she wanted to read and grow or listen to a topic we were discussing, she could discuss it honestly. The best place she could do that was in community with other girls and with a leader who could help disciple them.

"As a leader, I put more emphasis on training quality adults who met with the kids on a regular basis and helped them grow.

"Eighty percent of the kids will give up their faith when they come out of a student ministry and go to college for four years, then they may come back when they get married and have their first kid.

"We encouraged student-led worship because we wanted them to assume as much responsibility as possible. By the end of the first year, we had three worship teams rotating for the evenings. The main teaching, usually about 20 minutes, was done by myself, another pastor, or a gifted adult leader. Then we would use some time to apply the teaching in the smaller groups."

Karyl: "Do you remember anything specifically about Renee?"

Don: "What I remember was that she was fairly opinionated and strong, not in a bad, disrespectful way, but wanting to know truth, probably questioning.

"At first, I remember that Renee was tough to win over. Maybe that was an outer shell. Once she saw that 'I think you are for real,' then there were good questions. That's probably where Brenda came in. She could look at Brenda and see, 'Spiritually, she is the real deal. So, I will trust her. I will go to her house. I will listen to her.' But, it may have taken some time."

"She was fun-loving and enjoyed life."

Interview with two friends and youth leaders

I was fortunate to interview two of Renee's closest friends (Kelly and Mandy) who also participated in the Youth Ministry;

also Brenda and Marty, both youth leaders. Their memories and insights related to Renee were precious; it gave me a peek into her life with her friends and with the Lord.

Brenda worked with youth for many years and is incredibly knowledgeable about the Word; for years she also attended Bible Study Fellowship (BSF), an in-depth Bible Study of the Old and New Testament books of the Bible. Her practical knowledge and unflappable, upbeat, and positive personality were a blessing for the D team.

Karyl: "Tell me a little bit about the Sunday evening youth activities."

Brenda: "We had an all-youth group meeting with music, worship, and some kind of a skit from Don, the youth pastor. Then, we would break into our own small discipleship group. We would have some kind of life issue, consistent with the evening skit/program. The girls would discuss it using what they learned from the scriptures. Then, we would have prayer requests. We would ask, 'How can we pray for you? How can we help you be strong?'"

Karyl: "In the D teams, you studied the Bible. I remember Renee coming home talking about scriptures and the Bible. One time, I remember asking, 'How is Renee doing?' You said, 'She always asks the hard questions.'" (Kelly: "She always did.")

Brenda: "She would not jump up and answer questions. She would just sit back and you could tell she was thinking about everything. She was not going to swallow everything hook, line and sinker. She would question it sometimes, which was good."

Kelly: "She would really have to think it through and make sense of it. If she didn't, she would question it and push back a little."

Brenda: "She would definitely push back, but I would have to say, with respect. She was not gullible and would not say, 'OK, you are older and teaching the Bible, so I believe it.'"

Karyl: "I think this reality-based Bible study grounded Renee in scripture more than the average teenager in high school."

Brenda: "Yes. A lot of our purpose was to help the kids grow spiritually. We saw this much more out of the building than in the building. Don said this and Rick H said it a lot. 'What we did in the D teams was to prepare the kids to go out and put into practice what they learned.'"

Karyl: "Brenda, how did you prepare for the D team?"

Brenda: "Karen, one of my prayer warriors, encouraged me, 'Just keep one step ahead of the girls. That's all you need to do.' For example, for the study of the book of John, we had some topical questions and a deep study of culturally relevant questions and the Word. Bible Study Fellowship richly poured the Word into me. That's why I could pour the Word into the times with the girls."

Mandy: "One thing I remember from D team was that you, Brenda, always told us to remember to be 'Jesus with skin!'"

Karyl: "I really believe that our church had an important role in developing Renee's value system. I am sure our family did, too. But the activities of the youth groups – going on the youth mission trips, the prayers, discussions, friends and you, as leaders of the D team, had an important role in Renee's life. Thank you for all you did for these young women."

Brenda: "When Renee stood back, she was checking, too, to see if we were authentic (Mandy: "Yes"), which was really good. Howard, the previous lead pastor of our church, always said, 'Don't just believe what I am saying. Check and see what the Bible says.'

"I don't know what other youth groups were like. We obviously had a lot of fun and did crazy things, but I don't think we were 'shallow fluff.' (Both Mandy and Kelly: "NO!"). We didn't do 'fluff stuff.' Everything we did had a Biblical foundation."

Brenda: "I remember my hardest lesson was challenging the girls to pray out loud."

Kelly: "I remember this ... I remember where we were standing when you taught us how to pray out loud. (Brenda: "You do?") You were standing at the bottom of the stairs almost underneath the stair well. You said, 'Let's do it right now. You taught us to pray out loud!'"

Karyl: "Cool. I wondered, 'Is there something that happened in youth group that explains Renee's grounded faith?' We, from minute one, got Renee and Mark into Sunday school and the youth ministry activities. In fact, we chose TPCC because of their excellent youth ministry. But it had to be more than that."

Kelly: "We did a lot of hanging out, outside of church, in 'get-togethers' or unofficial parties. After the D team, we went somewhere all the time – our home, your basement, Mandy, Steak–n-Shake or something. The D team invited the youth leaders (Brenda and Marty), too!"

Karyl: "Did Renee go with you?"

Mandy and Kelly: "Oh, yes, oh, yes."

Marty: "No iPhones (Mandy and Kelly: "Nope"). It was great to see the close connection between the girls from as many as six different high schools. Most of the girls went to Pike High School."

Spiritual Happening Week

Renee's freshman year, the youth participated in something called 'Spiritual Happening Week.' Kelly said, "I loved it!" Mandy's perspective was, "It was awesome."

Brenda: "This was another one of those 'Outside of the Walls' activities. We stayed at somebody else's house. We just lived there for a week during school."

Marty: "We got up and had the same responsibilities as a family (Mandy: "Like cook or clean up breakfast."). We worshipped and had Bible Study and great speakers. The coordination of getting everyone to their different schools was the biggest logistical problem."

Brenda: "Rick H started this many years ago. The idea was that we would get the kids together after school, almost like a retreat. Then, when they went back to school the next day, they would be talking to their friends, 'Oh, we are doing this and we are doing that.' It was a witnessing tool as much as a discipleship tool. The coolest thing was that after school, we had two rooms that were all-homework rooms – the dining room and the living room."

Kelly: "Yeh, snacks and homework. We would have to clean up after each other."

Mandy: "It was very intentional. It wasn't like we were just 'hanging out.'"

Brenda: "Very intentional, like Spring Break or Mission trips!"

Kelly: "Each night we would gather in the living room for worship. Someone would lead worship and give a message, related to the theme for the week."

Other Youth Trips

Another trip that consisted of youth from three churches, including TPCC, was a ski trip to Colorado. Renee, Kelly and Mandy all went on this trip. The weather was terrible, freezing cold with fifty mile-per-hour winds.

Kelly: "We went down the bunny hill first and then rode the ski lift to the top. An ice storm hit. As soon as we got to the top, everything was frozen over. It was awful getting down! Mandy could ski; I couldn't ski. I was probably on my rear end most of the time.

"Renee was one of the few snowboarders but she hung with us. She was a good snowboarder."

One of the Youth Sponsors posted on Renee's tribute page, "Renee was always so sweet and kind in the Youth Group and had such a peacefulness about her. Although I didn't see her much after high school, I did have a chance to catch up with her at a wedding. I am in awe of all she had accomplished in such a short span of time and also that she remained such a sweet spirit."

Chapter 16

Reaching Out to
A Young Man

*Then the righteous will answer him, 'Lord, when did we see
you hungry and feed you, or thirsty and give you something to
drink? When did we see you a stranger and invite you in, or
needing clothes and clothe you? When did we see you sick or in
prison and go to visit you?' The King (Lord) will reply, 'Truly I
tell you, whatever you did for one of the least of these brothers
and sisters of mine, you did for me.' (Mathew 25:37-40)
Renee demonstrated how to love all of mankind
without fear, pride, or selfish ambition.*

The Lord works in amazing ways. We prayed and prayed
for Renee's protection and deliverance from harm or evil –
drugs, unhealthy relationships, and friends, all of the pulls
of peers and the world. We always met the parents of her friends
and kept close tabs on where Renee was, who she was with or
what she was doing. Renee was not always happy about this. Only
later did I realize that Renee, as a young adult, was really glad
for this.

Gene listened to Renee and tended to give Renee what she
negotiated for, such as a pool table for one birthday. That was a
pretty big gift. In retrospect, the pool table was a blessing. All her
friends came to our house to play pool, so we knew where she was

and who she was with. Again, we saw an answer to our prayers for her safety and blessings with friends.

Well, one friend that Renee met on the soccer field was Yves. He played boys' soccer in high school and was really, really good. Yves, his father, and his brother were refugees from Haiti. They landed in Florida with nothing but the clothes on their backs. They left Haiti in the fall of 1991 to avoid the political turmoil of that country. According to the father, "Yves' mother and two of his brothers were killed for supporting a pro-democratic government."

In September 1991, a surprise coup in Haiti overthrew the first democratically elected President of Haiti, Jean-Bertrand Aristide, triggering a flood of refugees. Within six months of the coup, the U.S. Coast Guard intercepted more than 38,000 Haitians at sea; 10,747 were eventually allowed to pursue asylum claims in the United States following screening by immigration officials on board the ships or at the US naval base at Guantanamo Bay (https:// www.hrw.org/reports/1992/WR92/AMW2.htm, pages 1-2).

In the aftermath of the coup, Haitian troops killed at least three hundred and maybe as many as one thousand civilians in random shootings and targeted massacres of residents in impoverished neighborhoods suspected of being supporters of President Aristide (https://www.hrw.org/reports/1992/WR92/ AMW2.htm, page 2).

North United Methodist Church sponsored Yves's father, Yves, and his brother as they settled in Indianapolis in 1992. Praise the Lord for the alive and active faith of those on the United Methodist Mission Committee. They walked many miles with this family and assisted them in obtaining permanent residence, learning English as a second language and obtaining housing, schooling, and work. In the first years, the church provided a stipend to assist with housing and some living expenses.

Since one of our hard-and-fast rules was to meet and know the parents of all of Renee's friends, we met Yves's father, Andre. Yves's family lived in a very modest, humble apartment. When we were visiting with Andre, he pulled a book off a shelf titled, *75th Anniversary of the North United Methodist Church* and showed us a photo of him and his two sons. As he was turning the pages to find the picture, I noticed a picture of Gene and me with Anna Lee, the pastor's wife, teaching the two-year-old children. Surprise of the century!

Indeed, we even knew several of the parishioners who were assisting Yves's family. Before moving, we were actively involved in the Mission Committee of the church. The Lord works in amazing ways. As I learned later, the members of the mission committee were praying for this family's adjustment, integration into the American way of life and healthy relationships for Yves and his family. In retrospect, we realized that perhaps Renee was an 'earth angel' in Yves's life and an answer to their prayers.

In many ways, Yves and his father were not accustomed to the culture and life in America, even though Yves was a great soccer player. Renee's friendship with Yves spanned eight years through the last years of high school and several afterwards.

When Yves's family came to Indianapolis from Haiti, they entered a vastly different world. Yves's father did not understand English; neither did Yves or his brother. They had to learn a new language, develop new relationships and friends, and learn all new ways of living.

Renee helped Yves realize the importance of completing high school in a preparatory school and gaining entrance into college. These were big steps for Yves. During Yves's high-school years, Renee urged him to obtain a driver's license and learn to drive. While she was working as a bank teller at Charter Bank, she encouraged Yves to apply for a bank-teller's position.

Only years later did I realize the significance of Renee's friendship and the impact she had in Yves's life. The documentary film 'Lost Boys of Sudan,' shown by the Leadership in Adolescent Health Program at Indiana University, vividly chronicled how difficult it was for the Lost Boys of Sudan to acculturate into the American way of life. They entered into an incredibly different world from the Sudan. This film opened my eyes to how much they had to learn: living in a "house" when they were used to huts or minimal shelter, learning to live and work together in a city, learning to work for money, budget and buy food for sustenance, learning to drive and buy an automobile and finally, understanding the cultural values and unspoken rules of relationships.

It was astonishing to realize how the Lord used Renee in reaching out to Yves. Yes. I realized that the sponsorship of North United Methodist Church and Renee did more for Yves, with healthy, positive relationships than lots of money and some social-service programs could do. Wow!

God is good. Renee was a divine gift. For us, the biggest blessing was coming to realize the full significance of Renee's gifts of compassion, caring, and non-judgmental attitude.

Renee was thrilled to watch this young man come from a guy who loved soccer to one who had a banking career. Amazingly, he continued his banking career as a loan officer several years through the extremely challenging downturn of the market (2008) without losing his job.

I watched Renee experience God's sacrificial giving and care through her friendship with Yves. It was such a blessing to realize how God worked through all those years that I was concerned about her. God works through people in amazing and unbelievable ways! His agenda is not ours. Only when we get to heaven will we fully know all the ways God has been working. I can hardly wait! Wow. It is so exciting to realize Renee's impact in retrospect. Indeed, it is more blessed to give than to receive.

After Renee's funeral, I visited with Yves who shared, "Renee helped me become a responsible young adult, urged me to complete high school and enter college, encouraged me to read the Bible and even recommended me for a bank-teller position in the Charter Bank. When I learned of her passing, I was so upset I had to leave work."

In a later interview, Yves shared more about his relationship with Renee.

Karyl: "So, let's shift back in time. How did you meet Renee originally?"

Yves: "In school, we both played soccer. I was always quiet. Renee would talk to me. It's one of those things, when you don't talk much; you find few friends take interest. We became friends through soccer practices and seeing each other in the halls at school."

Karyl: "What do you remember about her?"

Yves: "She was very free-spirited and always wanted to do things. I wouldn't say stubborn, but she wanted to do things the way she wanted to do them. She was very smart and stood for people when things were not right.

"That was one thing about her, if someone did something she did not agree with, she would say something. That is important. You don't find a lot of people like that. She would go out of her way to make people feel comfortable. She was well-liked by a lot of people in high school because she always was a caring person."

Karyl: "Interesting that you say, 'She was well-liked.'"

Yves: "Yes, well-liked by people who played sports and people who didn't, just every-day students."

"She did well. She played an instrument and played a sport so she had friends on both sides of the aisle, academics to sports. She got along with everybody. It's rare that you find someone who gets along with almost everyone."

Karyl: "So, as she got to know you, I know she had lots of conversations, ones encouraging you and helping you with school."

Yves: "She tried to encourage me with school because, when at Pike, all I cared about was playing soccer. That encouragement – to do the best that I could – helped. I wish I had listened better.

"She tried her best to guide me a little bit because I had a lot of things I was stubborn and stupid about. She knew a lot better. When she was at Purdue, I went there a couple of months to clear my head because I had a very nasty breakup. I could always depend upon Renee."

Karyl: "So, talk a little more about Renee. I think Renee encouraged you to get a driver's license."

Yves: "Yes, she did. I didn't get one until I was a little older because my dad never drove. It was a different process. Yes. She encouraged me. Eventually, I did it.

"She was encouraging in a lot of ways – in high school and as we got older in college – to make myself better in school, to make myself better in a lot of ways. That was very beneficial. That was very helpful."

Karyl: "I remember you were at Purdue. You helped her a lot."

Yves: "She was going through a tough time at that time. We both were. We both were friends for a long time and we both went through tough times."

Karyl: "Tell me about other things you remember about Renee."

Yves: "When you spend so much time with a person, it's a lot of details that become part of that person's personality. And, for Renee – Renee was Renee! She was honest. She would tell you the truth. She wasn't good at beating around the bush – not in a mean or cruel way – but she would tell you the truth.

"We were like all teenagers, trying to grow up, doing the best we could. I think she had it figured out better than a lot of us did. She made sure she studied and did what she liked. Music was important to her, too."

Karyl: "If I had something to say relative to you, what is it that you would want me to say?"

Yves: "I think Renee was more of a mother figure. To be honest with you, since my mother died when I was a very young kid, Renee was that kind of a person – with a kick in the behind when it really was needed. That's who she was."

Chapter 17

Off to See the World

Have I not commanded you? Be strong and courageous.
Do not be afraid; do not be discouraged, for the Lord your
God will be with you wherever you go. (Joshua 1:9)
Renee was strong and full of courage; her
inner peace was from heaven.

O ff to see the World. Yes. That was Renee. She wanted to see everything, first hand, fresh and fabulous, living full out. Renee wanted to see all seven of the Wonders of the World before she was 30 years old. That seemed pretty out of the box, for a young lady just beginning her college and career.

When Renee was a junior in high school, a career counselor evaluated her interests and abilities with a 500-question tool. The only other information Renee gave him was that she was a junior in high school. No grades. No discussion regarding interests. At Renee's follow-up visit, when she was coming into his office, the counselor saluted Renee as an officer in the military. She looked confused – dumbfounded. The counselor said, "Your personality and interest profile matches those in the military or police officers."

Gene and I were shocked. We both are scientists; this was out of our realm of reality. It was hard to fathom a military or police career for our bright, charismatic young daughter.

With Renee, we explored various military options – fast, since many of the college decisions had to be made the next fall. Renee was planning to attend Purdue University, participate in the band and continue some of her Spanish studies. She passed the tests that would allow her to skip the first two years of Spanish courses at Purdue.

Now what? How was Renee to pursue a military career? Renee decided to check out West Point Academy (army) and the Air Force Academy. As a non-military family, we knew almost nothing about military life. That fall, we scrambled to learn eligibility requirements and visit the academies.

Big-time prayers went up to the Lord for divine guidance in navigating this new territory. Thankfully, we met an academy counselor, someone from the Air Force Academy, who coached Renee regarding what to do. Pass the physicals. Pass the fitness test. Submit an application with academic information and lots of information about Renee's sports activities.

Academically, Renee was quite eligible (thirty-two of thirty-six on the ACT [American College Testing] Exam). She participated in the Extended Learning Program (Gifted and Talented Program) for Pike Township Schools from the second grade through high school and completed nine Advanced Placement college courses in high school. She was a starter for the women's soccer team early in her high school years; she was perfectly cast for soccer. She loved to run and, especially, be in a team sport that encouraged and supported one another. We visited the Air Force Academy and learned about the culture and expectations. The Admissions Coordinator was very interested in Renee and very forthright about the admissions process. Renee always was up for a challenge.

We just kept praying that if this were what Renee was to do, she would be accepted into an academy or military program at a university. When we visited West Point, the Admissions Coordinator misread her transcripts and almost dismissed her. Perhaps that was a sign from the Lord. She ate lunch with one of the sophomore cadets who was 'called out' during the meal; both left without finishing lunch. Renee also was possibly interested in pursuing soccer but the West Point soccer team already was set. All in all, this was a very disheartening trip for Renee. Perhaps the Lord sent angels to tell Renee this was not the place for her.

Renee was inspired by her visit at the Air Force Academy and decided she would apply there. Senator Lugar and Congressman Burton from Indiana interviewed Renee for the Air Force Academy. She passed the physicals and was nominated for an Academy appointment. Unbelievably, Renee sprained an ankle in a spring soccer game so she was unable to complete her fitness tests until June. Finally, she completed the fitness tests with one deficit, not enough upper body pull-ups and submitted her application due June 30.

Very exciting news! Renee was accepted for the Air Force Academy Preparatory School to pass the upper body pull-ups. Shortly after beginning, the prep school asked her to become a tutor for other cadets with their science and math courses. She was more than happy to assist her fellow students.

As parents, we did everything we knew to support Renee during Basic Training, both at the Air Force Academy Preparatory School and at the Academy. We sent many letters of encouragement during Basic Training. We were available for precious one to two-minute calls from Renee once a week. We came for the Parent's weekend with an Academy Football game and met her friends' parents.

On the day we were unloading Renee at the Academy Preparatory School, thankfully we met a family who loved the Lord and generously shared their faith, their walk in the military, and the blessing of their friendship. The father was a colonel in the Air Force and the mother was a nurse, both with incredible testimonies and great family relationships.

We cherished the time with Renee in Colorado Springs. With permission, we brought Renee and a few friends off base for supper at Texas Road House. These were really fun times of sharing, meeting her friends and hearing about the life at the Academy. Pretty amazing! Thankfully, Renee had really wonderful friends, two of whom had much more background in military culture than Renee.

Renee completed the prep school with academic honors, passed the fitness test and became familiar with Academy/military expectations. On to the Air Force Academy the next year.

The Academy was rigorous and demanding. Renee passed Basic Training with flying colors. This was her second Basic Training; the first was at the Air Force Academy Prep School. The inspections were numerous and the course work demanding but doable for Renee. She eventually chose a major in Foreign Affairs.

Many of the Academy courses were memorable. She became a sharp-shooter. One course in "Survival" included several days in the wilderness, in the midst of snow with little, if any, food provided. On one of the days, only a baby rabbit was provided for food. Oh, no...not that! The thought of eating this little rabbit was painful for Renee. Another was a parachuting course. Renee said, "I'm going first, then I do not have to watch everyone else jump!" She did several jumps and finally, at the end of the course, she said, "That's enough for me."

The swimming course was like "falling off a log" for Renee. She passed the swimming and water survival evaluation the first day of her swimming class. According to Renee, "I swam two lengths of the pool underwater with a heavy backpack, heavy clothes and heavy boots. The only other person who passed the survival on the first day was a six-foot-tall cadet." No easy feat.

She joined the Air Force Academy Bands, playing the trumpet for Academy basketball games. During the fall, Renee was chosen by the flag team to be one of the leaders of that team for the football games. Little did I imagine that Renee would ever use the essentials taught in our baton twirling lessons during an early school year. God is good and uses everything!

Renee was the Manager for the recreational Girls' fast-pitch softball team at the Academy during her sophomore year. Additionally, one year Renee was assigned to provide leadership for the cadet team who hosted Vice President Dick Cheney when he came to give the inaugural address for graduating seniors. He wrote an email letter thanking Renee and the hosting team for their excellent service during his visit to the Academy.

The 911 attack by terrorists occurred during Renee's tenure at the Academy. The entire Academy was shut down with only very limited access that year. Renee received one of the coins that were minted and distributed at the Academy acknowledging this event. She was thrilled to have it. Evidently, the cadets collect these coins, given only for special occasions.

One summer during her Academy training, Renee was assigned to Guam. That was perfect for Renee. In addition to an introduction to military tactics and life on oversea assignments, she learned to scuba-dive in open water and was able to ride a water buffalo. Scuba-diving became so important to Renee that she convinced Mark, her brother, to take scuba-diving lessons so they could go to Curaçao and dive together.

Eventually, Renee decided that military service was not her mission and withdrew from the Academy. Renee had learned many lessons and skills that many older adults never learn. She learned to salute and march, to follow orders and to be totally aware of her surroundings. She learned the value of teamwork and supporting one another. Most of all, she came from a rather naïve understanding of what it means to "defend our country" to a much more realistic, practical reality of the importance of integrity, leadership, and working together. She learned much about herself through the Basic Training and her values, which were consistent with the Academy values – integrity first, service before self and excellence in all we do.

Renee still had her earlier goal in mind – to see the Seven Wonders of the World. During the Christmas holiday 2009, she and Jacqueline toured Machu Picchu (Peru), one of the seven wonders. Jacqueline was a long-time friend, over twenty years, through thick and thin. At this time, Jacqueline was back at Notre Dame, earning a Master's of Business and Law degrees. In their travels to Peru, Renee and Jacqueline were not concerned about safety. "We will be careful," they insisted. As parents, Gene and

I were concerned about the many possible dangers for two young women travelling alone in a foreign country. Yes. Both Jacqueline and Renee knew fluent Spanish from their eight-week course in Spain, when they could only speak Spanish with host families.

Chapter 18

The Funeral Week - Walking in a Daze

One who has unreliable friends soon comes to ruin,
but there is a friend who sticks closer than
a brother. (Proverbs 18:24)
Jesus knew the love and strength of a friend. I am so thankful
for His friendship and the earthly angels (friends) He
provided. God SHOUTS from heaven through a friends love!

Numb. Unable to process all that needed done this week. Stunned was the word.

"Now what? How are we going to get through this week? What do we need to do? Where will we put the body to rest? Who will assist with the funeral? We had to decide immediately so the funeral home could take the body to the morgue to be embalmed. We had never even thought about, let alone discussed, a gravesite and cemetery or funeral home. What about an honor service, similar to the one the police do for fallen troopers? Then, there was the obituary. The obituary was really important to us. We wanted to honor Renee with a wonderful, accurate obituary, one that was available for genealogical searches. Gene's mother and Gene spent ten years searching for the roots of the Rickard family history.

Later in the evening of Renee's passing, Maria and Jacqueline came to our home; Mark and Rorie arrived from Michigan. This was an incredibly difficult time – searching for names of people to call, figuring out what to do next, trying to understand what just had happened. Our dear Renee was not with us. My head throbbed. My heart was torn in two. Nothing made sense.

All I can remember was that a guy friend of Renee kept texting her iPhone. Finally, I said, "Someone needs to respond to this text."

The time just slipped away until finally we went to bed very late. The tears started flowing down my cheeks, not sobbing tears. Tears of deep, deep sadness – a broken heart. "Oh, Lord, this does not work. I need rest. I want to be able to function and do what is needed tomorrow."

I did not sleep at all. Finally, at 4:00 a.m. I got up and started walking and talking with the Lord. The night was eerie, pitch black with only a few stars visible and a street light on the corner of the street. Walking and talking to the Lord was something I have always done. In younger years, it was jogging and talking to the Lord, often first thing in the morning. So, getting up early in the morning was not unusual. But, getting up soooo early was very unusual.

That first morning, I brought more than my usual concerns with less of 'me' present to the Lord. I was exhausted, tired, numb, and unable to process my thoughts. I was not able to figure out what to do next. Most of all, I felt as though my heart had broken, my brain had stopped and I was just going through the motions of walking and talking. What if I was not able to get it all together tomorrow for the funeral director's meeting? Millions of questions with no answers raced through my mind.

Then, as the sun began to rise, I prayed with a dear prayer warrior and friend, Deb. True to the Lord's faithfulness, I felt a sense of clearing and peace come over me as we prayed. There was a miraculous clearing when I knew indeed that Renee was in heaven with Granny Mary, "playing" and having fun. But, oh, how I missed her. My deep, deep sadness was that I would not have more special times on earth with her; but I knew Renee was in good hands – she was fine.

The Lord was there with us during the first day of her passing and the week of the funeral. The prayers of our faithful friends in the Bible Study group and church were with us. They were praying – knocking on heaven's door – beyond anything we had ever known. The Lord's presence became very real.

We were left in shambles. Gently and lovingly, the Lord helped us pick up the pieces. The Lord's presence seemed like a miracle of gigantic magnitude. Miraculously, we could find the Lord, see the Lord, and know the Lord's presence in each moment of the funeral week. Oh, how we needed His amazing love as we floated through the week. I felt like I was in another world and literally being carried through the week.

As we walked this journey, I knew we did not walk it alone. God's presence was with us, as were so many good friends. What I saw from my limited perspective did not begin to encompass how the Lord was working behind the scenes. To me, this seemed stunning and amazing. Four of my closest friends shared their account of that day.

Ann's Version of the First Day

Ann was a retired nurse, one who was caring, compassionate and insightful. Through the Holy Spirit, she had an intimate personal relationship with the Lord, something we all need.

Ann, my close friend from our nurture group, relayed her story:

"That fateful Sunday morning, we greeted Gene at the 9:00 a.m. church service. He had just returned from Colorado, shared a little bit about his trip and that you were working with Deb. It was a light-hearted conversation.

"I said, 'We are glad you are back. Sorry to hear that Karyl is at work.'

"We shared our concerns about the mother of another dear friend in Christ, Eileen. I remember us standing at the doors to the sanctuary, saying 'Good-bye,' with no thought about what was to come.

"Before that morning, the Lord had said to me, 'Clear your schedule for the week.'"

"'OK, Lord.' The Lord made it very clear. This was not just a suggestion. It was a very direct command. I had no idea why. On that Sunday, I thought *Maybe this is for Eileen's mom.*"

"You called. With a broken and tense voice you said, 'Pray for Renee. She collapsed. They are taking her to St. Vincent by ambulance.'"

"I knew from my nursing experience that this was serious. Something in my spirit confirmed 'This is *really* serious.' A lump or knot came into the pit of my stomach. I broke out in a cold sweat.

"I immediately got down on the carpet on my hands and knees and put my face in the carpet. With all the intensity I could muster, I called upon the Lord, beseeching him to be with Renee, heal her and care for her. I knew my job was to pray until I heard more.

"You called a second time and said, 'They are working on Renee.' Again, I got down on all fours, face down and prayed. I knew it was extremely serious.

"Before you called a third time, I felt God release me from praying. I had no idea what His answer was to my prayers. I still wanted to know what happened. Rog, my white-haired husband of more than thirty years, knew I had gotten up from my prayers. The knot in the pit of my stomach stayed until you called and said, 'Renee did not make it.'

"After you called, I grabbed my purse and Bible and ran into Rog's office. 'Renee has gone home to Jesus. We have to go now,' I said.

"We drove quickly, in less than twenty minutes, to the Emergency Room, told the receptionist in a desperate voice, 'We are here for Renee,' and hit the metal button to open the swinging ER doors. Surprisingly, the ER was empty, except for you with Renee. Not another soul came in for emergency care the rest of that afternoon.

"The kind ER nurse, the one who was tall and had long dark brown hair, ushered us into the examining room with you, Gene, the chaplain and Renee.

"I saw the Holy Spirit hovering over you and Renee from the moment we went into the room. I recognized the Holy Spirit's presence because of my experiences in praying with some of my patients, ones who asked for prayer. We were not abandoned.

"The hospital chaplain and three others – Eileen, her husband Duane and Barb B – were in the room with you. They were all members of our Nurture Group. Everyone in the room with Renee prayed. Each prayer, forty-five seconds to a minute, was as beautiful and individual as the next. The prayers came from deep within each pulsing heart; they were not wooden or rote.

"People were continually coming and staying. Only a few were leaving. Our friends were all shocked, stunned, very sobered and subdued at the horror of losing your daughter. The scene in the ER was not what I would call emotional, with sobbing and hysteria. I was aware, though, that since almost all had children, there was a palpable feeling...'This could have been mine.'

"The atmosphere was very reverent, very hushed and grave. There was no chit-chat. People got that Renee really had passed on. After coming into the room with you and Renee, groups of two or three gathered and prayed in the ER waiting room. Everyone was in prayer; no one had to ask for prayers. They prayed fervently. They prayed for strength. They prayed for comfort. They prayed for God's love and presence.

"We held hands and went around in the circle that circled Renee's gurney and we prayed. Everyone's prayer was special.

"It wasn't a searching for words. We were crying out to God. The prayers all made sense. We were all connected in one prayer, lifting each other up, lifting you and Gene up."

In a voice that was choking up and with tears gently streaming down her cheeks, Ann added, "It was the unity of believers, in action, in real time...

"I remember how composed you were. You had a sober, quiet bearing, a calm demeanor, just as if you were doing what the Lord had called you to do. I knew it was the Lord's presence. I could see that the Lord was with you."

"I was reminded of one of my patients, one receiving acupuncture for pain management. I vividly remember her husband pointing to her saying, 'Looky... Looky there, Martha. She's got the Lord. She does not have to say anything. Look at her face.'

"I have seen the same thing in my country church with women who were the salt of the earth and not necessarily educated. When tragedy struck, they had that the same kind of calm, Holy-Spirit infused demeanor. It truly is a gift of the Holy Spirit. When you are in it, you don't see it.

"You looked purposeful. I took that as a direct answer from God Almighty.

"You were not alone. Not only did you have people praying for you, but also you had the Holy Spirit carrying you along, lifting you up above the paralyzing tragedy of losing your daughter.

"You and Gene were in the ER side room with Renee for what seemed a long time, maybe four hours, waiting for the pathologist and Reverend Jim.

"Around 5:00 p.m., we were ushered to a larger area that fits twenty or more. It was over-flowing, with people standing in the hall. For some of our friends who came early in the afternoon, that was several hours of incredible prayer.

"As a nurse, I focused on getting you fed. You had not eaten for more than eighteen hours. As ridiculous as it sounds, I could not find a dining room that served food that afternoon. That's a 'bone in my craw' – no food for a patient or family, ones who may come from a long distance. The only food was in vending machines. You ate the fruit salad and a little of the grilled chicken on the salad. You said, 'I am not hungry. I cannot eat any more.'

"God was still there. I kept seeing His answers...even though Renee was not there...although she may have been present in Spirit. We will not know until we get to heaven. That veil is so thin, a very thin veil between earth and heaven. At times, you just know. It seemed like heaven on earth, especially as I heard the many prayers and friends who were united as 'One in the Lord.'"

In Ann's words, "God knew that I needed to be free the entire week and even the following weekend. It was like God was just there. It was okay; I didn't miss a thing. I was supposed to do this. My husband, Rog, also knew that and supported me."

When Ann asked me, I had to say that I never felt anger. I am not sure why. Perhaps, it was because the Lord loves me and supernaturally protected me. God was *sooo* good. Looking back, I saw that it was the prayers of our friends and the peace of Christ that carried us through the afternoon. I was supernaturally loved and protected from layers of emotions way too much to burst wide open all at once. I was once again looking down from above... observing distantly, not able to access my emotions, but able to do what was needed.

Barb B's Version of the First Day

"I thought Renee had fainted. Someone from our small Bible Study called and said, 'Renee is on the way to the hospital.' I dropped everything to go to the hospital to support you.

"When I got there, she was already gone, just gone... I had to call Rick H and tell him she had passed. I ran into a closet since there were so many people everywhere and called Rick H. (Rick H was your neighbor and the youth pastor who baptized Renee. Rick H's children and yours grew up playing together.) He freaked out, just in shock, 'What, what, what...Renee Rickard!?' ... He dropped everything he was doing and came to the hospital.

"First, you and I held hands touching her forehead – your right hand, my left resting on her forehead. She had an intubation tube in her mouth. I was praying over her...everyone was.

"I remember when Brian (my husband) showed up at the hospital, after an hour of driving to get there. You and I were praying. The room was filled with people praying. Both Brian and I wanted to see God supernaturally raise Renee from the dead. I wondered if we should have prayed for God to raise Renee to life again. I just wanted her to live.

"You had the peace that passes all understanding. I never have seen that kind of peace on your face except with one other. It reminded me of my friend who lost her nine-year-old. As Renee was looking up with the intubation tube, she was being ushered into heaven right at the moment the angels and the Holy Spirit were comforting you. I was so humbled. Only a few people were in the room. It reminded me also of the stoning of the first martyr, Stephen, stoned to death for his faith. The Bible says he looked up and saw Jesus standing. He had the face of an angel. You must have been given grace and strength just like Stephen.

"It felt Biblical, like the body of Christ (the church is referred to as the body of Christ), you and I with Renee and all who were there. We felt like we were one with so much love abounding!!!

"We were all in shock, just grieving with you, not knowing how to minister. You were just a rock. We did not know what was the right thing to do. We went back to a small room and prayed. We wanted to do as much for you as possible. It was so difficult to just be present. When you feel that much love for someone you want to fix it.

"God helps us through all our trauma. Jesus cried when Lazarus died. He loved his friends. Renee is in heaven. It's for God's greater glory. Ultimately, this book will be for God's greater glory because of who God is. God says, 'All things work together for good for those who love the Lord and are called according to His purpose.'

"Phil Wright, bereavement pastor for our church, came and wanted to know if you needed assistance in finding a funeral home."

Deb's Version of the First Day

Deb is the colleague and friend who was working with me when I got the call from Gene about Renee's collapse. Her version of the last day of Renee's life and the Lord's whispers were amazing. The amazing part was seeing, from another perspective, how the Lord puts everything together.

Deb said, "The whole day was horrible.

"I had just had surgery on my big left toe on Thursday. It was actually the second surgery for the same problem since the first surgery was unsuccessful. I was told not to put any weight (walk) on my foot, even to go to the restroom. They had put pins in the joint to hold the toe in place. At first, you planned to drive to my home, an hour's drive. We needed to complete the preparation for the online course and student retreat. Rather than coming to my home, at the last minute we realized we needed to work at the medical center since all the content and materials were there. That was the Lord's grace and mercy. You were much closer to St Vincent's Hospital, where Renee was transported.

"I was annoyed. I had to crawl from my car to our office. It was stressful and humbling. I could not tell if it was you or me, but we were not connecting and flowing. When one is in physical discomfort, their thoughts and the world revolves around their needs. It didn't seem like you were taking the course preparation seriously. You would not be available the next day because you were to have a colonoscopy. Usually, we prayed before beginning our work. You did not even come into my office and ask me to pray. You missed the first call from Gene.

"You, Karyl, finally came into my office and said, 'Gene left a message. He wants me to come home and help with Renee.' Then, you were quiet...and then you said 'Well, I don't know what's going on, just help me pray.' I could tell you were uncertain about what to do. I wondered if it was because of the low blood sugar from you not eating in preparation for the colonoscopy. Internally, I was wondering why Gene called. This was out of character. It was very odd. Gene always respected and supported you in your work. Looking back I wish I had been more present and sensitive to the moment.

"I could not imagine anything that was an emergency with Renee, a healthy young adult. Just a month earlier, Renee had you (Karyl) and I do 'cross fit' exercises in fifteen-minute intervals. She was not fazed but I could hardly move for several days (weeks). I was having a hard time comprehending what was going on.

"My reaction was, 'Get in your car and go, if this is so important, if your child or husband needs you. Why are you still here?'

"I felt totally out of control; we would not get our work done. Then, I overhead the second call to Gene. I asked, 'What is going on?'

"You said, 'I have to go right now. Something happened to Renee, she has collapsed. The paramedics are on their way.'

"I froze instantly. I felt worthless. I couldn't do anything. 'Karyl, do you need me to drive you?'

"Then, you left. I felt horrible. I knew now in my spirit, I needed to support you. I went north to Lowes' parking lot, near the hospital, my foot throbbing. I sat there and prayed intensely, nonstop. It was rough, waiting for you to call. The whole time there were no thoughts of Renee dying, only that Renee was sick and everything would be okay.

"Finally, you called. I could not capture what you said, 'No Deb, she did not make it.' After the third time, when you said, 'No Deb, she died.' I realized the painful truth. I just sat there in total shock and disbelief. Then you asked, 'Can you go get Mary Bess?' Mary Bess is your older sister who lives independently but she walks with a walker. I knew Mary Bess well and was happy to be able to attend to her needs.

"In retrospect, it is somewhat easier to understand how the power of denial keeps you functioning through such devastation. Everyone reacts differently with horrific events that come unexpectedly and unwelcomed. We desire goodness for those we love; in the moment when your best friend loses their daughter, how do you describe it?"

"Denial and anger become your friend. In my world that day, I was trying to survive my own needs; clueless to the events that were taking place in your life. My agenda was: get to work with a left foot bandaged from surgery, complete work for student presentation and assist Karyl with preparation for colonoscopy. Nothing else was on my radar but God had me there for such a time of need. He knew I could handle what was part of His plan.

"Picking up Mary Bess, who lived close to the hospital, was eventful. She walked with a walker. It required love – which is both patient and kind – due to her immobility and slowness in getting around. It was like the blind leading the blind!

"My foot was bandaged with a medical foot boot and her with her walker. I helped stabilize and get her into the car. It seemed like a very long time from the time you called to the time we arrived at the hospital. I helped Mary Bess figure out where to go in the emergency room to see her beautiful niece.

"There were police everywhere. I could hear them talking. I asked one of the officers 'Why are there so many police in the emergency room?'

"He said, 'A call went out – "officer down" We always respond to our own!' I thought, *What incredible faithfulness and respect these men and women were displaying.*"

"At the hospital, I went into Renee's room, looked at Renee lying there and you, then whispered 'God, is this what you want?' I went up and held Renee's cold, lifeless hand and started praying to the Lord. I still kept thinking she was going to come back alive. She did not.

"People came in, too many people to be in the room at the same time; some went to the waiting room. They were calling those in your Bible Study groups. Then, the rest of the day for me was calling people other than those in your Bible Study. There were lots of tears and anguish. Eventually, my cell phone ran out.

"Every person I called, I had to repeat 'Renee passed away' a number of times, five for Jackie, the Director of our program. Finally, they asked 'What can I do?' It seemed it takes time to process this kind of devastating news. Finally, the chaplain came to the hospital. I stayed until the very end, early evening. I remember thinking I didn't want to leave Renee.

"The only other thing I remember that brought joy to my heart was a conversation we had earlier in the week (Wednesday evening). I remember feeling overwhelmed and urged you to go home early and do something with Renee.

"I said, 'Karyl, this is insane, working late. You may not have the opportunity to go out with Renee again.' I was so happy that you took her to Texas Roadhouse and had the most perfect evening with your precious daughter, Renee. Here is your description of the evening:"

"Texas Roadhouse was Renee's favorite place to eat. She loved the wafting smell of warm soft rolls plastered with cinnamon butter. Yum. They melted in her mouth. Then, there was the juicy sirloin steak, hearty, flavorful, and a great value and the house salad and steamed vegetables. Yes, those were Renee's favorites."

Deb continued: "Renee and you had an incredibly wonderful time at Texas Roadhouse. You told me later that as always, it was such fun to be with Renee; her life and friendships were always interesting!

"You also shared the following with the joy of a mother: 'Renee just shared whatever was on her mind, sometimes something that happened with her work or more often what was going on with her friends and activities outside of work. Indeed, this was a high privilege and gift that I now treasure, the times that Renee shared from her heart. I felt trusted. I was like a bedpost, as she updated me on her many friendships and her work as an Indiana State Capitol Police Officer guarding the State Capitol, the Governor's Mansion and downtown Indianapolis.'"

Deb continued: "The Lord knew how important it was for you (Karyl) to just listen to Renee and have this quality, special time together. That's all you wanted to do with your Mother – listen to her many family stories and thank her for the incredible gift she was in your life. When you were twenty-eight years old, your mother died from a pulmonary embolism during hospitalization for pneumonia. For you, this was a sudden shock, totally unexpected. You regret to this day that you did not make more time to just listen and be present to your mother."

"You (Karyl) continued to share, 'For this reason, being present to Renee at the Texas Roadhouse and the night we just hung out and watched TV was meaningful. Getting to spend this special time with Renee the week of her death were further whispers from God. He knew I was going to need these precious memories.'"

That conversation stayed vivid in my mind and helped me know that God loved Renee, you and Gene and somehow we were going to walk through this painful journey."

Maria's Version of the First Day

Maria's version of what happened the day of Renee's passing was just as interesting. I tried to call Maria all afternoon, at least eight times. Finally, when we reached home after 6:00 p.m., I called Maria one more time. Thankfully, Maria answered.

Maria leads a "Christ Renews His Parish" weekend retreat and was in a closing session. She was shocked.

Maria immediately called her daughter, Jacqueline. On that Sunday, Jacqueline, a law student, had come to Indianapolis from Notre Dame for a Colt's football game. She planned to meet Renee afterwards.

Maria left several voice mails and texts for Jacqueline, "Sweetheart, please call me immediately. You will want to leave the stadium so we can talk.

"Jacqueline just happened to glance down and finally saw the text. Jacqueline knew something was seriously wrong. I (Maria) never call her while she is at a football game.

"Jacqueline left the stadium, called me and asked, "Is something wrong with Dad?"

"No."

"Is something wrong with you?"

"No."

"Then what is it?"

"I (Maria) said, 'Sweetheart, I am so sorry to tell you, Renee passed away.'"

""What??? What did you say?' Jacqueline just couldn't wrap her mind around this.

"After the third time of asking 'What?' she asked, 'What do I do?'"

Both Maria and Jacqueline immediately came to our home. Mark, our son, and Rorie, our daughter-in-law, arrived from

Midland, Michigan. The four of them were a Godsend. Jacqueline had her law books from Notre Dame with her, thankfully, so she stayed the funeral week and assisted with many of the preparations.

By midnight, Jacqueline and Rorie recovered phone numbers of Renee's friends from her smart phone. On Monday, the next morning, Rorie and Jacqueline made the many calls to all her friends.

On that Monday, the obituary for The Indianapolis Star newspaper with Renee's picture was due by noon. Maria, who knew Renee so well and who was a superb writer, came to mind. I called her, asking, "Maria, I cannot even think of the first line for Renee's obituary. My mind is blank."

She said, "Let's write this together."

Praise the Lord! He sent a divine earth angel in the midst, one who knew Renee well and loved her as her own daughter. She helped me write an accurate portrayal of Renee. It was a gift.

I remember my mother's obituary, fraught with errors. Mother was the daughter of the owner and editor of a newspaper, the *Torrington Telegram*, in a small Wyoming town. My Grandfather Loomis took great pride in accurate reporting. Mother wrote her own obituary and shared with me its location in the corner of her desk. Unfortunately, I did not get home quickly enough for my father to use it.

Maria writes beautifully, a writer after the Lord's heart. She not only helped write the obituary but also a tribute to Renee, captured in a beautiful poem written just for Renee.

Gene, Mark, Rorie and Others

Gene and Mark thankfully worked on what seemed like a million details. What pictures shall we use? Where are they? What is the passcode to Renee's computer? What are the passcodes for her bank accounts? We were all going through the motions of taking care of things but it was surreal. Empty and void.

Gene was incredible with knowing what needed to be done. I do not know how I could have done it without my husband. His ability to understand details and the planning involved were enormous. Our son, Mark, was right there supporting Gene and walking with him through each step.

Rorie, Mark's wife, endeared herself to us. She was a warm, positive hostess. A million calls, it seemed like, came. She answered them all with kindness and graciousness. Rorie said, "I do not know most of your friends so here is a log of all the calls and contacts."

We needed that. She was organized and warmly welcomed family and friends who came from distant locations. Best of all, she was focused and able to be present to each person and all that was going on. We so needed that, too.

I was numb but knew many details had to be arranged in three short days. Early in the afternoon of the first day, we met with Jay R, the Funeral Home Director, the Indiana State Capitol Police Chaplain, the Commander of the Indiana State Capitol Police and the Commander for the Indiana Police Honor Guard at the Flanner Buchanan Funeral Home. I was astonished when I saw all these police officers meeting with us at the funeral home. Maria, who had been twenty years in bereavement ministry for her church; and Jacqueline, Renee's best friend, also met with us. Gene, Mark, Rorie and I were at the funeral home, too.

We made many decisions instantly – I can't even remember, there were so many. I wanted Renee to be honored and the guests to be graciously received. My brain was not capable of "executive function." It seemed "erased, empty, null and void." I was in a fog. I couldn't think. Normally, I would be grounded, organized, and have a plan for managing the days. I was so grateful for the early morning intimacy of the Lord and a friend whose prayers were powerful. I remember the peace, the calming effect that came.

The major decisions were made with suggestions from the Honor Guard Commander. The visitation was to be Wednesday evening at the Washington Memorial Chapel and the funeral was to be the day after, September 23, 2010 in the Main Worship Center of our church, Traders Point Christian Church. With some gentle guidance from Maria, we selected gravesites at the Washington

Park North Cemetery for Renee, Gene and I, with space for a bench. With suggestions from Jacqueline, we selected two non-profit organizations for those who wished to make contributions in Renee's name, one related to saving dogs and cats and the other an emergency fund for police officers fallen in action. Both of these were perfect for Renee.

The Lord sent what I call "earth angels" to assist us through all these details for the funeral, taken care of in a flash, it seemed. I will always be grateful for those who so graciously helped us behind the scenes through the whole week: Mark, Rorie, Ben (my brother), Mary Bess, Deb, Ann, Maria, Jacqueline, Barb B, Police Chaplain, the police officers (Indiana State Capitol Police Officers), the Funeral Home Assistant and Director, Louise, Nancy, Anne SF, and other Sisters and Brothers in Christ as well as those who actively participated in the funeral, Honor Guard and graveside service.

Monday afternoon, Louise, a former nutrition faculty member at the University of Delaware and housemate during my graduate school years at the University of Wisconsin, arrived from Newark, Delaware. She was a dear friend of both Gene and I who dropped everything to come and walk with us through the funeral week. She was a great comfort and blessing. Louise towered over most people, being six foot tall and in her late 70's, was also very wise and a pillar of strength. She was with me at the kitchen counter when I hung up from talking to Maggie. I had just seen a "vision of heaven – a glimpse of glory" with Renee there.

Louise said, "Saturday evening (the evening before Renee died), I saw a large box turtle on our cement patio, the one facing our woods. We always enjoy the 'wild life,' but in fifteen years, we never have seen a turtle. I called Arlette (her housemate) to show her."

The Lord works amazingly. Instantly, I knew the Lord was reminding me in one way or another, either with Louise's box turtle or Maggie's dream (Chapter 3), that Granny Mary was in heaven "playing" with Renee. Remarkable.

Wednesday evening, Nancy, a dear friend from my college days at the University of Wyoming, came. A special neighbor, Barbara W, generously opened her home to Nancy (and loved her!). Barbara W, a devout Christian, said she never had done this before but felt called to do so. For many years, our family lives have touched each other. I worked with her husband, Dr. Robert W, and she was the president of a preschool cooperative. She knew many options for preschool programs in northwestern Indianapolis, ones shared with me when considering a program for Renee. As well, Gene shared a garden with Dr. Robert W in their backyard.

Anne SF coordinated (I might say perfectly!) all the food from so many generous and wonderful friends, neighbors and the Bible Study/Nurture groups. Anne SF came to our home each day to determine the number of people we expected in the coming days.

She said, "I am way out of my comfort zone since I do not know most of these people. But this is something I can do for you as a 'Sister in Christ.'" Just writing this brings me to tears. More whispers from heaven.

A Peek into Renee's Photo Album

Renee Allene Rickard, May 26, 1982 – September 19, 2010

My family, the Rickards

Smelling the roses with Dad

Mark and I catching water bugs

Duber, my best four
legged friend

My first horse show when I was 6

Fun at the Magic Kingdom

Junior High girl power. I am
in the middle row, right.

My precious cat, Mufasa

Memorial Day parade

Jacqueline and her
mom, so special

We are the champions! I am on the right.

Snowboarding in Colorado

I'm a cadet at US Air
Force Academy

My oldest and closest
friend, Jacqueline

Rocky Mountain High,
12,000+ feet

Kingdom Mixed Martial Arts (MMA) competition team: I am front left

Snagging the tractor tires for MMA training

Machu Picchu, Peru, with Jacqueline

Curaçao, scuba diving: Mark's underwater photography success

Best Woman" and keeper
of the ring (thumb) for
Mark's wedding

Police Honor Guard
at my funeral

Honored with a police
memory pin

Enjoying my life
(and she did!)

Chapter 19

Renee's Visitation

For great is His love toward us,
and the faithfulness of the Lord endures forever.
Praise the Lord. (Psalm 117:2)
The stories of Renee's friends confirmed the promise that
the Lord's faithfulness to Renee and myself will endure forever.

L iterally, hundreds of people came to the visitation and
funeral. We were deeply touched by this outpouring of
love from friends, family and colleagues.

Maria, my dear Maria, who knew Renee so well, was an earth
angel! She was there for "such a time as this." Her bereavement
ministry of more than twenty years was amazing. Maria led the
prayer and the hour for sharing near the end of the visitation.

Special stories were shared, ones I had never heard. Many were
about the influence Renee had in their lives. A common theme
was, "She is compassionate, caring, incredibly calm, and effective
as a problem-solver in a crisis. She had lots of fun. Laughter was
a hallmark of Renee! She was laid back with an attitude of compassion and acceptance and inclusion of everyone: those young
and old in the Kingdom Martial Arts, fellow troopers senior to her,
colleagues and friends. Loyalty, compassion and teamwork were
strong values of Renee."

Jack G's sharing

Jacqueline's dad shared a story about Renee with their family.

"We invited Renee to come with us on a Pennsylvania vacation. Renee just obtained her driver's license. She convinced me to let her practice driving on the hilly roads of the Pennsylvania Mountains.

"Renee said, 'Hey, Jack G., can I drive? Can I drive?' So, I let her drive on these small, windy roads with no guardrails up the mountain. In our van, she was hugging the outside of the road. When you looked down, there was nothing but air to fall into.

"I kept telling her, 'Move over towards the center of the road. The sides of the road are VERY steep!' I kept saying, 'Move over. Move over a little bit more.'

"Finally, I was so tense I said, 'Pull over. I am driving.'

"Renee pouted, got out and let me drive.

"At some point, we were headed back to Grandma Betty's house. We stopped at a gas station-convenience store to make a phone call to Maria to see if she needed anything. (This was before cell phones.)

"I went into the gas station, came out and got into the car. I noticed the dash was rearranged and looked over at the passenger side. There sat another lady with wide eyes. 'Whoops – wrong car!' I apologized and hastily retreated."

According to Jacqueline, the girls were having the following conversation:

"Dad made the call and came out of the store. We were in a green Chevy Astra minivan. There was a dark greenish bluish Ford Explorer, somewhat similar to ours several cars back. Dad came out and was going the other way.

"We were like, 'Where is he going?' Then we realized he thinks the other car is ours. He went toward the car, 'Oh, my gosh, he is going to get into that person's car.'

"So, it's weird ... like in slow motion. We were trying to reach the doors, trying to get our car door open to yell, 'Dad, Dad.'

"Renee is like half out the door, yelling 'Jack G!'

"Dad opens the door to this other car, gets into the car and closes the door. We are like…'ahhhhoooooooh, no,' still trying to get our door open.

"He then comes out of the other car quickly and starts walking toward us. We are like, 'Dad, what are you doing?' He gets in our car, closes the door.

"Renee is dying laughing. 'You got in the wrong car!' She was literally doubled over in laughter, like laying out over the back seat. Tears were streaming down our faces."

"Dad said, 'Promise not to tell anyone, especially not your mother.'

"What he told us was, 'When I got in the other car. I thought … Hmmm … this doesn't feel right. I looked over to the side and there was a woman in the car I didn't recognize. 'Oops … wrong car.' I opened the door and she went 'AAAAAAHHH…'

"Later, Renee said, 'Well, Jack G, I may not be a very good driver, but at least I know which car is mine.'"*(Laughter. Tons of laughter.)*

Erin's sharing

Erin, a friend from second grade through high school, shared her story with tears streaming down her face. "I was very timid and awkward in elementary school and not included in other children's games and play on the playground. Renee invited me to play with her and her friends. That changed my life. I was included, felt loved and welcomed by Renee and her friends. This opened the door for me to make friends with others in my class." Erin is an attorney now.

Then, in high school Erin and Renee went canoeing in the Boundary Waters Canoe Area Wilderness (northern Minnesota) with others from the Pike symphony orchestra. Erin recalled, "Renee and I were buddies. We portaged the canoe over dry land, shared a canoe and laughed the whole time. We had a wonderful time. We swore we would come back together. (*They did, two years later!*). Regardless of what happened, we laughed all the time.

"In our free time, we went exploring. I remember one time we found a bunch of wild blueberries, picked some and brought them back for blueberry pancakes later in the week. That was really neat!

"Another time, we were on the lake with a big storm blowing in. The wind was fighting us paddling to shore. It seemed like we would make two feet forward, then go back three or four feet. Finally, we got to land totally exhausted.

"All of a sudden, one of the canoes was picked up and flying into the air like a leaf blown into the water. That was an amazing site – a heavy canoe flying in the air like a leaf!

"The whole situation was ridiculously hilarious. Renee and I, the strongest swimmers in the group, were imbued with new energy. We were back in the lake bringing the canoe back.

"It was all the more funny because Renee was a part of it. Renee had a knack for finding humor in everything, it seems. Whenever Renee and I were together, we were nearly always laughing. She was always so funny and so fun. It was a joy and it was like vacation being around her."

Erin's pseudo name was 'Moonshine' in the Boundary Waters journal given to me at the visitation by Mr. Ed S, who organized the trip. At the end of the first day her post was: "I feel like running a marathon! I have so much energy. It is absolutely gorgeous here. (Happy face.) My back is going to break tomorrow but I'll get over it. I'm all good for Canada Dry but dying for some carbonation – Mountain Dew! But the hamburgers were super 'delish', all three of them. Look for me when the moon is full. (Star) Moonshine (Star)"

On the last day of the trip, Moonshine posted: "Well, I had a wonderful trip! I wish I could have stayed forever! But, I missed the carbonation too much! I really began to love portages in the end. I like carrying the canoes alone! I will miss all of my sisters. But I have all those wonderful memories to cherish, so it won't be that bad! Thank you, Mr. Ed S, for this wonderful opportunity! And, I'm glad we were all able to pull together in the end!"

It was amazing how the Lord gave us this peek into Renee's life with her friends.

Mandy's sharing

Mandy was a friend who played spring indoor soccer for many years with Renee and travel team soccer (Indy Burn team) with Renee her senior year. Both Mandy and Renee were in Sunday school during their early years, church youth groups and a small high school 'D' (Discipleship) team Bible study together. They also went on several youth mission trips together, one to New York and one to the beaches of Florida under the sponsorship of our church.

Renee was maid-of-honor in Mandy's wedding. The day of the wedding, she joined the other bride's maids as each had their hair styled, put on makeup, and painted their nails and toenails.

Mandy said, "Renee had never painted her toe nails, so she just painted her nails and the end of her toes, with a good sense of humor. The other girls were cracking up with laughter."

After the wedding ceremony, Renee said, "Now, I'll wear more comfortable boots, not these painful killer heels."

Mandy's response, "Oh no, each of you bridesmaids will be presented at the reception!" So, Renee wore her heels a bit longer.

Dr. Joan L's Sharing

Renee decided to take an Indiana University-Purdue University Indianapolis course from Dr. Joan L, a nationally recognized expert in mental illness and brain disorders. She has a PhD in Physiology with a unique physiological and experiential understanding of brain disorders.

The course "Biology of Mental Illness" was for teachers, police officers, and others in public service who interact with people who may have any one of a variety of brain disorders, such as schizophrenia, Attention Deficit Disease (ADD) and Attention Deficit Hyperactive Disease (ADHD), bipolar spectrum, autism, or depression.

At the visitation, Dr. Joan L shared, "Renee enrolled in my 'Biology of Mental Illness' course to become a police officer certified to serve those who have brain disorders."

Later, Dr. Joan L shared, "When I talked to the person at IU responsible for grades, I told her that Renee died and asked, 'How can I withdraw this student from enrollment in my class on her behalf?' Her response was, 'Did she withdraw from the class?' I responded 'No, she died suddenly.' She just couldn't seem to understand."

Dr. Joan L said, "I thought, *Lady, I can almost hear Renee laughing in heaven. No one would have appreciated that as much as Renee.*" Dr. Joan L knew Renee well.

Angie S's sharing

Angie S was a member of a Mixed Martial Arts program. Angie S was the one who Renee worked-out with often, so she knew her well. The day after Renee died, Angie S, in tears, called, saying, "Renee was my best friend. I want to do something special for her at the funeral service."

She, with Rorie and Mark's behind-the-scene help, made available 200 circular metal buttons with Renee's Indiana State Capitol Police picture and the words 'In Memory of Renee Rickard, 1982 to 2010.' Many police officers put these on their sun visor to honor fallen officers.

She shared, "Renee influenced me to become strong as a woman. 'Women can become cops,' she said. I was the softer voice, very friendly, smiling a lot going down the street. Renee would say 'What are you doing? Reserve yourself. Don't be too nice and let people walk all over you. As a woman, you can carry yourself well without conceit.'

Chapter 20

Police Honor Guard, Funeral and Graveside Service

But we do see Jesus, who was made lower
than the angels for a little while,
now crowned with glory and honor because He suffered death,
so that by the grace of God He might taste
death for everyone. (Hebrews 2:9)
Death is a time where we all take a peek at our mortality.
It means many things to people: pain, separation,
loss, finality, grief, and sorrow. This moment filled
with shock, disbelief and great sorrow was also a
moment where I reflected on the life of Jesus,
who died at thirty-three years of age and paid the price of His life
as a sacrifice so my daughter Renee would have eternal life.

Indiana State Police Honor Guard

O ne of the questions I asked the police officers in the emergency room was, "Is it possible for Renee to have an honor guard for her service?" not realizing what this really entailed.

Indeed, we were awed that an Indiana State Police Honor Guard attended Renee's body during the entire funeral week. For a family not used to a military and police formality, we were very humbled. Humbled beyond imagination, especially when we realized the significance and extent of the Honor Guard's service.

The Honor Guard escorted Renee's body from the downtown central Indianapolis embalming location to the funeral home, Flanner Buchanan Washington Park North Funeral Center, near Kessler and 56th Streets. Several of the police officers who worked on Renee's shift chose to escort the body. There were eight police officers riding motorcycles and four police cars escorting the hearse to the funeral home. Jay R, the Funeral Director, was told by the lead police officer to stay close as they travelled to the funeral home. They travelled the distance in eight minutes, zooming through streets and back roads closed for the hearse's travel.

Those who knew Renee well knew that she would be thrilled to go for one last, high-speed ride. Renee was one of the top high-speed/fast chase drivers during her Indiana Law Enforcement Academy training. I could just see Renee flying atop the hearse, laughing and loving every minute of her final thrilling ride. When the hearse arrived at the funeral home, the motorcycle police officers circled behind the hearse holding their motorcycle helmets under one arm while saluting with the other as Renee's casket was being removed. I was so humbled by this show of respect for Renee. I know she was, too. Only the funeral director and police officers were there, so no need for fanfare – just deep respect. Thank you Indiana State Honor Guard for showing Renee such respect and honor.

The only reason I knew about this deep show of respect was because the funeral director shared the story. He was thrilled to drive the hearse with Renee at top speed. A nickname for him was "A. J." after A. J. Foyt, an Indy 500 racecar driver.

From then until Renee was laid to rest in her grave, an Honor Guard stood with Renee's body, at the Funeral Home, at the church, and then finally at the graveside, with a great show of respect and honor for her. The color guards marched, a trumpeter (from St. Louis) played *Taps* and several honor guards folded the flag draped over Renee's casket. We have that as a reminder of Renee's police service.

Perhaps the thing that impressed us most was the family of police officers who came to Renee's funeral, more than 100 police officers in thirty-six police cars and nineteen motorcycles. The police officers coming into the funeral together were spectacular, very heart-warming. One of the staff with the funeral home who graciously facilitated the funeral activities (behind-the-scenes) said, "I have never seen so many men sobbing in the gymnasium before the funeral began." Evidently, a police grief counselor was in the gym with the police officers.

One of the Indiana State Capitol Police Officers, Sergeant Jeremy Roll, gave a eulogy related to Renee's police activities. That was very special, since the officers who worked with Renee told the head of the Indiana State Capitol Police that they preferred to escort Renee's casket to the funeral home. We will always be grateful for the men and women who humbly honored Renee, in her death, for her service to the Indiana State Capitol Police.

Funeral Service

As we entered the church for the funeral service, I noticed four men in a corner of the entrance area, none of whom I knew personally. They appeared to be in prayer. My heart was deeply touched. Before the service began, they came to Gene near Renee's casket and shared some words of comfort. They were from a Bible Study that Gene participates in every other Monday morning. To this day, my heart is warmed knowing that these men cared for Gene and were there when he needed them.

God is good, all the time. Indeed, He sends his caring angels to look over us, just when needed. Another couple from Renee's friendships at the Air Force Academy came from Colorado Springs. We were pleased they were able to come and be present that day. It was their great wisdom that helped oh-so-much in the days ahead, walking through the grief journey. They encouraged us in several ways: "Join a grief-support group, write in a little journal whatever comes to mind, carry a little notebook so you don't forget (a hallmark of grief), talk about Renee comfortably in your family as you are reminded of her by some antic of her Chihuahuas and things that make you smile."

The funeral service began after a short time of viewing Renee's casket and our family welcoming those who came to the service. It was beyond anything I could imagine when I saw more than a hundred officers in uniform join us at the funeral. Renee would have been overwhelmed, knowing so many officers came to show their respect.

What an honor. We were overwhelmed by the support of the police family. Renee had a wide network of friends among the police officers. Tears came to my eyes as I realized how incredibly loving and wonderful the Lord had been to allow such a close family and special relationships.

When everyone was seated, the guards standing at Renee's casket left, stomping their rifle to a cadence. Wow. That left an indelibly printed impression of the gravity and seriousness of Renee's life and passing.

Funeral Service Welcome and Participants

Reverend Jim Craig, as a bittersweet privilege, welcomed all to the Traders Point Christian Church.

"We have a befitting tribute to Renee, her coworkers and friends. I invite you to worship with us as we love and adore God and provide honor and recognition for Renee and her life."

Those serving for the funeral included:
- Reverend Jim Craig gave the homily and accompanied the vocal soloist on the guitar.
- Jana Wagner provided beautiful music with the piano.
- Maria Pimentel-Gannon, a dear friend of the family and Renee, wrote an original poem for Renee, to be read first.
- Pastor Ben Kohrs, Renee's uncle from Oklahoma, opened with a prayer.

- Mark Rickard, Renee's brother, read scriptures to honor his sister.
- Jacqueline Pimentel-Gannon, a dear friend of Renee; and Jeremy Roll, an Indiana State Capitol Police Officer on Renee's shift, provided the eulogy.
- Judith Ernst, the soloist, accompanied by Reverend Jim Craig on the guitar, sang as the Spirit led.
- Father Daniel Coffey gave the committal prayer. He is the primary chaplain for the Indiana State Capitol Police, the one who came to the hospital to be with our family and friends on Sunday.

Maria's Poem

I Am Not the Same written "with love to my sweet Renee:"
"Where are you My dear Renee?" you ask. "I cannot see you."
You don't recognize me because I am anew.
I am different – I no longer look or act the same.
But it is still me; yes, you still know my name.
God called out my name – since day one, He had called me.
Today, I heeded His call; in His Presence He called me to be.
"Come be with me, my child," He invited.
I accepted the call. My spirit became excited.
In obedience I answered, though I hated to let go.
Praying He would lead me, the path to Him He'd show.
In His infinite mercy, kindness, forgiveness and love,
He showed the grandeur and majesty that comes from above.
Now, it's time for me to go home – to return.
Toward my "new home" I surely will turn.
He'll keep me safely under the protection of His Son,
Holding me forever, for the good race I have run.
I know that as long as He is with me, protected I'll remain.
Though saying good-bye is hard, His
Kingdom I want for my domain.
"God, please take care of my brother, my mom and my dad.
They'll miss me greatly; their precious love I always had.
Your timing was not mine, I had no clue.

It happened so quickly; I didn't know what to do.
Even though like a thief in the night death did come for me.
Fully surrounded by angels. You let me be.
"Please remind my family that I'm with
You and let them know I'm okay.
That I'll always love them and will
watch over them day after day.
Dear God, help us all be strong and to let go, I pray;
And always stay at our side at the end of each day. Amen."

Pastor Kohrs' Prayer

"Lord, this is a troubling time and hurting time. Yet, I know that Renee is looking down, pleased at what she sees. May we remember the fullness of life and joy that came from her living and doing what you called her to do. You have called her home. Be with us, Lord, as we worship today that you might be honored and glorified. In Jesus' name, Amen."

Mark's readings

Ecclesiastes 3:1-8
A time for everything
There is a time for everything, and a season
for every activity under the heavens:
a time to be born and a time to die, a time
to plant and a time to uproot,
a time to kill and a time to heal, a time to
tear down and a time to build,
a time to weep and a time to laugh, a time
to mourn and a time to dance,
a time to scatter stones and a time to gather them,
a time to embrace and a time to refrain from embracing,
a time to search and a time to give up, a time
to keep and a time to throw away,
a time to tear and a time to mend, a time
to be silent and a time to speak,

a time to love and a time to hate, a time
for war and a time for peace.

John 14:1-4

Do not let your hearts be troubled. You believe in God; believe also in me. My Father's house has many rooms; if that were not so, would I have told you that I am going there to prepare a place for you? And if I go and prepare a place for you, I will come back and take you to be with me that you also may be where I am. You know the way to the place where I am going.

Reverend Craig led the singing: *How Great Thou Art.*

Reverend Craig's Homily

"The scripture I have chosen is not usually one used for funerals, but it applies here."

Romans 13:1-10 (NABRE)

Obedience to Authority. [1] Let every person be subordinate to the higher authorities, for there is no authority except from God, and those that exist have been established by God. [2] Therefore, whoever resists authority opposes what God has appointed, and those who oppose it will bring judgment upon themselves. [3] For rulers are not a cause of fear to good conduct, but to evil. Do you wish to have no fear of authority? Then do what is good and you will receive approval from it, [4] for it is a servant of God for your good. But if you do evil, be afraid, for it does not bear the sword without purpose; it is the servant of God to inflict wrath on the evildoer. [5] Therefore, it is necessary to be subject not only because of the wrath but also because of conscience. [6] This is why you also pay taxes, for the authorities are ministers of God, devoting themselves to this very thing. [7] Pay to all their dues, taxes to whom taxes are due, toll to whom toll is due, respect to whom respect is due, honor to whom honor is due.

Love Fulfills the Law. [8] Owe nothing to anyone, except to love one another; for the one who loves another has fulfilled the law. [9] The commandments, "You shall not commit adultery; you shall not kill; you shall not steal; you shall not covet," and whatever other commandment there may be, are summed up in this saying, "You shall love your neighbor as yourself." [10] Love does no evil to the neighbor; hence, love is the fulfillment of the law.

"Renee was tenacious. The word tenacious does not come close to describing the complexity and beauty of Renee. I thought of words like softhearted, compassionate, kind and giving. She was that, as well.

"More than a decade ago, some fifty of us flew to San Diego and hopped onto a van that took us to a little town in Mexico, Roso Rito. We spent a week building homes for poor people in that community. I was one of the adult sponsors and Renee was on my team.

"With tenacity, she helped cart cement bags, water, gravel, lumber, and other building supplies up to the building site. We had to go up a steep, barren, rocky hill strewn with glass and inhabited with wild dogs. Renee did her part, carried her weight, picked up those 100-kilogram bags and managed to get them up the hill.

"During her break, instead of sitting around and panting like the rest of us, Renee was playing football with the locals and bending down to show kindness and compassion to the little children hanging around the construction site. Because of her kindness and because the oldest son, for whom we were building a home, quickly fell in love with Renee, we were invited to their church that evening to participate in a worship service. Most of the people were tired from working in the heat all day, so they chickened out.

"But I grabbed a guitar and we (Renee and two others) went with the family to worship in a Mexican church. It was a blast. We sang. We played. Afterward, we did what friends and family should do after church – go out and eat.

"We went downtown and had quesadillas. I told Renee very clearly, 'Only order things cooked. Stick with cooked foods.'"

Renee replied, "Right. Got it.'

"Five minutes later, I looked down at the end of the table. She, with Mexican children, were dipping into salsa fresca and I am thinking 'oh, oh.' Even though it steamed me a little bit, it endeared Renee to that family and we had a much better mission trip as a result.

"We have an older gentleman in our church who was in the Marine Corps. I heard him speak often about the very thin and tenuous line between civilization and barbarism. Police officers understand this better than the rest of us. They form what has been called a 'thin blue line,' a very visible human shield that separates chaos from that which is creative, which keeps the predator away from his prey, which punishes the perpetrator, and seeks to protect, redeem and, in the words of the scripture, 'avenge' the victim.

"In the words of the apostle Paul, a police officer is an authority ordained by God. In fact, the word *diakonos*, which means servant or minister, is used a number of times to describe the work of a police officer with the admonition that, 'if we do what is right, we have no fear. But if we do what is wrong, then it is right to fear because that is what God intended.'

"In 20-20 hindsight, God created Renee to be ordained into the police 'ministry.' I already talked about her being tenacious and being compassionate. She received instruction in her home, in her school, in her church, Pike soccer team, U.S. Air Force Academy, Purdue University, Indiana Law Enforcement Academy, her employment for a short period of time in a bank, her close friendships and the proverbial school of hard knocks. We see that God prepared her well for her life's work. He prepared her for her ordination. He prepared her for her ministry.

"Then, she joined that thin blue line of the police ranks and willingly served to protect us and, in doing so, to minister to us in an honorable and tangible manner.

"Young people die too young, suddenly, because we live in a fallen and sin-sick world. Sin is not just something that we do but an inescapable condition that afflicts every one of us. From the moment we are conceived, we are afflicted in this way. While this inescapable condition that is in our world is significant and troublesome, this shrinks when compared to the resurrection of Christ.

"The fall of man and all the wrong doings of sin and sickness of disease is not as important as 2000 years ago when Jesus died on the cross, was buried and raised to sit on the right hand of God. The apostle Paul in Romans, declared that 'I am not ashamed of the gospel, the power of God urging us to believe, urging us to accept the righteousness of God available to those who will live by faith.'

"Ironically, that same power empowers us to live eternally with Christ. Whether God is training us to be good citizens of this earth or heaven, they are one and the same. Renee was ordained into that ministry.

"With certainty, we release Renee this afternoon into God's care. We know that He will care for her. We know that He will give her a new body. Like all Christians, we will wait for that day impatiently and we will cry out Maranatha. Come, Lord Jesus."

Jacqueline's Eulogy

"My name is Jacqueline Pimentel Gannon or Bobby to my family and Renee. I will start by reading the following personal letter from Renee to me:

> October 12, 1995 - Don't let anyone see or read.
>
> Dear Bobby,
>
> "How ya doing? I talked to my parents about doing all those things next week. They said 'maybe.' It is an improvement because I probably get to see him two times next week.
>
> "This is the first time in my life that I will say this. What should I wear? Should I wear a tank top? Help me out here. Jump in any time now.
>
> "Oh, that's right. I am writing a letter.
>
> > "Best Friends, Nay (Renee),
> > 'as though I didn't know.'

"By the time that note was written, Renee and I had been best friends for five years. We met and became fast friends in the second grade. Renee always was more of a sister than just a friend.

"Although way back in the second grade, we had another relationship. Renee was my daughter. We were performing the play Cinderella. I was the evil stepmother and Renee was the evil stepsister, my daughter.

"I could continue all day and all night with memories and stories about Renee. One memory was when, in high school, we scheduled all eight periods together. Then, we were mad at each other half the semester. When she would be gone a day, the teacher would ask me where she was. I was so frustrated; I said, 'I didn't know.'

"Other memories were playing King Arthur with our wooden swords out back at the Rickard's, the ones we got living in Spain for a summer. We've been through a lot."

"I can just imagine hearing Renee say, 'Jacqueline, don't make this too long.'

"My response, 'Well, whatever you want to hear about yourself. So, Renee, I will make one more compromise. I will share some qualities that you have and only share a story or two.'

"First of all, Renee was generous with her time. Renee would always pick up someone if they needed a ride and be generous with her money. She always was willing to treat friends to lunch or to the movies. Anything that was there to give, she gave.

"Her sense of humor was so funny. We all loved it so much. A couple of anecdotes: One Halloween when we were really too old to go trick-or-treating, we decided at the last minute that we wanted to go. The only thing we could find was a big sheet and two masks of pigs. Renee comes up with the idea, 'We will be the ghost of a two-headed pig.' So we were!

"She laughed so hard, she made others laugh. One time at my house, I told her a dumb joke. She had just taken a big swig of milk. The milk went everywhere, even coming out of her mouth. I swear there are still stains of milk on the fridge today. That laugh of hers – the high-pitched giggle or the one where she would be laughing so hard her shoulders would be moving, with no sound coming out – I will miss for sure.

"She was a good sport. When she was home, she swore her name was MarkRenee. I think she actually liked it, especially when she was getting in trouble, because the blame actually went on Mark.

"Renee was forgiving. Sometimes, we fought for long times. No matter what happened – boy problems or homework troubles, when either of us needed to talk, we'd call and immediately all was forgotten and we'd just pick up where we last left off.

"Renee loved to buck tradition. Renee thought a maid of honor was silly, so she told me I could be her 'Best Maid.' At your wedding, Mark and Rorie, it worked out so perfectly when she was the 'Best Woman' for Mark.

"Similar to that, you know most people do not ask for honorary things. Well, Renee didn't bother with any of that. She informed me a long time ago that she would be Godmother to my children. I didn't have much of an option in that. Certainly, I don't have any kids now but I can assure you they will know their 'Aunt Nay.'

"When we went to Peru, who but Renee would make friends with the police officers who had the big guns. Renee ended up going to them and talking to them (in Spanish). They ended up giving her a piece of their badge. We came home with something few others would receive.

"Renee was adventurous. Just looking back at this year, for example. Renee and I went to Peru. We were biking down this mountain with mountain bikes. Here I am walking my bike down among the rocks to a place more manageable. Here's Renee, 'All right, here I go over the biggest rocks ever!'

"We decided to go on a bike ride across Indiana on a ride called RAIN (Ride Across Indiana). I gave her about two weeks' notice. She says, 'Sure, I'll go.' She hadn't been riding her bike until then. Oh, my gosh, she made it halfway through, much longer than many others. She said 'I just can't go on. But we're riding again next year.' She must have told me five times, 'We are going to do it next year. We'll finish then.' So, I might just have to do it in her memory next year.

"Then again, even though she didn't finish the bicycle ride, two weeks later she goes and does a sprint triathlon in downtown Indy – swimming in the canal, running, and then bicycling.

"There wasn't an adventure that Renee turned down. Think of how many of you had Renee convince you to do something that you probably would not have done. It's just hard to resist her and her convincing manner.

"Renee was kind and loving to others, both people and animals. She couldn't stand to see a living being hurt. From her days wanting to be a veterinarian before knowing that blood would be happening, she absolutely could not pass up a creature in need without doing something for it. All of her animals – Comet or Comet 2, her guinea pigs from long ago; Duber, an adopted dog; Mufasa, Simba and Scar, her cats; and Lily and Stokley, her Chihuahuas – were the most spoiled pets.

"I cannot imagine anyone loving their animals more. In fact, Renee didn't like to share straws or cups with people but she had no problem whatsoever eating after her puppies had taken something from a fork. I would gross out. She would say, 'Jacqueline, their mouths are so much cleaner than ours.'

"I don't want to ruin Renee's image as a 'tough girl' but Renee was kind and respectful to the people she had to arrest and to those she came into contact as a police officer. She had a special place in her heart for all those in need. It was an inspiration for me.

"Renee was loyal, trustworthy, dependable, and always there when you needed her, not just for me but for all her friends. You could always count on Renee. I never had a choice about being her best friend. That was a given to me. 'Yes, you are.' There it is. I wouldn't have had it any other way.

"And, then working nights worked out very well. I am in school and she would call when I needed a wakeup call at some ungodly hour, like 3:45 a.m. There she would be, an alarm clock who called whenever needed.

"Lastly, Renee was a teacher. In so many ways, she taught me things. I learned to shoot pool, checking the angles. Not that I am any good. I learned how to ride a motorcycle. My life was threatened if I let it fall over. So, I was very careful. I learned how to be a good friend to others, as Renee was a good friend to me. I know so many of you have learned from Renee, as we have heard in the past seven days. Renee had so much more to teach me – how to shoot a gun, not that I was sorry I missed that, how to scuba-dive and other life lessons. I guarantee that I will always be learning from Renee the rest of my life.

"All these memories are wonderful, but I think more than anything, I will remember Renee's presence. She didn't even need to be there to feel her presence. Just seeing her phone number come up would bring a smile on my face, no matter what time of the day. I am so thrilled that her presence is so strong because it will be with us, even if Renee is not.

"Thank you, Renee, for twenty years as my best friend. Through you, I gained not just one friend, but also the entire Rickard family. During holidays and birthdays, Renee brought us together. I believe she will continue to do so.

"Few people get to have twenty years with a friend like Renee. I would have liked another twenty years with her. For these past twenty years, I am grateful – every whop or punch on the arm (how we showed affection rather than hugs), every joke experienced, even every fight we had, every meal eaten, every movie watched, every prayer spoken and dream shared. I miss you very much, Renee.

"Although you would yell at me for being so sentimental, I love you, Renee. You've touched the life of everyone in this room in some way. I speak for everyone: Thank you, we will miss you and we will look forward to seeing you again one day."

Sergeant Jeremy Roll

"My name is Jeremy Roll. Renee came to us October 6, 2008. From the beginning, she wanted to see everything. Believe me, she did. There were a lot of things that Renee knew that she might not have let others know. For example, she knew that two drinks always meant four. She knew that grass should not smell as bad as the gas in the car. She knew that the little baggie of white powder probably was not sugar from your neighbors. She was good at that.

"Renee was a communicator. What she would do is bring the level down. We never had an altercation with Renee on our shift. (No one else had this record.) Renee was outstanding at bringing the level down, at getting people to do what she wanted them to do. You need to know that. We owe you for her. She was a wonderful, wonderful person. She worked with me pretty much continually. Our third-shift family stuck pretty strongly together. There were only seven of us. She was part of the seven.

"Every time you rolled up when she made a stop, when things were OK, you would get a 'thumbs up' but she wouldn't smile. Once she had something she would turn around with a smile. OK, let's get him out of the car. Let's go. She loved doing it. She was good at picking up those 'Operating a Vehicle While Intoxicated (OWI).' We all tried to compete with her. She works Monday, Tuesday, Wednesday and Thursday. She can get three OWIs in one week. I work Thursday, Friday and Saturday and I didn't get even one last week or the week before. They must be picking a different road, picking her road.

"I would like to thank you for our time with her. You did a wonderful job. We owe you for her. You need to know that. She was special. She always spoke highly of you and loved you. She's part of the police family, also. We will greatly miss her. She will never leave us.

"Thank you for her."

Judith Ernst's Solo, Reverend Craig accompanied with a guitar. *The Lord's Prayer*

Chaplain Coffey's Prayer of Committal

"For Renee working the third shift, Psalm 130 is especially appropriate:.

"Let us pray. Oh, God of grace and mercy shown to Renee and all your servants who, having finished their course in faith, may rest from their labors. May they also be faithful unto death and receive the crown of life.

"We are thankful for the service Renee rendered to Indiana; to the 6.2-million residents and citizens of this state. They owe her a debt of thanks. For in her vocation as a minister of righteousness, she provided safety to the government of this state. Those who bear responsibility for this state – the governor, the legislators, the judges, the peoples of Indiana who serve the state – were protected by her vocation, her profession, by her daily activities.

"We ask, oh Lord, for blessings upon the work she has done. We pray also for Renee's coworkers – the Indiana State Capitol Police and their coworkers – that you would bless the intentions of their hearts and the work of their hands. We pray for their safety.

"We place Renee in your hands, for you are our Creator and Redeemer. Into your infinite love, we place her family, asking for your support and your blessings.

"Remind each one of us of your continual presence, hold each one of us in your hands of mercy. Encourage us with your words of peace. Holy God, Holy God, Mighty and Merciful, Hear our Prayer. Amen.

"The Lord bless you and keep you. The Lord shine upon you and be gracious unto you. The Lord lift up his countenance upon you and grant you peace. Amen."

Judith Ernst's Solo, with Reverend Craig accompanying:
On Wings of Eagles.

Following the funeral service, the police officers exited first, then the chaplain, then the casket was removed, then Gene and I, our family, Ruth, Louise, and Karyl's brother, Ben, were ushered out.

The pallbearers were: Mark Rickard (brother), Richie Rickard (cousin) and Richard Rickard (uncle), Jay Rickard (cousin), Jacqueline Pimentel-Gannon (friend), Jenica Kohrs Long (cousin) and Jim Schammerhorn and his son James Schammerhorn (friends).

Graveside Service

At the cemetery, Pastor Ben Kohrs (uncle) and Chaplain Daniel Coffey (Indiana State Capitol Police Chaplain) led the way, with the casket following; then, Gene and I, Rorie and Louise were escorted by police officers to our seats. Ruth (adopted grandmother) with Mary Bess (aunt) sat in the front row. The police officers formed several rows behind the rest of the people.

Pastor Ben Kohrs Graveside Homily

"We thank each of you for being here, especially the police officers and Police Honor Guard. Every one of you put your lives on the line to protect us. We can't thank you enough for that.

"The third shift calls Renee a part of the family. I've seen that as I have talked to the fellow officers. Renee was a unique person, one who thought outside of the box. When she did, she got positive results. In the funeral service, we've heard of her character. We loved her for that.

"David, in the Old Testament, was a man who thought out of the box, too. In Psalm 139, David talks very much about the creation, what we are, and what we became. Here is Psalm 139:13-18:

For you created my inmost being; you knit me together in my
   mother's womb.
I praise you because I am fearfully and wonderfully made;
your works are wonderful, I know that full well.
My frame was not hidden from you when I was made in the
   secret place,
when I was woven together in the depths of the earth.
Your eyes saw my unformed body;
all the days ordained for me were written in your book
before one of them came to be.
How precious to me are your thoughts, God!
   How vast is the sum of them!
Were I to count them,
   they would outnumber the grains of sand—
when I awake, I am still with you."

"Renee is with the Lord now. I sit back in awe at how she was able to do her mission, what she was called to do. She did it to the best of her abilities. Outstanding. Awesome. God put her together and wove Renee, a person that lived life to the fullest, a person that loved life.

"The term maverick was invented in the West where cattle ran wild, millions and millions of them. They drove them north to Kansas to railroads. The lead steer would be out front leading them. Guess who was out front – Renee, a wonderful leader. God put Renee together. We have had the wonderful privilege of living with her twenty-eight years. Guess what, we get to see her again when we go to heaven. She will be waiting there with our parents. As we commit her body to the ground, we worship and celebrate her life.

"Let us pray. Thank you Lord, for Renee, the way she lived her life. She got every ounce out of that. Thank you for knitting her together and bringing her to us. She loved life and she loved You. She had that compassion and sweet gentle heart to go along with it. Thank You for that. As we commit her body to You, we know she is already with You. Amen."

The color guard with three flags – U.S. flag, Indiana State flag and Indiana Police flag – marched off and the rest of the honor guards were dismissed. A trumpet player, a police officer from St Louis, Missouri, played *Taps*. The final event in the graveside service was the folding of the U.S. flag draped over Renee's casket. The Honor Guard Commander presented the U.S. flag to Gene and me.

When the flag was handed to us, we knew ... *RENEE IS GONE*. The finality of this hit, with a punch in our hearts and minds and souls. We were running on fumes ... from exhaustion.

The funeral and graveside services with all the police officers, the Honor Guard and the trumpet player were most humbling. Renee would have been surprised to see this much honor given her.

Chapter 21

Animals and the Week of the Funeral

The righteous care for the needs of their
animals. (Proverbs 12:10a)
Renee loved animals! She brought so
many animals into our family.
These precious pets were God's whispers from
heaven that He loves Renee and us.

Mark and Rorie brought their golden retriever, Shiloh, with them when arriving for Renee's funeral. One golden retriever, two cats inherited from Renee when she left for college, and two Chihuahuas of Renee's left behind. Shiloh was the dog Renee helped Rorie choose at the Humane Society. More animals than adults. Yes, Renee loved every single one of them.

While Renee was working as a bank teller in Lafayette, she adopted a gray Chihuahua, "Stokley," who she named after a Colt's football player.

Later, she decided, "Stokley needs 'company.'"

So, Renee found another gray Chihuahua in Michigan, just six weeks old. Renee was so excited about Lily that she asked, "Mom, please come to Lafayette so I can show you this dear, very little puppy, the size of my hand."

Lily, to this day, has a sweet, positive personality. She is happy to meet everyone, with her little tail almost wagging off her bottom. She literally saw Renee as her mother and followed her everywhere she went.

Renee was loving and so gentle with her dogs. She was a great "mother" for them. As a priority, she fed them each in their own dishes just the right amount of dog food and took them outside to "potty" three times a day.

Lily and Stokley were her "children" and were treated with "luxuries" – special dog tags and leashes, doggie coats, a pink one for Lily and a black one for Stokley, Christmas and Halloween costumes and a shoulder, carry-on travel bag with netting on the sides for the pups to see out.

Yes. Lily and Stokley travelled everywhere with Renee, even flying to our Colorado cabin. They were great travelers. No yapping. No flight sickness. No "accidents." Thankfully! They still travel with us to this day.

One evening, I picked up Renee at the airport in Indy. She was on her way home from our Colorado cabin with the puppies. It was almost midnight; as most travelers came through to the waiting area, they looked bone-tired, almost dead. Suddenly, I saw several families with children smiling broadly. Then, Renee appeared smiling and laughing with Stokley and Lily on a leash; the children were so happy to see and pet Lily and Stokley! That pretty much represented Renee's character – love, vibrancy and energy, a charismatic effect on those around her.

Then when Rorie, our son's wife, said, "I want to adopt a dog," Renee was all for helping her. Renee searched the Humane Society dog posts and found several possibilities. Off they went to the Humane Society in Indy that afternoon to check out the dogs. They came back for supper, with no dog, just one possibility – Shiloh, a one-year-old, golden retriever who was already trained.

Rorie and Renee both wondered, "Why does he seem so depressed in the dog kennel? What is he like with young children?"

After their rather thorough psychoanalysis of the dog, I urged, "Maybe you should go back this evening and see if you can find the answers to these questions."

I went with them! After all, this was very important to both Rorie and Renee.

As we entered the Humane Society, we saw Shiloh in the entrance. A little girl ran up to him and put her face square in his, "This is Shiloh, Mom. See how nice he is." It seemed miraculous. Shiloh just wagged his tail and let her pet him. Wow. That was an answer to one of the concerns.

Shortly, one of the Humane Society personnel came to the large entrance area. Shiloh raced to him with great joy, jumped into his arms and licked his face. He provided more information about Shiloh's history, his younger days and why he came to the kennel.

The Humane Society worker shared, "I took care of Shiloh in my home during the past three weeks. Shiloh came to the kennel because he was left on a leash outdoors. The owners had not given Shiloh loving attention and care."

Several months before Renee's passing, Renee gave Gene and me a magnetic paw for the refrigerator that said "My grandchild is a dog." Indeed, that was prophetic. She left us two Chihuahuas as a continual reminder of Renee, her love and gentleness.

Now, Lily and Stokley are ours to feed, care for, worry about getting them outside regularly, travel with and take to the vet. Hmmm. Our dogs see the veterinarian more often than we ourselves see a physician. It's not that the dogs are sick. They just need routine care. The veterinarian, Dr. Gail G, knew Renee well, because Renee shadowed her in her teen years when considering a career as a veterinarian.

Stokley is a healing comfort to Gene. He adores Gene and snuggles on his lap while Gene is working on the computer. God is good, all the time.

Lily, sensitive little Lily, was "lost" with Renee's passing. Rorie carried her everywhere during the week of the funeral, snuggled in her arm – answering the door, answering the phone, coordinating all that needed to be done. Yes, there was little Lily snuggled in Rorie's arm for that week.

When Mark and Rorie left the Saturday after the funeral, Lily just stood. She literally would not move.

"Oh my, Gene. Now what? Lily won't move. She is just standing, like she is in pain, frozen. This is the last thing I want on my watch – something wrong with Lily, Renee's favorite little companion. If something happens to Lily, I can just see Renee in heaven 'croaking.'"

So, off to the Emergency Veterinary Clinic we went with Lily on that Saturday night. Lily still would not move. The veterinarian could find nothing wrong in a physical examination but gave us a prescription for pain medicine, in case Lily needed it. When we returned home, Lily snuggled with us on the couch, just like she did when Renee watched football games and movies. Lily finally was moving around and kept going downstairs to Renee's bedroom. This broke our hearts.

When Renee was here, Lily even followed her to the bathroom. Losing Renee was a shock for Lily. Lily must have been mourning, especially after Rorie left.

Yes. Renee's animals were her heart and soul. They brought great joy, great comfort and great love to her and she to them. These animals were the best things that happened to Renee. Whenever she was upset, sad, disappointed, or concerned, she was brought almost instantly out of the funk with her animals.

Smile. Renee would say "Mom. You need to greet Lily and Stokley when you come home!" Indeed, they were always at the door waiting to be greeted.

Chapter 22

Jacqueline – Faithful Beyond the End

*But show me unfailing kindness like the
Lord's kindness as long as I live,
so that I may not be killed, and do not ever
cut off your kindness from my family,
not even when the Lord has cut off every one of
David's enemies from the face of the earth.
So Jonathan made a covenant with the house of David, saying,
"May the Lord call David's enemies to account." And Jonathan
had David reaffirm his oath out of love for him, because
he loved him as he loved himself. (I Samuel 20:14-17)
Jacqueline and Renee had a friendship
similar to David and Jonathan.
Mutual friendship and loyalty continue with our families today.*

Jacqueline's interview

Jacqueline and her mother, Maria, were long-term friends of both Renee and me. This friendship seemed destined to last a lifetime. As already mentioned, Renee and Jacqueline met on the soccer field. Here is Jacqueline's interview:

Soccer

Jacqueline: "We started playing soccer together in the first grade. My folks remember better because they were talking on the sidelines to you guys. Dad talked about the freezing cold rain at some of the spring games. One really cold, rainy day, we wore sweats under the shorts and T-shirts of our uniforms. Yes. Rain or sunshine, we played all the soccer games.

"We both continued to play soccer through the second and third grades. Renee played a lot longer in the recreational leagues and joined a spring travel team, Carmel Dynamo, her junior year and the Indy Burn team her senior year."

Swimming

Jacqueline: "Both Renee and I swam on the Westchester Swim team. Our family joined several years before your family joined. The Westchester team practiced in the COLD (brrrr-r-r) water early in the morning. Renee was a very good swimmer. Half the time we were in the same age group (e.g., seven-eight or nine-ten years) and half the time we were not because she was a year older than I was. When we were in the same group, she would 'kick my butt.' We did a couple of relays together. Swimming at Westchester went through high school (fifteen to seventeen years old)."

Band

Jacqueline: "We both started playing trumpet the summer before the sixth grade. After the seventh grade year, we were allowed to do summer band camp with the Pike High School marching band. Renee and I roomed together several years. The days at the band camp (St Joseph's College, Rensselaer, Indiana) were incredibly hot and sweaty. After practice, the greatest thing was going to 'Wally World,' the Wal-Mart across the street, to be in air conditioning. Sometimes, we got water balloons!

"On the first day of the Indiana State Fair, marching bands from around the state competed with drill formations. We did that all the way through high school. During the year, we played in the concert band, the pep band, and the symphony orchestra. Oh, yes, Renee's senior year, she also played in the pit orchestra for a musical. That was a lot of rehearsals!"

Tennis

Jacqueline: "Renee ended up playing tennis with me for a year in high school. This was super fun. At the beginning, Renee said, 'We have to play in this – a tennis skirt?' (Renee was not into wearing skirts). Yes. Renee wore the skirts for the team. (*Laughter*).

"Renee had never played tennis so we were able to play doubles together in several matches. We had a blast. But, we had little decorum. 'Oops…I can't believe you missed that one.' The other team didn't know what to think of us."

Godmother

Jacqueline: "When we were younger, Renee told me that she was going to be the Godmother for my children. Too funny. As a Catholic, you are supposed to have a Godmother who is Catholic. The Godmother is supposed to help raise them in the Catholic faith."

"I told her, 'You are not Catholic.'

"Renee answered, 'I am more Catholic than some of your Catholic friends. I have been to more masses.'" (*Laughter. More laughter*).

Pennsylvania Trip

Jacqueline: "My dad shared some about our family Pennsylvania trip with Renee at the visitation before the funeral. That's one of our favorite memories. I still remember Renee, Veronica, and I laughing our heads off, almost falling out of the car as we saw my dad get in the wrong car. Tears were streaming down our faces."

Spain

Jacqueline: "Those going into the senior year of high school could apply for the summer Indiana University Honors Program in Foreign Languages. Renee and I were included in the thirty chosen for the Spanish immersion program. We were the only two students from Pike High School. There were others from around the state. We lived with host families in Spain for eight weeks. We signed an agreement to not speak any English.

"Both Renee and I were selected for the same city in Spain, Ciudad Real (Royal City in English), an hour and half south of Madrid where there are lots of windmills. This was in the La Mancha area, the setting where Don Quixote lived.

"We both went to Spain that summer which meant that we missed our band trip to Hawaii. A bummer. We just couldn't do them both since they overlapped a bit.

"We flew out June 10, the day before my birthday, so excited to go to Spain. We had separate host families but we had classes all day every day and saw each other lots. It was so great. But, we did end up getting into a big fight over some silly thing at one point. So we were not talking to each other for a while. Whenever we needed to, we would still chat. Like we were in little groups and would go over to each other's house.

"Then, for a big final presentation, we did a program for the host families. Part of the program included singing. So Renee and I were in the choir singing different songs in Spanish. For some reason, no one could remember the words to the second verse of a song. Renee whispered, just say the words of the next line before we get there.

"We also were in a play together. This reminded me of the Cinderella play in the second grade. In this one, I was a wife of another guy. Renee was a sister so we had all our Spanish lines. It was a lot of fun. We both brought our trumpets so we played those, too.

"When we came home, our 'speaking' Spanish was much better. Renee and I used the Spanish when we got back as a secret language. We were in the fifth-year Spanish class with only a handful of students."

Peru

Jacqueline: "Renee and I really wanted to see Machu Picchu. Renee said, 'Let's go.'

"Since I was in law school at the time, it had to be over winter break. Finally, we decided to go the end of December, 2009 and beginning of January, 2010. The New Year was spent in Cuzco to become acclimated to the altitude. Cuzco is a city in Peru at a super high elevation. We stayed in a crazy youth hostel, one that was an inexpensive lodging place for young folks on bicycles or hiking. It was on the side of a mountain so we had a great view of the fireworks going off all over the city.

"We scheduled our own tour. It was great! The first night was scheduled and after that, we said, 'We will figure out what to do as we go.' We had two Machu Picchu biking and hiking trip books. The Inca trails were many, many trails spread all over. The Peruvian tour guides drove us in trucks to where we started biking around the Inca trails. We biked the Inca trails for a couple of days.

"At one point, we just started hiking on an Inca Trail, 'Let's see where this goes.' No phones, nothing to tell us where to go. We had all our stuff in hiking backpacks, clothes and all. Along the way, we came to goats on the trail. We skirted around them in some bushes. Finally, near the end of the day, we came to a little town.

"Then, the tour guides helped us get tickets to the bus and train in the town of Aguas Calientes (Hot Waters in English), the town at the start of our trip to Machu Picchu. We took the bus and hiked up to Machu Picchu on a horrible, rainy, foggy day. Finally, the rain broke and we were able to get pictures at Machu Picchu.

"We spent a day at a great hostel in the town of Nazca. That's where we rode in this tiny prop airplane to see the Nazca lines, lines cut into the earth that make pictures of animals only visible as animals from the airplanes.

"In Cuzco, we explored the town and practiced our Spanish by going up and talking to people. Spanish is the native language. At first, Renee deferred to me and then she started her own conversations with a police officer. He ended up giving her part of his badge. Their police officers have big guns so we did not want to inadvertently say something we didn't mean!

"At the end of our trip, we flew from Cuzco into Lima. The sister of a family friend of my mom welcomed us with a meal and wonderful hospitality. She took us sight-seeing on the coast and different beaches and then back to the airport."

Football

Jacqueline: "Renee wanted to come to Notre Dame for a football game. Since this was my last year at Notre Dame, we planned for her to come to a game the weekend after she passed. That never happened, of course, but we did a lot before that.

"Renee loved football; a few of her girl friends liked football and knew the names of all the players. Many Saturdays and Sunday afternoons, Renee would be sitting on the couch with her puppies beside her, watching college and NFL football. We always had a lot of fun chatting about football, the players and teams."

School Projects

Jacqueline: "One time, during a Labor Day weekend, Joy, Jenny M, Renee and I acted out the play, Romeo and Juliet while Veronica, my sister, videoed it for us."

Karyl: "Yes, Jacqueline, I remember that time. You were having such fun and laughing as you created the play with whatever props were around our house, like an angel food cake pan for a queen's hat. Your teachers definitely knew how to create fun, memorable learning experiences!"

Jacqueline: "Oh, yes, Marlene, Renee and I did a commercial one year of the 'Lifestyles of the Rich and Famous' for a social studies class. We filmed it at Marlene's house. It was really funny. Again, we had a good time laughing. It was great!"

Other Activities

Jacqueline: "During Renee's last year, it was really fortunate that we did a lot of things together. The summer of 2010, Fourth of July weekend, we went to your Colorado Cabin (10,300 feet altitude). It snowed on the Rockies on that Fourth of July weekend. We did some crazy Jeeping on those mountains (12,100 feet) and almost got stuck in the snow. Unbelievable. Brrr-r-r, we were in sweatshirts and shorts with snow on the ground. In a few short days, we hiked, played cards with your friends and Jeeped all over the mountains.

"Then, two weeks later, we did the RAIN – Ride Across Indiana bike ride. The RAIN is a 165-mile bike ride. Renee did not even have a road bike or hybrid. Her bike was a mountain bike so she rented one that never quite fit. But she stuck it out. We rode our bikes together, talking to each other. When we were yelled at, we said, 'We are not trying to win.' We made it all the way to Plainfield (sixty-five miles), our lunch stop. That's where Renee ended. So, that was awesome."

"The same summer, the first Sunday in August, we did a sprint triathlon, the Tri-Indy: 500-meter swim, a 13.5-mile bike ride and a 5-K run. We started at the same time swimming. Renee was a faster swimmer. She waited for me at the transition center. On the bike ride, we were yelled at for riding together. By the 5-K run, I thought Renee was ahead of me. I was running super, super slow and then would speed up. She actually was just a little behind me. She said, 'Every time I would get close, you would speed up!' We both finished our first triathlon."

Karyl: "Jacqueline, what do you remember most about Renee?"

Jacqueline: "Oh, that's tough. So much. Probably, she was more like a sister than a friend, always there. I don't fight with other friends. I just fight with family. *(Laughter)* That was true for Renee, too. She was very diplomatic with others."

"When it's people who are not as close or just normal friends, I might say, 'OK, sure, if that's what you want, go for it.' For me, it's not worth my emotional energy to get into an argument or bicker. But with Renee, we definitely did, more like sisters than friends, knowing that she was always there for me."

"We would be in the middle of a fight, then there would be some kind of boy drama. We would drop everything and ask, 'Okay, what's wrong? He's such a jerk.' Then, we would go back to, 'We are still mad at each other.'"

Karyl: "Jacqueline, how did Veronica fit into the picture?"

Veronica's Interview

Here are excerpts from Veronica's interview:

Veronica: "Renee was definitely like a sister to me. She was the closest thing I had besides my blood sister. So, I have lots of memories with her. We did lots together on vacations, at water-parks and theme parks like King's Island in Ohio and Holiday World in southern Indiana.

"We went on the rides. I always wanted to ride with Renee or my sister but they rode together so I was very much the little sister. Renee always made me feel included even though I was the little sister. She made me feel valuable, even if it was just sitting with her in the middle on a ride.

"She really liked roller coasters and the water park slides. I picture her with a laugh on her face, hands up, always not afraid. Yes, she liked the risky rides, always daring. She made me feel braver. She had the best laugh. Even if I didn't know it was funny, I wanted to laugh around her. She always made things more fun.

"When we played at your house, we built forts and other things with the large blocks that looked like bricks in your basement. When we played outside, we played King Arthur. That was one of the most fun games. Renee was King Arthur, of course. She would knight us, 'I knight you once, twice, thrice' (I think thrice is a word!).'

"Renee made me feel good about myself, exactly as I was without having to change, to look different, to have different inter-ests. She loved me for who I was. I remember one day she com-plimented me on my eye makeup. To this day, I have not changed it. She was very sensitive and picked up on details a lot. When we were having a conversation, I felt like she cared and was really listening.

"When Jacqueline called to tell me about Renee, it was single-handedly the worst day of my life. She is the only person I have lost that I really loved."

Veronica posted this on the Memorial Tribute page:

"For the last twenty plus years, Renee, or 'Nay', as I have called her for as long as I can remember, has been my second sister. She was 'Nay-Nay,' I was 'Hey, Vee-Vee' as in 'Hey, Boo Boo' from Scooby Doo. She and my older sister, Jacqueline, met in the second grade and have been best friends ever since, their spirits inseparable, their collection of bizarre inside jokes a world record and their loyalty stronger than any other bond I have ever had the pleasure of witnessing first hand.

"I learned and laughed with Renee as much as I did with my real sister. A true part of our family, I can barely remember a family vacation without her with us. Like any older siblings, I remember Renee and Jacqueline whispering when I walked into a room and intentionally leaving me out of a conversation to the point where I would get frustrated and stomp away. They held me down and pretended to tickle me until I almost wet my pants. They chose the seats together on a roller coaster and made me sit in the single seat."

"But any time I dated a guy, Renee was the first one to make sure he was a good guy and the first to threaten to beat him up if he ever hurt me. She laughed harder at my stupid jokes than anyone else. She noticed my first attempt at makeup when I was eleven years old and complimented me even though I looked like a clown. When we all swam together at Westchester, I could see her cheering on the side of the pool every time I took a breath.

"One time she came to New York in that red Altima she had for a while. We were driving with the windows down and she turned on a country song. She said, 'Just listen to these words.' The song was *It's a Great Day to Be Alive* by Travis Tritt. The song reminds us that this is a great day to be alive, even though there are troubles in the world. Why can't every day be a great day with the sun shining?

"That song has framed my life ever since that day and I picture Renee cranking up the radio, the wind blowing and the words coming from her mouth that it IS a great day to be alive. I think she believed this every single day she was alive. I miss her already. Renee was a part of my family, my childhood, and my world. Now, she'll continue to be part of me, until we meet again."

Veronica (Friend/Surrogate Little Sister)

Chapter 23

Our Family's Journey Together and Parenting

*You have been taught the Holy Scriptures from childhood,
and they have given you the wisdom to receive the salvation
that comes by trusting in Christ Jesus. All Scripture is
inspired by God and is useful to teach us what is true and
to make us realize what is wrong in our lives. It corrects us
when we are wrong and teaches us to do what is right.*
(2 Timothy 3:15-16, NLT)
*Gene and I understood the responsibility of raising our
children to know God and obey His commandments. It is
beyond our understanding how God answers prayers and
keeps our loved ones close to Him even at the time of death.*

Family Activities

Our family's journey together was important to us. That's why we moved to a more rural area on the outskirts of Indianapolis. Mark and Renee were in their element playing in the woods, the creek, and the sandbank behind our home.

Thanks to Dr. Robert W, a colleague at work, and his wife Barbara W, we were introduced to this area. Since our home was located in the woods, there was little sunlight, not enough to support a garden, one of Gene's favorite hobbies. The W's generously offered to let us use a part of their garden plot.

The garden was a great family project. Mark, Renee, and I worked with Gene and his garden: helped plant a wide array of vegetables, watered them during the hot summer, weeded and picked whatever was ripe. Some of the seeds planted were: corn kernels, summer squash seeds, carrot seeds, little tomato plants, little green and purple pepper plants and some seeds for beans. One year, we had a bumper crop of colored Indian corn. Renee and Mark filled a wagon with the corn and pulled the wagon around to the neighbors and asked, "Would you like to buy some colorful corn?" Renee was the mouthpiece. Mark was quite willing to help as long as Renee did the talking!

Many times when we gardened at Dr. Robert W and Barbara W's home, young Renee (four years old when we moved) played with Sumi, a big black Shepherd. Sumi loved chasing an old bicycle tire tube and bringing it back to Renee.

One Christmas, when Renee was a little older, we made warm, delicious orange rolls for the W's. When we rang the doorbell, Barbara W answered the door. Sumi saw Renee and started running in circles around the house. He was sooooo excited to see Renee. Barbara W said, "I have never seen Sumi act like this." Yes, Renee was magical with animals. Sumi remembered Renee!

Every summer and Christmas we travelled to the farm of Gene's parents, a thirteen-hour trip to Andover, near Wichita, Kansas. This continued through Mark and Renee's high-school years.

Renee loved the farm, especially the visit when there were four little kittens. On one trip, when Renee was younger, she hid one of the fluffy, little white kittens in the car and tried to bring her home. Bummer. "Sorry Renee, we just cannot have kittens with Mark's severe allergies to cats (at a young age)."

Many times, Renee's cousins (Gene's brother Richard's children) from Vancouver, Canada – Franziska, Julia, and Richie – were at the farm as well. The older two girls were similar in age to Mark and Renee. Renee really looked forward to playing with her cousins. This turned out to be a great gift for our children, the gift of knowing their cousins. Renee and her cousins loved to go almost anywhere on the farm with Grandpa – to the pasture in an old 50's pickup, fishing, or watching him milk the cows. One summer, the girls pitched a tent and slept in the backyard.

Just about everything on the farm had play value. Renee and her cousins pretended to drive the old tractor and farm equipment, threw the hedge balls that fell from the hedge trees and picked beans or pulled carrots to assist Grandma with her garden. Renee loved to feed the cats, mostly wild, except for the one who had the four kittens.

Franziska, Renee's Cousin

Franziska was the oldest daughter of Richard, Gene's younger brother. On the Memorial Tribute website, Franziska posted the following:

> "Dear Renee,"

> "I have so many memories. I guess I will start at the farm in Kansas. You were the cool older cousin; Julia and I always looked up to you. I remember how you, Julia, and I used to chase cows and the one time we climbed into Dotty's stall because we were scared we had pissed off the bull. You were the bravest and climbed out first to make sure it was safe for us.

> "I remember the summer we spent camping in the yard and the kittens we each adopted from Midnight's litter. We snuck those kittens into the tent almost every night. There was also that fort we built in the barn out of hay bales. I had so much fun playing in there that I did not even care about the rash that covered most of my body for a week.

> "I remember you, Julia and I taking turns learning to drive in Grampa's old pickup.

Then there was the Sedgwick plaza when we were older, the assisted-living facility where Gramma and Grampa lived after his stroke.

"It's horrible that you were taken from us before your time, but I am grateful to have such fond memories to remember you by. I will miss you with all my heart.

"Franziska"

Barbara F R, Renee's Aunt

Barbara F R, the wife of Richard, Gene's younger brother, was a wonderful aunt for Renee. She was always interested in whatever Renee was doing. Even when Renee was at the Academy, Barbara F R and the girls met us for dinner near Denver. Our family visited Richard's family in Vancouver and their cabin northeast of Vancouver several times. One of the times, the 'girls' decided to go trail riding.

Here's Barbara F R's story:

"It's a hot day sometime in 1997 or 1998. Renee, her brother Mark, and her parents are in the Far North, Canada, visiting her uncle Richard and his family in Vancouver. Richard's family just purchased a cabin three and one-half hours northeast of Vancouver in the Nicola Valley. Both families are spending the weekend at the cabin on a hot summer day. This is range country. The 'girls' – Karyl, Renee, Barbara F R, Julia, and Franziska – decided to leave the 'boys' to do their own thing at the cabin and go on a trail ride, guided by a wrangler at Stoney Lake Ranch, about thirty miles away. Complicated arrangements were made: at an appointed time, we were to meet the wrangler waiting at a locked gate somewhere at the end of the road to let us in to another road leading to the ranch.

"The trip to the gate involved a good ten miles on a 'not-so-good gravel road,' the kind that leaves you with a car caked in dust, a cracked windshield and a flat tire. And a flat tire is exactly what we got.

"Stranded in the middle of nowhere and I mean NO WHERE. Barbara F R proceeded to unearth the jack from somewhere in the depths of the car, trying to figure out where the spare was so she and Karyl could get to work changing it.

"Then the realization hits: We are going to miss our riding appointment if we don't make it to the gate where the wrangler is supposed to meet us. Renee suggested that she and Franziska walk there, so they can warn the wrangler that we will be a tad late. Off they set, down the gravel road while we worked on the tire.

"Time passes; we are still fiddling with the tire. A pickup truck with two natives in cowboy hats approached, slowed down, and came to a stop, enveloping us in a cloud of dust. The guys offer help, but we decline: The tire is almost on. Then it occurs to us to ask, 'Have you seen the two girls?'

"'Oh, yes,' they say, 'we gave them a ride. They are waiting for you at the gate.' Karyl's jaw drops. She was not happy but forced a gracious smile.

"A little later, we pulled up to the gate where a beaming Renee and excited Franziska greeted us. Karyl asked, 'How did you get to the gate?'

"Renee explains, 'I thought we would never get to the gate on time if we walked. So, when the opportunity arose, we caught a ride – in the MIDDLE of NOWHERE. I thought it best to hitch-hike to save our riding date.'

"That's exactly what she did. Being the older cousin, Renee made an executive decision, which, thank God, turned out to be okay. The girls were safe and our riding adventure was saved, adding a little adventure of Renee's own to it! Renee was quite in control of her horse and even galloped. I had never ridden a horse before."

Later Barbara F R shared the following:

"When Mark and Renee were teenagers (16 and 14 years), they visited us at our cabin. They helped dig out the fire pit at the cabin.

"After Renee passed, Richard made a wood burning sign at the fire pit honoring Renee. They call the fire pit 'Renee's place.' He ripped a piece of pine log, made a flat surface, sanded it, then wood-burned Renee's name, her birth and death dates on it. It is still hanging there today."

Jay B R, Renee's cousin

Jay B R was Renee's cousin, the son of Gene's older brother. Jay B R was one of Renee's favorite cousins. He was incredibly fun for the girls (Julia, Franziska and Renee). Jay B R was perhaps 20 years older, an electrical engineer who finished his degree at California Institute of Technology and worked at Apple.

Jay B R: "I always felt like more of an uncle to all my cousins since I was so much older. One of the memories I have of Renee was at Grampa's farm. We were playing around with Mark, Franziska, and Julia. For some reason, Renee was looking at my foot – my little toenail. She said, 'That's really ugly.' *(laughter)*

"'Yeah, I can see it. That's a really ugly little nail! I think she just was trying to tease me and get a reaction out of me by saying 'Your toenail looks really bad!' I think she painted it!!

"Renee always wanted to play 'piggy back' and 'rough house.'

Karyl: "I remember you even allowed her to pretend you were a bucking horse...."

Jay B R: "Yes, I bucked her off several times!"

Barbara F R: "I remember the girls climbing up on you ... like you were a gigantic monkey tree."

Richard: "All the girls wanted to play with their cousin Jay B R, especially Renee and Julia. Jay B R was pretty patient with them." *(laughter)*

Gene: "Another thing I remember was you and Renee played Connect Four."

Jay B R: "Yes, we definitely played games if they were around."

Karyl: "I remember that when she was in the eighth grade, she won a Connect Four game. I asked you if you let her win. (Jay B R was a National Merit Scholar) You said, 'NO!'" *(laughter)*

Jay B R: "NO ... I DID NOT let her win!!"

Jenica, Renee's Cousin

Jenica was Renee's cousin, my brother's daughter, about two years younger than Renee. She lived in Indianapolis from her kindergarten through second-grade years. We had Sunday dinners together, so Jenica really got to know Renee. Jenica now loves teaching science classes in a small rural high school in Oklahoma, bringing cutting-edge modalities to her curriculum.

Here is Jenica's interview:

"From an early age we knew each other and spent a lot of time together. Renee and I had a bond. The three years I was in Indianapolis, I went to soccer games with you and birthday parties. I specifically remember the ice-cream cake for my birthday one year; I think you gave me a stamp-making kit.

"Renee also was my introduction to video games. I didn't know much about video games because we didn't have any. That was in the era when they were just coming out. It was something fun and new. I think there are some benefits such as hand-eye coordination."

"I remember one time it snowed and we had a snow fight with shovels of snow, throwing snow at each other. These times were a great introduction to what it would be like with siblings, since I did not have any. Renee was like a big sister. Those three years were a ton of fun.

"She and your family often visited us in Kansas when we lived in the country (after moving from Indy). It was kind of neat to share my country life with Renee. You came to Lincoln, Kansas, the day I was actually showing my lambs in the County Fair. Renee loved animals and was happy to hold the halters, walk the lambs, get in and help feed them.

"Renee was really awesome in making sure I was involved and included in whatever she was doing with her friends, both at Mark's graduation (1999) and her graduation (2001). Mark's graduation was the same weekend as the Billy Graham crusade in Indianapolis. Renee took me with her and the Youth Group from her church to the Billy Graham crusade. She included me in the conversations with her friends. It was just really cool because this was the first time we connected more as young adults than as young children. That meant a lot to me. I felt important to her.

"When she graduated in 2001, she took me with her to several of her friends' graduation parties. Renee introduced me. Her friends were amazing because they would talk to me, too. It was really cool that she included me.

"That same weekend, we went to the movie *A Knight's Tale* starring Heath Ledger. It's about a pauper of a kid (peasant squire) who works for a knight. He takes care of his horses and equipment. His master, the knight, dies. The peasant squire creates a new identity for himself as a knight. I never would have watched it except for Renee. Now, it's a fun favorite of mine.

"The weekend after Renee's graduation, I needed to be in Wichita because I was part of the Youth Ambassadors, an honor band that spent three to four weeks in Europe. I played a clarinet. We started in England. We practiced and then had a concert. The next two or three days, we toured the country. We saw Buckingham Palace and the guards at the gates. We tried to get them to smile!

"I remember visiting Aunt Mary Bess in Chicago a couple of times. Renee was always there. Chris, her husband, was always joking around and having fun. Usually, Chris had all his family, over 25 people at Thanksgiving and Easter with a food feast."

"Indeed, Chris was a gourmet cook who always created mouth-watering, delicious feasts. For Thanksgiving, we had a huge, juicy and tender turkey, wine-based stuffing, mashed potatoes and gravy with other unique and delicious sides such as the fresh cranberry relish. For Easter, we had a spit-roasted whole lamb, small red potatoes, peas with caramelized onions and other gourmet fruit and relishes. The dessert that topped the chart was the 'Death by Chocolate' flourless cake."

Thank you Jenica, for reminding me of these fond family traditions. One of the best gifts was that Chris tutored Mark with all the special gourmet tricks of the trade as he was supervising the preparation of the meal.

Other Family Activities

When we travelled, we soon learned that sibling rivalry was at its finest – well, worst, when both were in the back seat. We even tried travelling through the night hoping the children would sleep. No such luck. That only resulted in all of us dead-tired when we arrived.

Finally, we got a van with bucket seats in the front and middle rows. This was a dream come true for travelling to Kansas. No more squabbling. No more arguing over who was in the other's space in the back seat. Mark and Renee were separated. Travel was much more peaceful.

Counting cows or white horses, spotting something a certain color or guessing travelling games only lasted a little while. Then, it was back to reading a great book. Mark and Renee loved to have me read as we travelled.

On our trip to Yellowstone Park and the Tetons, I remember reading the Newberry Medal winner *Rats of NIMH* (National Institute of Mental Health). We stayed in log cabins at Coulter Bay in Teton National Park just below Yellowstone National Park. We purchased wood for the real fireplace and rented sleeping bags. Definitely, this was more like camping.

The book was so good, Mark and Renee pleaded, "Mom, please read more." They both crawled up with me onto the top bunk with their sleeping bags. With a flashlight, I read. They avidly listened to the end of the book. Midnight. But worth every minute of shared suspense together. Books were a gift for our family and still are.

Another summer vacation was over the Fourth of July at Estes Park, Colorado. We all enjoyed the beautiful mountains of Colorado. Cool crisp breezes and hikes in the beautiful woods were the draw. Campfire singing and a chapel service in the mountains were a real treat. Probably, most of all, Renee and Mark were thrilled to tromp through running streams of water, ones where they could wade and splash with abandonment, laughing as they created water games that tickled their fancy!

Indeed, one of Renee and Mark's favorite activities was playing in the water. Any kind! I remember the fun and joy they had when they went to Marott Park Nature Preserve in Indy and waded, with water up to their waist, down Williams Creek where it joins White River. In fact, Mark's preschool teacher brought Mark and Renee's classes to Marott Park for an outing. The kids loved it! Yes. They and their clothes were soaking wet when they came out of the creek, but OH SO HAPPY!

Mark and Renee's swimming skills proved to be a huge gift. When our family went to Hawaii for our 25th Wedding Anniversary, Mark and Renee snorkeled and dived with the fish, just like two fish swimming in the coral reefs. They were thrilled to see the beautiful bright colored fish – bright yellows, fluorescent blues, and oranges.

The vacations that were some of the most memorable were to Tincup, an old mining town 10,000 feet-high in the Rocky Mountains. Gene's college friend and family, Jim and Glenda S lived in Tincup during the summer. Their two children, James and Lydia, were similar in age to Mark and Renee. Mark and Renee really enjoyed Jeeping up from 10,000 feet to around 12,000 feet at the base of beautiful mountains that rise gloriously, and then hiking to the top. The 360-degree view of mountains was spectacular. Eventually, we purchased a cabin on a mountain overlooking Tincup.

Parenting

The Lord knew our concerns and great struggles during the 90's to make sure we knew Renee's friends and were making wise decisions as parents, ones consistent with the Lord's will. We had clear expectations related to Renee doing her best with integrity and honesty. We knew, with the right values and the Lord's wisdom and guidance, she could do almost anything she decided.

We had clear expectations related to friends, i.e., where she was and what she was doing. We made every effort to know Renee's friends, their parents and families. This was relatively easy during the elementary years, since I created and implemented, with the teachers, "Food for Fun and Thought" projects for their classes. The children participated in cooking/food preparation, tasting/

eating and nutrition education games through the fourth grade. They loved these enrichment activities and I came to know each of the children well. Most of the children continued with Renee in enrichment classes through high school.

In high school, when Renee was invited to extracurricular activities and parties, we always checked with the parents and those in charge. Renee was not particularly happy about us checking with the parents and let me know "You are the worst mother." Renee was allowed to have group dates when she was sixteen years old. We always had to know where Renee was going, with whom, and when she would be home.

The closest thing to acknowledgment from Renee came when she was telling me about a single young man with a six-year-old daughter. He asked Renee to marry him. Then, after the date was set, he texted her and said, "The wedding's off, my daughter says 'no.'"

Renee was shocked and devastated. He made decisions related to dating and his relationship without communication with his daughter and then, based on his daughter's desires, whom Renee had not met, he was ending the relationship with a text message. Whew. That was a shocker. My view was, "Better to find out now then later."

Renee's reaction, "Just wait until his daughter gets into high school. She will be running the show."

My reaction, "Renee, you know we prayed non-stop for you in high school."

"Oh, no, Mom, you always had a hold of my shirttail. I was one of the few, if not the only one, who got through high school without doing drugs, alcohol, and sex." That was a huge acknowledgement to Gene and I (and the Lord!) for years of praying, listening to her desires, yet holding the boundaries during her earlier school years.

Chapter 24

Mark, Renee's brother – A Twinkling Star

He determines the number of the stars;
and calls them each by name.
(Mark, a twinkling star). (Psalm 147:4)
We are each a Star
Sometimes we shine with the other stars.
Sometimes we twinkle alone and sometimes....
When we least know it ... we make someone's dream come true.

Mark is a twinkling star in so many ways, not one you would necessarily notice mainly because he quietly goes about everything he does. When Mark was born, the Lord was with him. The Lord brought this twinkling star into our lives and the world. We welcomed him with great love and joy! He made one of our dreams come true.

Mark is a handsome young man, mid-height with shorter brown hair and hazel eyes. He is well built, now in adulthood, trim and physically fit. Mark is solid and reliable. If he says he will do something, he does it and even better than one expects.

Mark was always efficient and effective in everything he did. He played intensely. He read voraciously, a book or more every week. He worked, with every second productive. So was Renee (if the activity was a priority) and she had lots of fun along the way!

In many ways, Mark was different from Renee. As a strong introvert, he processed internally before he spoke. Everything he said was targeted and purposeful. No extra chit-chat. In his pre-school years, however, he made all the noises of the engines and cars that he was playing with!

Mark loved the science classes – math, chemistry and physics – and did well in them in the Extended Learning (EL) Program. Renee also did quite well in them, but they were not her favorite. She was more interested in negotiation and topics such as foreign affairs, where she learned the customs, culture and political climate of different countries. She always was caring and compassionate, concerned about the well-being of others and the least of these.

When playing or working together, Mark and Renee were like two peas in a pod. Mark was more reserved. But he was loyal, considerate, kind, and generous. He had a small group of loyal friends, ones he came to know well from his early years in school through high school. One family, the D's, had two children the same age as Mark and Renee, both in the EL Programs. Luke and Marlene and their parents became fast friends of our family. Our families went to Chicago together for an adventure-filled day.

Mark excelled not only in the sciences but also in debate. It seemed like a miracle that Mark, an introvert, was willing to debate in high school. It was Luke, his friend, who encouraged him to take the debate course as a sophomore. Indeed, the more comfortable Mark became speaking publicly, the better he would later be at explaining to others the value of the work he was doing. Policy debate was a phenomenal boost to Mark's self-confidence and security in sharing publicly. Mark was destined to become a scientist. Indeed, he did.

Debate was the beginning of transformation for Mark in speaking. Yes, a big transformation. He, with his friend Joe Z (also in the EL program), began to debate in regional policy debates and continued beyond their sophomore year. This was the first time that any team from Pike High School ever debated in regional competitions. During the summer of Mark's junior year, he and Joe Z went to a seven-week National Debate Camp at the University of Michigan. They prepared for the next year's policy debates related to U.S. policies with Russia.

Since Mark needed a debate judge to go to regionals when Mrs. Donna C, his debate teacher, could not go, he begged me to become a debate judge. Yikes ... that was a wakeup call, way out of my comfort zone. My response? "Surely you can find someone else. I know nothing about debate."

Indeed, parents will do things for their children they never would consider otherwise! With a huge gulp, I said "Okay, Mark, if I am to judge so you can compete, I need to know a lot more about debating and how to score debates."

Back to school I went. Mrs. Donna C loaned me a debate text, gave me the rules for debating and invited me to her high-school debate class to see real debates, the class Renee happened to be in. Renee welcomed me! She was taking debate her sophomore year (Mark was a senior). This was a reversal; I was attending Renee's debate class!

Attending this class was an amazing experience. These kids were debating some hot topics like abortion and other simpler topics like "Is an elevator better than an escalator?" and "Is a pen better than a pencil?" I also attended an Indy all day debating session led by one of the national debate champions. He discussed the year's policy debate topic: "Are there any U.S. – Russia policies that will work?"

Bottom line, my prayer was that I *never* had to judge a debate! Thankfully, I did not need to judge and Mark was able to participate at all the regional competitions. The debating had another advantage. Since I was taking Mark and Joe Z to the competitions, I had the opportunity to visit with them and heard their perspectives about many aspects of their lives. They were captive audiences!

As a senior in high school, Renee was quite happy to give up her study period to assist Mrs. Donna C in her debate course. Through debate, Renee learned to view both the pro and con sides of an issue and developed persuasive skills, not that she was lacking in these areas! Her writing skills improved, as well.

Mark's Younger Years

He was extraordinarily active, alert, and inquisitive as a young boy. Yes, ALL boy! He loved playing with the big Tonka trucks and "heavy" equipment – the front loader, the big dump truck, the scoop, the mighty crane and the trencher – perfect for the sand bank at the creek.

In Mark's younger years, he was not saying words; that was not important to him. He clearly communicated his wishes and happily went on his way. Finally, at three, we had a speech and hearing evaluation. My dear friend, a speech and language pathologist for early childhood, was the one who suggested this. This was a gift but I was very concerned. The speech therapist said, "You are doing everything correctly. He clearly understands what you are saying. His receptive language is excellent. Keep speaking words directly to him, repeating in words what he is doing."

Shortly after, he began speaking in sentences, well, at least in combinations of three or more words that accurately reflected the situation. Interestingly, that heralded some of his later behaviors. Only when he knew something was accurate and correct would he do it.

Mark also was thrilled to have me read books to him. Reading twenty to thirty library books every three weeks became common for Mark. He savored and wanted to read all of them. He gained a love for reading that continues to this day. It is not unusual for Mark to read two or three books a week. Thankfully, the library provides a great variety of science-fiction books, his favorite.

By the time Mark began the first grade, I was reading Keyhole Mystery books to Mark. These stories of young school-age boys – detectives who solved mysteries – enthralled Mark. The boys had a hideout center for the detectives in one of the Uncles' junkyards.

They hired a chauffeur to drive a Rolls Royce. This was the ultimate joy for all the young boys, to have their own hideout with a secret entrance and a fancy Rolls Royce to solve mysteries.

The Lord has favored Mark through all his years of school. It seemed like he was destined to get the best teacher in his preschool cooperative classes – Mrs. Connie R – the teacher for all the other preschool co-op teachers. She was wonderful! Mark had the advantage of having her for the 4's preschool and the 4/5's. This extra year allowed him to go from being the youngest in the class to the oldest. He became quite comfortable with social interactions with the other five-year- old boys. They built forts with huge blocks and bridges to the moon. One of the girls complained because the boys would not play with her. So, with Mrs. Connie R's encouragement, the boys let her play with them. They allowed her to go to the moon on a rocket they built and left her on the moon. Smile...such is the life of a young boy!

Behind the scenes, Mark is thoughtful and considerate, very observant. When Mark was younger, a big issue for me was remembering where my car and house keys were. When Mark was in the first grade, he gave me a key ring holder for Mother's Day. No more problems with keys. I just put them in the key ring holder by the door. This was a simple solution! That's Mark – very considerate, very caring and very observant – doing just what was needed for the moment. He was that way during the funeral week, working with Gene to find whatever was needed and a calming, competent influence for Gene. That's what he does with whomever he is around – simply and thoughtfully meets the needs of others.

Mark entered the EL program in the fourth grade and continued through high school. Mark just seemed to skate through the toughest courses and shine like a twinkling star for those who knew him.

DePauw University

Mark was focused, centered on what he needed to do and did what was needed (very well) in the science field. He went to DePauw University in, Greencastle, Indiana, primarily because of the Science Research Fellow program. Mark majored in both chemistry and physics.

Interestingly, the topic of debate was what Mark used for an essay for admissions into DePauw University. He developed all the reasons why learning debate was beneficial and then at the very end said, "Debating is fun!" Smile. My last words of wisdom and advice for Mark when he left for the National Debate Camp were "Have fun. It's not worth doing if you are not having fun!"

When Mark was being interviewed for the Science Fellow program, at the end of one of his interviews, I heard the interviewers laughing heartily. That was odd because Mark rarely told jokes. So I asked him, "What was the laughter all about?"

"They asked me, 'How did you come up with the research project idea?'

"I told them, 'For one Christmas, I gave my mother a present of *Learning to Search Computer Websites.* I handed her a hard copy of the directions for searching the web. She said, "I need a little more help ... please *show and tell me* what to do!" *It was clear that my mother and I learn differently.* '

"I, an introvert, process internally, however, my mother, an extrovert, processes and learns through conversations." That provided the idea for the proposed research project: Determine the effectiveness of two approaches to educating companies about newer computer technologies, based on whether the employees were extroverts or introverts. This was during the late 90's when computer skills with websites were just coming into being.

Mark entered DePauw with a full-tuition scholarship in the Science Research Fellow program, a select group of seven or eight students interested in a career in research. Several science disciplines were represented: chemistry, physics, computer sciences, psychological sciences, math, and geology. Every fall and spring, the Science Fellows participated in a team research project with the guidance of a faculty advisor in the area of study. They worked together to design the research project and methodology, collect data, summarize data and present the project as a presentation. For Mark, who knew that he wanted to go to graduate school in the sciences, this was a fabulous opportunity to participate in a research team.

Another area Mark participated in was debate at DePauw. Amazing. I could hardly believe that my son was debating. During Mark's initial days on campus, he met a young man who debated at DePauw. He invited Mark to debate and then to join his fraternity, Sigma Nu. A particularly appealing aspect of the fraternity was that he would have his own room for the four years at DePauw. We assisted Mark in making the room comfortable for him, with a piece of rug that perfectly fit his room, several on-sale bedspreads and pillows and a rolling chair we found on sale at Staples.

I later asked Mark, "How is the fraternity going, especially the drinking issue?" He said, "No problem. I just tell the guys I don't drink."

While Mark was at DePauw, he was a teaching assistant for his advisor's course, Physical Chemistry. Physical chemistry is known as one of the most difficult courses in chemistry. Mark barely mentioned to us that he was awarded an outstanding chemistry-student award his junior year and an outstanding physics-student award his senior year. Mark's undergraduate chemistry advisor guided a chemistry research project that he presented at American Chemical Society (ACS) meetings both as a junior and senior. His senior year, he was selected as one of the top student researchers at the ACS meeting.

University of Wisconsin

It was pretty miraculous that Mark went to the University of Wisconsin at Madison for his graduate studies. He did not go because Gene had gone there. Nope. He said, "It was the friendliness and interest of the professors in having me come. They sent emails that shared their interests and the opportunities that were available at the University of Wisconsin."

Our guess was that the emails came from the Department Chair of Chemistry, the one whom Mark later chose for his research advisor. The Lord works in amazing ways. The Department Chair happened to call Gene seeking support for a new chemistry research building named in honor of Gene's major professor. This was just at the time Mark was deciding where to go to graduate school. We told him about Mark and asked if there was anything he could do to encourage him to come to Madison. The emails sent from the faculty persuaded Mark.

Mark and his friend from DePauw, who was entering the physics PhD program, went to Madison the summer before beginning graduate school to find an apartment for rent. After looking two days at every possibility, Mark came home very discouraged because his teaching/research assistantship would not support the cost of the only available two-bedroom apartments ($1200/month).

This was one of the few times I have seen Mark in tears. Mark was certain there was nothing available since they had searched all sites and newspapers that advertised available apartments for students and found nothing.

My suggestion, "Why don't I call one of my favorite teachers, Dr. Dorothy P, at the University of Wisconsin and ask her if she knows of any reasonable rooms or possibly a house for rent?"

Dr. Dorothy P's answer, "The house next to mine has a graduate student who is completing his studies this summer. That might be available."

This home was very close to the university campus. It seemed like a miracle. A son of an older lady owned and was renting the home. He never advertised. Dr. Dorothy P contacted the son, a nurse who lived in Chicago. The son met Mark and his friend and when he learned that Mark's friend's father was a physician, he rented it to them for $400/month.

Mark and his friend literally renovated the house during the four-and-a-half years they lived there. With permission of the owner, they totally cleared the garage filled with all kinds of junk, old furniture, cars, and squirrels. They replaced the flooring and updated the kitchen with their own labor. The owner purchased the supplies.

One weekend that we were visiting, we noticed one of the French doors was not closing correctly. Sure enough, Mark and his friend were looking at it and figuring out how to fix it. Wow. This was great for the owner of the house and Mark and his friend.

Dr. Dorothy P lived next door. She enjoyed getting to know the guys. In fact, she came to Mark and Rorie's wedding. We were thrilled!

The first two years of graduate study, Mark was a teaching assistant. He was not thrilled about teaching, but the assistantship paid the bill. The Chemistry Department at the University of Wisconsin is one of the biggest in the United States; it provides chemistry courses to 13,000 undergraduate and graduate students a year. By the time they graduate, 55% of the students who enter as freshmen will have taken a chemistry course while on campus. In 2014, U.S. News and World Report ranked the graduate-study program in Analytical Chemistry at the University of Wisconsin sixth in the nation.

Mark, with undergraduate degrees in both physics and chemistry, chose to work with his advisor, who had a PhD in physics. His advisor had just stepped down as the Department Chair of Chemistry and was updating his own laboratory for laser research. Mark was thrilled to assist in setting up all the computers. Mark's research was published as the first article in a chemistry journal (a coveted location in a highly rated journal). Since his advisor was not able to go to Switzerland to present the work, he sent Mark, saying, "Mark can present this work as well as I can." Mark received an award for his outstanding doctoral work. Perhaps the most heart-warming comment from his advisor was, "Mark is like a son." Mark completed his PhD in four-and-a-half years.

After graduation from the University of Wisconsin, Mark began work as an analytical chemist with spectroscopy expertise at Dow Chemical. He later transitioned to DuPont after the Dow-DuPont merger and spin-off and remained in Midland, Michigan.

Getting to Know the Lord and His Love

One day as a young child, Mark and I were reading together. I noticed Mark's toe had an open sore that was not healing. That concerned me. We wondered whether we should take Mark to the doctor. Finally, I said, "Mark, let's pray for healing of this toe." The next evening, it began healing and within several days was totally healed. Wow. That was an amazing answer to prayer for Mark, the beginning of faith for a child who saw and believed in the power of prayer. That and the reading of the *Children's Bible* were the beginning of a long, faithful journey with the Lord.

Mark accepted Jesus as his savior when he was 12 years old and was baptized. In the sixth grade, Mark began a national Bible Bowl program at Traders Point Christian Church (TPCC). Bible Bowl has a quick recall quiz format where student teams compete over their knowledge of scripture. A selected book or books of the Bible is determined as the text that season, alternating each year between the Old and the New Testaments.

In preparation for monthly competitions and the national Bible Bowl competition, Mark's and other teams from TPCC met weekly and reviewed a chapter or so of one book of the Bible. Many of the children memorized scripture; all learned applications of the scriptures to their daily lives. Rather than memorize the scripture, Mark read the assigned chapters every night so he became very familiar with them.

Gene was a quiz master for the weekly practices and monthly competitions during the fall and spring. The quizmaster reads questions (referred to as "toss-ups") to the players. The first player to buzz in and answer correctly gets a series of "bonus" questions for that player's team to answer together.

Integrating the Word into his life through Bible Bowl was a very important part of his growing years. That really grounded him. The Fire Chief for one of the Indianapolis townships was the team coach. He was exceptional, a great inspiration for all the guys. The lead team from our church frequently placed in the top 10 of 250 teams nationally.

At the University of Wisconsin, Mark found a Holy Spirit-filled church and finally joined a graduate Bible study sponsored by InterVarsity. InterVarsity at the University of Wyoming made a huge difference for my walk with the Lord. Miracle of all miracles. That is where he met Rorie, his future wife. She was a teacher, who returned to Madison to obtain a Master's in Special Education. We love her. Rorie and Mark were married in 2008. Renee was thrilled to stand as the "Best Woman" in their wedding.

Renee got to know Rorie in a very special way. Rorie assured Renee that she was not taking her brother Mark away from her, and ultimately, began to do fun activities with Renee like playing Mario Kart on the Nintendo. They laughed hilariously and were competitive from the get-go. Such fun.

While Mark continued at Dow Chemical, Rorie taught alternative education for five years in Midland. The fifth year, the joy of their lives and ours came – Rachel Renee. In another three years, Peter Mark was born.

Now, Mark and his family are actively participating in a church in Midland. He and Rorie are treasurers for the church. Rorie assists with organizing children's church. The best gift is Mark's faithful reading of his Bible. Rorie participates in Bible Study Fellowship (BSF) with Rachel and the Community Bible Study preschool program with Peter. BSF is a blessing, a program that Gene and I participated in for more than twenty years.

We visited Rorie and Rachel the fall that BSF began the study of the book of Revelation. Rachel, sitting in her chair waiting for breakfast, out of the blue said to me, "Grammy, I can talk to Jesus. All I need to do is lay down on my pillow and pretend it is a cloud and talk to him."

Indeed, that's what John did in Revelation. He was caught up in a cloud and heard the Lord sharing "what must soon take place." Revelation is a book of the Bible that brings prophetic good news about the second coming of Jesus. Wow, a precious sharing from little Rachel, three years old at that time. This was an answer to one of our closest held prayers that Rachel and Peter will grow to know Jesus personally.

When Rachel was seven years old, we were reading from a little book called *Dear God*. This was a book of prayers for young children. The prayers centered around one truth from the Bible with the Bible verse given at the end of the prayer. When we finished one prayer, as I was beginning to share the Bible verse, Rachel said, "Wait, just a minute."

She got her children's Bible from her bookshelf and showed me where to find the scripture in her Bible. She knew the books of the Bible and how to find scriptures in them. That was sooooo exciting … so amazing. A big thanks to Rorie and all the BSF teachers for doing amazing work!

Little Peter began Bible School in the Community Bible School program when he was three years old. When Peter was four, Rorie and Mark would ask him what he was thankful for during the evening prayers. He always said, "Bible School."

After the prayers, I asked. "Why are you thankful for Bible School?"

He said "fishy crackers!" Smile … yes, the Lord has a great sense of humor … and we are grateful that he was so positive about Bible School!

Chapter 25

In the Pits – Searching for a New Identity

For we are God's masterpiece. He has
created us anew in Christ Jesus,
so we can do the good things He planned for
us long ago. (Ephesians 2:10, NLT)
God created a special career for Renee that was not fulfilled
at either the Air Force Academy or Purdue University.
As parents, we waited patiently for Renee to come to
know and fulfill the purposes God planned for her.

Renee was in the pits searching for a new identity after leaving the Air Force Academy. She was blessed in many ways during her time at the Academy. When she decided this was not her calling and mission, she had some tough transition years.

She transferred to Purdue and wanted to continue in a Foreign Affairs curriculum. Since Purdue did not have this major, she enrolled in Political Science with a Spanish minor and rented an apartment near the campus. Renee soon realized that her conservative political views were not similar to her professors and she became disillusioned with political science. Renee was searching for a new identity and purpose for her life. She did not find it there. In her heart, she still was committed to keeping our nation's people safe and making a difference in people's lives.

Chapter 26

Bank Teller

Always be humble and gentle. Be patient with each other,
making allowance for each other's faults because of your love.
Make every effort to keep yourselves united in the Spirit,
binding yourselves together with peace. (Ephesians 4:2-3, NLT)
Life is much easier to understand when you look at the past. The
time when Renee lived under the same roof as us was potentially
challenging. Yet, when this season of time was over, we viewed it
as a precious gift from God. Our relationships were strengthened.

While Renee was in Lafayette, Indiana, she began working for the Charter Bank as a bank teller. They soon had Renee closing the bank and in-line for advancement to Assistant Bank Manager. After the funeral, I had the opportunity to visit with the Bank Manager who hired Renee. She said, "I soon realized that Renee was 'Managerial' material."

Renee was transferred to Indianapolis as a bank teller and assisted in closing the Nora Branch Bank in a Marsh supermarket. She moved into a rental home across from us – the only one in this section of Pike Township. It was a divine miracle that this became available just as Renee transferred to Indianapolis.

Several months later, when we began remodeling our home, we moved into the rental home with Renee. Our biggest concern was how to manage the 'guidelines' and expectations for each of us. We had heard some stories about adult children who were living unsuccessfully with their parents. Our main guideline was mutual respect and good communication. Renee knew all our hot buttons. God answered all our concerns and gave us so much more grace. The biggest gift was ongoing conversations that allowed us to come to know Renee as a fun, respectful, and considerate young adult.

One day, I asked Renee, "What do you say to your friends about your living with us?" Her answer, "Oh, it's no problem. I just tell them, 'My parents moved in with me.'"

Renee rented the house across from ours for more than two years. Then, as she was transitioning to her own home, she stayed with us. Those almost three years were clearly a gift from the Lord. My mother died when I was twenty-eight years old. The Lord knew my immense sadness at not being able to listen to her wisdom and stories. Amazingly, the Lord allowed me to listen to two years of what I called 'bedpost' conversations with Renee.

Renee shared many of her 'action' stories when she came home early in the morning from police duty, just before I left for work. These sharing times, as good friends, were precious. Renee never repeated her stories. No time. She was onto the next adventure. The Lord knew my sadness from not having the time with my mother but granted it with my daughter. God is good, all the time!

Chapter 27

Finding her Niche – Becoming a Police Officer

Bring my sons from afar and my daughters
from the ends of the earth,
everyone who is called by my name, whom I created for my glory,
whom I formed and made. (Isaiah 43:6b-7)
As a mother, I had my own thoughts about
what Renee's life might be.
As I look back over her life, I can hear the
sweet whispers from Heaven saying,
'I created Renee to bring Glory to God.'

The Lord favored Renee with fruit of the spirit – kindness, goodness, and righteousness – as she came into her own as a police officer. The Lord must have had this in store for Renee all along. She just took the long way around to find it. We never imagined her becoming a police officer and never dreamed she would attend a Military Academy, either. Now, the options for women are many. The Lord had a special plan for Renee and for me, too. Walking the journey provided adventures beyond anything I could have "made up."

In finding her niche, Renee considered becoming a veterinarian. She volunteered to work with our local veterinarian, came home very knowledgeable and used that for her cats. That would have been a good fit. But, the summer she volunteered for the Humane Society, she saw some animals not adopted, but put to sleep. Ugh. For Renee's heart, that was unthinkable.

Renee was destined to have a career outside. She loved being outdoors, loved being physically challenged, running, working together in team sports such as soccer and riding her own motorcycle. Many guys who saw her riding drooled over her motorcycle. It was 'hot,' went fast and was a gorgeous royal blue Yamaha with all the extras (2005 Yamaha YZF-R1).

The bank-teller position was an important transition position, one that testified to her integrity and honesty, customer service, and organizational skills. But the job was indoors. The cattiness and drama of the women she was working with were not her cup of tea.

One of her Purdue friends asked, "Renee, do you want to be a police officer? Let's take the test to be one."

Both she and her friend took the fitness exam. Unfortunately, the night before the exam, her friend sprained a wrist. Though he participated in the fitness exam, he did not pass.

Renee passed the physical examination and completed the rest of the tests and interviews successfully. She eventually became an Indiana State Capitol Police Officer, guarding the Indiana State Capitol, Governor's mansion, and downtown Indianapolis. She was in her element; all her past years at the Academy proved valuable.

She loved the late-night shift because "there is more action!" She respected the guys on this shift and the shift supervisor. Renee said, "They work hard, work together, and enjoy their work."

Renee was laid-back but totally in charge with stressful or potentially harmful situations. Her fluent and persuasive personality was uniquely effective in making stops related to "following the law." For her two years as a policeman, Renee had no altercations (resisting arrest) with any of those arrested. According to Renee, a record with no altercations was unusual for police officers.

In fact, she had the most OWI (operating a vehicle while intoxicated) pickups for downtown Indiana State Capitol Police

Officers. The OWI in Indiana is the same as a DUI (driving under the influence) in other states. Both refer to drunk driving.

At her passing, one person who Renee stopped posted on Renee's tribute page, "I didn't know Renee at all, but she did happen to pull me over downtown one time and arrested me for a DUI offense. I just found out today at court about her passing. She was extremely nice to me and very understanding. We should hope for more officers just like her! It was bitter-sweet when my charges were dropped today because of her passing. In all honesty, I would rather have faced the problems with my case than to have heard the news about Renee."

When I mentioned that this was posted on Renee's tribute page, the Director of Human Resources for the police cringed and said, "I am so sorry."

"Oh, no. The tribute was an amazing tribute that helped me come to know who Renee was, even for those stopped and ticketed."

When Renee was working the night shift from 10:00 p.m. to 8:00 a.m. she usually came home before I left for work. That was a gift for me! I had a chance to regularly ask, "So, how did the night go?" I got the lowdown firsthand, like a bedpost. I listened and never repeated what she said.

It was the perfect way to see how Renee problem solved problems, her maturity, and her sense of humor. Most clearly, I saw Renee's commitment to keeping downtown Indianapolis and the Capitol safe, working together and being accountable for her partner's protection. I soon learned that her number one issue was being "dismissed" as a female police officer.

Renee said, "Sometimes women are considered not to have courage and the ability to handle tough situations." Not Renee! She handled her work responsibly, unflappably, and with a wry sense of humor. And covered the backs of the other police officers.

The men who worked with Renee were close in their collegial relationships. She definitely knew how to be professional, get things done with ease and simplicity, and still have a fun, positive attitude, one that often had others laughing – the officers, too.

After the funeral, her shift supervisor shared, "Renee was very organized and got all the other guys on the shift to work together as they completed their paperwork. She typed very fast, errorless, and talked at the same time."

Renee's supervisor further shared, "Renee is very professional, very bright, laid-back but handled things well in difficult and stressful circumstances."

Chapter 28

Night Shift – Stopping a Person Who Potentially Committed a Homicide

He has shown you, O mortal, what is good.
And what does the LORD require of you?
To act justly and to love mercy and to walk
humbly with your God. (Micah 6:8)
Renee always knew the right thing to do and did the right
thing; yet, she showed mercy to others and had a disarming
humility. As a parent of a woman police officer, her stories
took me by surprise and kept me devoted to prayer.

R enee chose the night shift for the Indiana State Capitol Police in downtown Indianapolis because there was more action. Indeed, there was action. More than I could imagine as a mother.

One morning, Renee came home absolutely thrilled, hardly able to contain herself. "I just picked up a potential homicide last night."

I am like, "Homicide? Do you mean murder?" My heart stopped. All I could think was 'Oh, no.' My dear daughter. With eyes wide open, I asked, "So, how did this go?"

Renee answered, "He was downtown around 2:00 a.m., weaving in and out of traffic and speeding. I stepped up my pace without turning on the rotating police lights. Suddenly, he made a sharp right turn. I turned with him and turned on my rotating lights. He pulled over. I went up to his rolled down window and said:

"'I am Officer Rickard with the Indiana State Capitol Police. The reason I pulled you over was because you were changing lanes without using a turn signal and you were speeding. Do you have your driver's license and vehicle registration?' He had to hand his license outside the window (so I could see if he was shaking).

"When he was getting his vehicle registration, I ask a second question. 'Where are you coming from?' He was not able to handle two questions, suggesting that he had been drinking excessively.

"Then I asked, 'Do you have a gun?'

"Yes."

"If you do what I say, things will go better for you. Please step out of the pickup and sit on the curb. I handcuffed him."

"I radioed the license number in and soon realized from the police dispatcher that this was a person who potentially had just committed a homicide."

"Immediately, several backup police officers and my supervisor came. My supervisor said, 'I can take over now.'"

"Thanks, but I've got it handled."

Renee took him to Wishard Hospital to have his blood alcohol drawn. Evidently, this suspect had been drinking excessively. He was clearly impaired and over the legal limit for blood alcohol. Renee completed the arrest for operating a vehicle while intoxicated.

Chapter 29

Fellow Policemen as Colleagues

Two are better than one, because they have
a good return for their labor:
If either of them falls down, one can help the other up.
But pity anyone who falls and has no one to
help him up. (Ecclesiastes 4:9-10)
God whispers through our "communities." Renee
was an integral part of her third-shift colleagues and
supervisors. Those who bonded with Renee
expressed deep respect that set her apart from others.

Matt W – Fellow State Capitol Police Officer

In the Indiana Law Enforcement Academy (ILEA), Renee met several young men in training to become police officers. One, Matt W and his fiancé, Ashley W, became fast friends. Ashley W worked in an upscale pet store where Renee thoroughly enjoyed finding treats and fun Halloween costumes for Stokley and Lily.

Surprisingly, Matt W was on the same night shift for the Indiana State Capitol Police as Renee. He was one of the five or six on the night shift who became a collegial family. The following spring, Matt W and Ashley W were married. At the beginning of the wedding, they said "We would like to acknowledge the passing of a dear friend, Renee, who is unable to celebrate with us today."

Gene and I travelled to northern Indiana, a three-hour drive, just to attend this wedding in a small, beautiful park and the reception afterward. We only knew the bride and groom so we were a little out of the mainline conversation. After the bride and groom finished eating the wedding cake, we left the reception.

As we were leaving, the groom's parents rushed out and said with tears streaming down their cheeks, "Thank you for coming. We met Renee. She was a very special young lady. We are so sorry for her death. We want you to know that Matt W said, 'It was just not the same on the night shift after Renee's passing. Renee was respected by all the guys.'"

Jarett – Fellow State Capitol Police Officer

Another young police officer that Renee met at the ILEA was Jarett. He also worked for the Indiana State Capitol Police and often was on similar shifts and had duties similar to Renee.

Renee said, "We are so much alike in values. Jarett is a great friend, such fun. We could never date and be serious, we're just too much alike."

Jarett gave our family the following letter:

"Dear Mr. and Mrs. Rickard,

"I'm so sorry for your loss; I have felt an empty spot in my heart since Sunday afternoon when I heard that God called Renee to be with him. Even though it hurt me so much to hear about her passing, I was glad to see that God gained someone that would make him smile, laugh, and always be there to hear about His troubles. I can truly say that our loss will only be heaven's gain; I always knew there were angels that walk this earth helping, caring and watching out and over people and Renee was one of them.

"Renee was that person always there with a smile and quick joke if you needed a laugh or just there to hear your problems. You raised a great daughter and even better friend; she will always have a special place in my heart for the rest of my life. I truly cherish her memories and the conversations that Renee and I shared together. Since I left the Capitol Police, Renee and I always kept in contact with each other and made plans months in advance to see each other when I go to Indianapolis. I will truly miss your daughter and her wonderful sense of humor, great smile, and her great laugh.

"'In times of great grief, I remember Matthew 11:28-30 which states:

"Come to me, all you who are weary and burdened, and I will give you rest. Take my yoke upon you and learn from me, for I am gentle and humble in heart, and you will find rest for your souls. For my yoke is easy and my burden is light.'

"May God bless you and your family in this time of need. You are in our prayers."

"Sincerely,
"Jarrett"

Aaron – Fellow Capitol State Police Officer

A third policeman, Aaron, was an engineer who became a police officer during the downturn of the economy. He returned to engineering shortly before Renee passed away. Renee mentioned the many conversations she had with him regarding his future and the future of police officers. She said, "He is very principled, disciplined, and practical."

Two of Renee's roommates at the ILEA posted the following acknowledgements of Renee on the Memorial Tribute site:

Jennifer – Roommate at ILEA and Friend

"Renee was my roommate at the ILEA last summer. We became close, as is common when you live with someone a while. Renee was always smiling and laughing. I don't ever think I will forget her giggling that sometimes kept us awake at night. Renee was obsessed with her dogs. We talked all the time about her experiences at the Air Force Academy. Renee was a squad leader for her class for a period of time. She was very determined and goal oriented.

"During Traffic Law, Renee exposed herself as a bit of the class clown, cracking a lot of jokes. She was very generous and even let me borrow a pair of her khaki uniform pants when I accidentally forgot mine. We shared a lot of laughs and she was one of the only people I could talk to while I was going through my divorce. Renee hung out with me a couple of times after our time at the academy. She was so much fun, full of life, and a great friend. She will be sorely missed."

Ariana – Roommate at ILEA and Friend

"Dear Rickard Family,"

"I had the pleasure of meeting Renee just over a year ago. We were roommates while in the police academy in Plainfield. Renee was a wonderful person with a very bubbly personality. Having Renee as a roommate made things a little more bearable while at the academy. I remember we would see each other during our breaks and after we were done for the day. The majority of the time we spent laughing. There were many nights where we would be up late just laughing and cracking jokes. We thought for sure we would be in trouble for being so loud.

"Renee and I kept in touch after our graduation. We would text each other often when things weren't going so well, when we needed to vent or just catch up on things. I don't have many good friends and, unfortunately, I just lost a great one. The last time I talked to Renee she was telling me about her triathlon and her Mixed Martial Arts training. I told her I would go see her if she ever came to Fort Wayne. I had the pleasure of meeting you both and her two Chihuahuas. I know how much you all meant to her. I do want you to know how much Renee meant to me. Renee was a wonderful person and she touched many people. I am glad that I was given the opportunity to get to know her. I will truly miss Renee and will keep you in my prayers."

Several of Renee's shift supervisors also acknowledged Renee. One, Sergeant B, wrote the following letter following Renee's passing:

Sergeant B Letter

"Dear Mr. and Mrs. Rickard,"

"It was a pleasure to see both of you on Thursday, February 10.

"I will never forget the day I received the phone call that Renee had passed away. I was attending the Frankton Heritage Days with my two daughters. That call made me realize how important each and every day is on this earth. I do believe that God has a plan for each one of us; we just do not think that it will happen so early in life.

"I know you have heard many stories about Renee's love for her career, law enforcement. As stressful as my job was and hers, Renee always found a way to make even her fellow officers smile. She had a vibrant outlook on life and I know she enjoyed her time with family and friends. She often would sit in my office and talk about things that she did on her days off. I always thought, *Boy, I wish I had that much energy in a day!* Renee was full of life and energy and it was contagious when she was around.

"I can tell you that there has not been a day that I have not thought about an event or story that Renee and I shared. I also hear my officers talk about her often. My shift held a moment of silence in respect for Renee during our December 19, 2010 shift Squad Meeting. I am still amazed at how much Renee influenced her fellow officers. Her memories will live on in the police officers she served with and I know that she is looking over and protecting anyone that wears a police uniform.

"God bless both of you and thank you for sharing the life of Renee."

"Sergeant B"

Sergeant C Interview

Another one of Renee's shift supervisors, a veteran police officer for more than thirty years, was a mentor and like a "grandfather" for Renee, a much younger, less experienced police officer. Sergeant C shared much wisdom with Renee. Truly, this was a gift. The Lord, indeed, brings blessings and protection in the midst. God is good, all the time!

The following shares my interview with Sergeant C.

Karyl: "You were Renee's Shift Supervisor with thirty-five years of experience. She looked to you for wisdom and coaching."

Sergeant C: "It really never was a matter of mentoring or coaching Renee, it was just nudging her in the right direction. She was very quick to pick up things. She paid attention. I don't know whether it was because of my age or that some of the guys called me 'Grandpa.'

"Even though she was a little reluctant sometimes – I don't want to say headstrong – sometimes, she would look at me like, 'Are you telling me what you want me to hear or that I need to know.' I said, 'I am telling you what you need to know, because you can hear anything.'

"Renee was a very good officer. All the guys on third shift got along. It was a close-knit group on third shift with Brandon, Jeremy, Mike, Matt W, and Renee. Renee was one of the guys. That's just the way it was. We had fun doing what we were supposed to do.

"In 2008, she had her FTO (field training officer) program when she worked all three shifts. She would ask questions of other officers. If she didn't get what she thought were the right answers, she would come to me.

"My reaction, was, 'If you don't tell the truth, then don't tell it at all.' That's the way I did things. Renee picked up on that pretty quickly so we got along."

"Yes, she couldn't tolerate that. She couldn't tolerate lying at all."

Karyl: "Will you share a little bit about how the shifts went?"

Sergeant C: "Because I was older and more experienced, I did things a little differently with Renee and the rest of the guys. We did things the way we thought they should be done on third shift, contrary to the day shift and the second shift. The officers knew what they were supposed to do and how to do it. Bottom line – that was just what they were supposed to do.

"We all got along well. We all did our jobs. We had a good time. We covered one another and at the end of the shift, we all went home happy, having had some fun. So, it was great."

Karyl: "Sergeant C, can you talk a little bit how you divided the work up to get it all done on the shift without several hours overtime?"

Sergeant C: "It was not amazing. It just was the way things worked. There were four or five of us on the third shift at night. The one who made the arrest would start writing up the arrest narrative, someone else would start with the paper work for the tow truck, recovered property or whatever else needed done.

"In a little more than an hour, the person would be in jail and the paperwork done. None of the other shifts figured out how we were doing that. It was because Renee, Jeremy, Mike, Matt W, and Brandon all worked together. All the arresting guy had to do was to write his narrative; all the rest was taken care of by everyone else. My supervisors could not understand how we did our work without overtime.

"We had great cooperation on third shift and all the officers respected one another. We had our fun. But, we had our issues, every once in a while. We sat down and talked them out and would go from there. We had a nice work environment."

Karyl: "Sergeant C, you mentioned that the officers had some really great conversations."

Sergeant C: "I don't remember too many things that we did not discuss among the five or six of us – our relationships, our work, vacations. For instance, Renee talked about Tincup, going to Peru, and Matt W's wedding. You were there in Tincup, too. We knew more about Matt W's wedding than Matt W because of Renee's relationship with Ashley W."

"One night, we discussed 'Integrity.' What is integrity? Your word is your integrity. None of us like a liar or a thief. That's why we all got along so well on third shift."

"We also discussed faith and belief in God. Renee said, 'I believe in the LORD and that somebody up there is looking after me all the time. If not, I would not be here.'

"I told Renee, 'I've been baptized twice. Most of my life I went to Methodist churches but I've been to lots of different churches. I don't care what denomination you go to as long as you believe in the Lord.'

"Another time, we talked about Martial Arts and how Renee felt about that. She liked to achieve. She had very specific goals.

"Renee was all female and Renee was one of the guys. She never wanted to be known as a Capitol *female* officer. She would say, 'I am an officer – don't bring in male or female.' She wanted to be as good as all the others. In fact, she outshot some of the guys on the range. It was not a 'guy thing;' it was an officer against an officer.

"Renee never hesitated, never doubted her ability, what she could do or couldn't do. She never gave me reason to have concern regarding her stopping another car. There was no comparison of the other females to Renee. Police officers really are in the eye of the bullet. Not everyone can do that. Renee could be in the eye and more."

Karyl: "Renee mentioned that she was on Dispatch duty sometimes."

Sergeant C: "Dispatch was not something Renee was happy about but, when she was assigned there, she knew exactly what she was to do and she did it. Staying down there with the state police and the sergeant was not the most interesting thing in the world.

"After Renee was off several days, sometimes I asked to see her paperwork as she was going off duty. Her comment was, 'Don't you think I can do it?'

"My reaction was, 'Yes, you can do it, but there might be something we can do better.'

"There was mutual trust between Renee and the other guys on our shift. More than one of the other shift supervisors asked, 'Do you trust the officers on your shift?' My reaction was, 'Where are you going with this? If you don't trust your officers, they have no business being here.'

"I can't say that all the police officers were what Renee would call friends. She would talk to an officer and be very professional. Renee could size up people she didn't trust.

"With the OWI (operating a vehicle while intoxicated, same as a DUI in other states), Renee was more than a little competitive. It pleased her more than ever to have two OWI arrests on her shift while the others had not one.

"Renee never lost a court case. She never made a 'bad stop.' That's when a police officer stops a car and it was not what the officer thought was going on. So, he goes on a 'fishing trip' to find something wrong.

"In heaven, I bet you someone is laughing. Renee had a smile that could melt an iceberg. It got her away with a lot. She was as good at playing jokes as she was at receiving them.

"God does things on His schedule. We don't always agree with Him, but He's still there. If you believe in Him, you have to go along with that."

Chapter 30

Other Friends as a Young Adult

Love is patient, love is kind. It does not envy, it does not boast, it is not proud. It does not dishonor others, it is not self-seeking, it is not easily angered, it keeps no record of wrongs. Love does not delight in evil but rejoices with the truth. It always protects, always trusts, always hopes, always perseveres. (1 Corinthians 13:4-7)
John (the Baptist) answered, "Anyone who has two shirts should share with the one who has none, and anyone who has food should do the same." (Luke 3:11)
Renee's friends spoke about the love of Renee and her kindness to each of them.

Brooke's Interview

When working as a bank teller and then as an Indiana State Capitol Police Officer in Indianapolis, Renee had several close friends. One was Brooke, whom she met in Lafayette while in college. Brooke and she met regularly for lunch to discuss their dreams, their daily realities, and their boyfriends (relationships).

Renee often shared how much she appreciated Brooke, just a down-to-earth young lady who was practical, wise, and lived a life that honored the Lord. Her mother worked for the Catholic Archdiocese. Following Renee's death, Brooke volunteered to work with families who had loved ones in hospice.

Brooke shared the following:

"As different as we were, hands down, she was my best friend. No matter what I needed or wanted, she was that person for me. She and I had 'mothering' in common.

"I asked her, 'Is this your idea of dressed up?' I was always telling her how pretty she was. She said, 'Brooke, you are pretty!'

"One always thinks there is time, we don't rush it. One day I was crying, then the next minute laughing. Renee lived a full life. She's in an awesome place. I have to block her passing out of my mind. She's away.

"She used to say, 'When you have some kids, I'll come and take care of them.' I can't imagine that my kids will not meet her. She won't be there. My daughter will have Renee as a middle name.

"I let Renee be herself, there was no changing her!

"We were in each other's lives seven years. I met her in the summer of 2004 when we were working at Sears.

"Hands down, there was nothing in common. I was girlie-girlie, Renee the opposite. Out of all my friends, Renee was the closest to me. We talked about anything and everything and never got into an argument.

"Finally, I was introduced into Renee's world when she brought me to the gun range. She wanted me to go with her to the martial arts. Renee finally went shopping with me. She got two pairs of jeans and left.

"Since we were both working nights, we talked every single night. Both of us were busy and had hectic lives but no regrets. I could be honest with her. She was the kindest person I had ever known. If you knew her, you were lucky. She would give you the shirt off her back.

"Renee was kind and good to everyone. The more the merrier. When we were in college, she would say, 'I'll pay. You don't have to pay. I'm here so we are going.'

"Renee was always ready to go at the drop of the dime. We were both single, both had no children and both had good jobs.

"Our last full-day outing was last weekend at the State Fair. We pigged out with elephant ears, candy corn, sushi, and sugar! Then, we went to a Japanese restaurant in Lafayette. It was expensive, but good.

"We discussed our relationships with boys. I told Renee, 'I love you. I don't want to see a guy hurt you. I want you to be happy. You deserve it as good as you are to others. You want to do things for others, do great things for great people.' Cade, who knew Renee in preschool and later reconnected as a young adult, invited her to a dinner he prepared on the Friday before her passing. I hope she was happy.

"Many of her earlier friends – I don't think she thought any of them cared about her. I was angry at the wake. All these people came. Why couldn't you let her know you cared while she was alive?

"I talked about God all the time. God gives signs and also gives free choice.

"Both of us knew we had great parents. The sisters of both my grandfather and grandmother were nuns. We have several priests in our family.

"When I heard Renee passed, I felt like screaming, 'WHY Renee? WHY me?' I was angry. My mom came over and said, 'Let's just go to church.'

"I felt like everything was in slow motion. I felt like a piece of me was gone, never to come back, a void that will never be filled.

"I know God blessed me with her friendship. I will always remember Renee."

Angie S's Interview

Another friend Renee met at Mixed Martial Arts was Angie S. Angie S was a single parent with two young sons, six and eight years old. Angie S was in superb physical condition and often sparred with Renee at the Martial Arts sessions.

In our interview, Angie S shared the following:

"Really, she was an outstanding person. You don't meet people like her today. Lots of people could sense she had great character. That's important for Christians. They could sense that she had good character but she never talked about that.

"Maybe Renee was in my life to bring me back to God. I went back to church after the funeral. Now, I pray and really believe that God is in my life every day. Renee made a difference in my life. I now know you can't take things for granted.

"Renee influenced me to become strong as a woman. She believed women should be respected. No matter who you were, she would not let women put themselves down.

"Renee was very aware of things but you could not tell. She was so calm and cool. Renee was intelligent and knew how to read people well. She could sense their motivations and would not hang around with those she did not trust. She always tried to be good to everyone but never 'too nice.'

"Always, when I went on a date, she would ask about the guy. She was pretty on target about the guys. She 'cracked me up.' She said 'Men should respect women. If they take you out, make them pay for meals and be safe even if they are a police officer or a kick boxer!' I actually use one of her sayings now 'Be Safe.' She always said 'Be Safe.'

"Renee laughed a lot and giggled. I got to share some of that joy. She wasn't emotional in a 'girlie' sense, but deep inside she was very sensitive to people. She had lots of inner strength. She was very good at reading people. Renee – that girl – she could be really accurate! I do not know if it was that she was a cop, or just her personality. She was able to read people! It made her a good cop. She paid attention to details and did not have to try very hard.

"Renee was a wonderful person. She had a bright spirit. She made life joyful☺ She made things fun! Renee was into things that just come off as funny, very humorous. Humor and dry wit came easily but she never wanted attention on herself. It seemed like everything was an adventure. She was willing to sacrifice for others.

"For example, for the Martial Arts Academy, Renee and I went to get a HUGE tractor tire. We had to drive through trees, cross a creek and finally came to the tires, filled with black water. Renee convinced a 'laid back farmer guy' to help her get a large tire into her pickup truck. The tire was taller than the cab. While he was helping, the black water splashed on her. She was disgusted with the stuff. Yuk. She cleaned up a little bit and then decided that *the tires* needed a car wash! That was a sight to see. I can only imagine what people thought. We had a good time, laughing lots. It was an adventure!

"At least the tires were clean, that is, clean enough for us to use for 'conditioning.' We ended up training with the tires. To build up strength, we hit the tires with a sledgehammer and jumped in the tires, out of the tires and over the tires.

"Renee was very humble yet she had a great presence. She held herself well. She was very outgoing. Renee tended to be a people-watcher. She knew how to read people and be protected. She was more reserved with some people.

"In a way, the dogs, Lily and Stokley, were Renee's children. She treated them so well. She was amazing with children, especially my two boys (Peyton and Tyler), who were six and eight years old. She always would make them calm down and do the things I wanted. In a sense, they looked up to her.

"Renee would not 'take anything from anyone.' Maybe, this was something God gave her to fulfill her purpose. She used everything to the best of her ability. She used all of her gifts and talents. I always felt safe with her.

"One of our last texts said, 'I'll catch up with you another day.'

"I believe this was all part of God's plan. She was doing things, visiting old friends not seen in a while. Maybe it was God's way of letting her say 'Good-bye.'

"Maybe God knew. She lived a short time and had to do all these things – triathlon, ride a bicycle across Indiana (RAIN), Kingdom Martial Arts – because the Lord knew her days were numbered.

"I was very blessed to know Renee and have her as a friend, my best friend! I learned a lot from her. She was humble and non-judgmental. She knew what I was going through. Friends and relationships are what matter in the end, no matter what you do.

"I also learned to *not* take things for granted. I know that God had a plan for Renee. Now, I will push more to know God's purpose for me.

"Renee encouraged me to go on to college. In my position as the Program Coordinator for the Trade School Apprenticeships (Associated Builders and Contractors), I enjoyed building relationships and watching the apprentices succeed. This and my commitment to physical fitness ignited a passion to help people recover from illness or surgery with physical therapy and instill hope. I worked hard and prayed to be accepted into the Physical Therapy Assistant Program at the University of Indianapolis. I was!

"Just the time we shared, I will forever think about Renee, talk about her. It was part of God's plan for us to meet."

Chapter 31

Mixed Martial Arts Academy

Do nothing out of selfish ambition or vain conceit.
Rather, in humility value others above yourselves,
not looking to your own interests but each of you to
the interests of the others. (Philippians 2:3-4)
Renee experienced God's incredible love, hope and faith
while focusing on the needs of others who crossed her path.

For more than a year before Renee passed, she went to a Mixed Martial Arts Academy. Renee said, "Since I am going to the Mixed Martial Arts Academy, I feel great. I am in the best-ever physical condition."

She not only participated 'full out' (two hours a day, four times per week) but also assisted the Academy in upgrading their facility and resources. As mentioned previously, Renee retrieved a huge abandoned tractor tire perfect for strength exercises at the Academy.

According to Angie S, her friend from the Mixed Martial Arts Academy, "Steve, the Director of the Academy, was very in touch with God. The Kingdom Mixed Martial Arts Academy was a ministry, one like a family who cared and encouraged respect and self-discipline. The more you see God's Hand through caring for one another, the closer you come to God. The members of the Academy had T-shirts with a Bible verse.

"I actually met Renee through kickboxing. She made the competition team for the Mixed Martial Arts (MMA) program. We trained together (four times a week) and then ate at Applebee's in Greenfield. We giggled so much. She always made me laugh and found humor. She said that's how to be with the guys, 'just joke with them and make them laugh.'

"When I first met Renee, I was intimidated. She thought I was a 'prissy girl' with makeup and high heels. Renee was not all about that kind of stuff.

"Renee was brought there by God to help people. Renee's spiritual gift was encouragement. With me, in kickboxing, she would say, 'Try this and do this.' Her presence at the Academy was good for the other girls and guys. It felt like Renee always had joy in her heart.

Renee wanted to be in a MMA competition. To be sure Renee was ready for competition, Steve, the Academy Director, recommended that Renee participate in intense training in a sister school in Chicago. So, Renee and Angie S went to Chicago for three days of intense training with a well-known MMA instructor, Dion.

Angie S said, "We had three hours of workout, slept, then went back for another three hours of workout each day. By the third day, we were exhausted and completely sore all over."

"On the third day, Renee said 'Let's go to the Cheesecake Factory. We worked hard for this!' That evening, we went shopping at a mall and then back to Indy. Renee was not about winning; rather it was more about competing within herself."

Renee and Angie S stayed with me at the McDonald National Retreat Center in Chicago while I was attending a leadership conference. It was then that I really got to know Angie S. True to style, Renee and she had such fun together. It was always interesting to be a fly on the wall as they shared their experiences with the extra intense training at the MMA Academy in Chicago. Yes. They were stiff and sore and ached all over!

"We were supposed to go to the first UFC (Ultimate Fighting Championship) team competition in Indy. Renee got tickets months ahead. A week or so ahead, I asked her about it. Renee said, 'I am not thinking about it, just thinking about other things. I am kind of worried about what's wrong.' One of her sayings was 'No worries.' I am mad at myself for not asking her if she was okay."

Many children and young adults in the Mixed Martial Arts Academy came to the funeral visitation, none of whom I knew. At the funeral, I learned, with relief, that the Academy was the *Kingdom* Mixed Martial Arts Academy, in existence to further the Lord's Kingdom. The owner, Steve, said, "Renee had many conversations with me about the Bible. She asked the hard questions, 'What does the Bible say about 'fighting' and self defense?'"

The following shares an interview that I had with Steve, the Director of the Academy:

Karyl: "Your Academy, Steve, was the Kingdom Mixed Martial Arts (MMA)?"

Steve: "Yes, my Academy was a Christian organization. I did not quote Bible verses but I did teach Biblically based principles. That was God's call for my life: teach God's ways and His Word through the vehicle of mixed martial arts. That's what I am put on this planet to do."

Karyl: "What is Mixed Martial Arts?"

Steve: "Martial arts are the study of warfare, those who want to dominate and fight people. Ancient martial arts teachers gave mental and physical teaching. With great power comes great responsibility. Being a force for good was at the heart of martial arts."

"Mixed martial arts are for those who want to prevent fights and use it for healing. Bruce Lee, considered to be the Father of Mixed Martial Arts, brought mixed martial arts into mainstream America. He revolutionized street fighting – the art of self-defense and protection – by cross training, mixing the martial arts – boxing (hit people), judo (throw people), wrestling (grapple) and karate (use feet to kick).

"Bruce Lee believed that 'the best fighter is someone who can adapt to any style. That is, if you are on the ground you need to be a wrestler, if you are on your feet, you need to punch (box) and kick (kick boxing).' He called it Jeet Kune Do, the way of the intercepting fist. Or, it means stopping a fight before it starts.

"Lots of people think of mixed martial arts as a fighting style, but Bruce had lots of strategies where you can fight without fighting or avoid the fight without walking away. Just find other ways to diffuse things. It is a life process. It can influence your work ethics and life style.

"When you are fighting you need to be flexible. If my opponent pushes, I pull. Or, if my opponent retracts, I expand. You don't fight force with force head on.

"What comes at you determines what route you take. So you need to study all the routes. If you only are a boxer, then for every fight that's all you have. When you mix these martial arts together you become very flexible. You can harmonize with whatever comes at you. This is what Renee was learning to do, learning how to be flexible in defending herself and then how to protect others.

"The mixed martial arts were passed on through Bruce Lee's students, Dan Asanto, and Dion Riccardo. Both of them were my teachers. Bruce Lee only lived 33 years but he lived life to its fullest. Renee was the same kind of person. She did more living in 28 years than most people do.

Karyl: "Tell me more about how you worked out."

Steve: "A workout was two hours, about an hour ground wrestling and then an hour stand up punching and kicking because we were mixing the martial arts. We did multiple things.

"When the students came for class, everybody lined up. We talked about what we are going to accomplish that day. Then, we did some warm ups to get the blood flowing, the body warmed up. We might do some calisthenics or we might do a two-hand tag game, something fun to get the spirits going.

"Then, everyone gets gloves and pads and does a combination with a partner ... punch, punch, duck and kick ... a few times ... with music like aerobic workouts.

"They do a series of motions ... bang, bang, switch the pads ... hold up to hit, moving around, hit, hit, kick ... okay switch ...

synergy ... learning how to move their bodies with the enemy, defending yourself while having fun ... tag your face. After several rounds with pads, we would take a water break.

"Then, do several rounds with how to get one to the ground ... grab legs, learn how to fall ... and learn how to strategically wrestle. If both are on hands and knees wrestling, they are trying to grab and pin the other person or put his/her arm where it could break.

"Renee did lots of weapons training. With someone who had a knife, she played tag, she would tag the others shoulder with the tip of her fingers. She was training her body to move.

"Out of all the women, Angie S and Renee were the most inspiring. Before Renee, Angie S was running the kick-boxing classes for me. When they became a pair, it was unstoppable.

"I knew if Renee and Angie S were going to be there, it was going to be a fun day. Beyond that, Kingdom was a place where family grew up and kids were there. It was a joyful environment.

"We were moving and having much fun with high energy. Even the men recognized Renee as a powerful force.

"Renee inspired me to teach police officers how to defend themselves and protect others through mixed martial arts strategies.

"I got to teach several SWAT (Special Weapons and Tactics) or CERT (Critical Emergency Response Team) guys a couple of days ago. So, I started teaching knife fighting and stick fighting with them. They carry batons but do not know much about them. The baton or stick can get a knife out of a bad guy's hand. So, I had soft sticks and soft knives. If a bad guy is swinging a knife, you can step back and crack their hand. Then they drop the knife and it is over.

"I taught this in pairs, one had a knife and one a stick. 'Let's play tag.' If you can tag my body you win. If I can tag your hand, I win. So, it is a game. The guys loved it! As they were playing stick tag, they were moving around and gaining flexibility and endurance. Then they switched partners."

Karyl: "Many students from the Kingdom MMA Academy came to the visitation. I was amazed that so many came."

Steve: "That shows how impactful she was. Renee touched so many lives at the Academy. It was a family place where everybody loved coming. Lots of children looked up to her. Then, seeing her in a uniform, that was another level of respect. Wow! She's a police officer.

"When she came into the Academy, especially when she was with Angie S, she was always just cutting up and laughing. Giggling. It would break the ice. It made it so much better to have that happiness, that joy.

"She definitely brightened wherever she went, even the darkest places. You would see her show up and her smile; that alone melted you. We need more people like her.

"Renee found that silver lining and made it good. She always made us happy. Again, the energy was high when she was in that room.

"Renee inspired a lot of females. I have dealt with a lot of women who have gone through abuse, emotional and physical. A lot of rape victims do not feel like they were worthy of fighting back. They saw Renee as a focal point of strength. The women would open up to her. I would see her go off and just chat with these women. She was giving them a reason to fight, to do better, to do more.

"When I heard the news about Renee, I received calls from so many in the martial arts community. They were heart-broken. Everyone knew and loved Renee. She was woven into all the connections and families at the Academy. All these people loved her. Renee was very warm and welcoming. When I had to call people, they would just break down on the phone, even those in Chicago. It was devastating to so many people.

"A dad who was a single parent had three children who just were hanging on Renee. He was one who was pretty broken up. He called and said, 'Man, I cannot go to the funeral because the kids are really heart-broken.'

"I hate that Renee's life was cut short. She lived two or three lifetimes in the time she was here. Renee did a lot, man, inspired so many people. When she left us, our program in the MMA area was not the same. Her spark was gone."

Karyl: "Dion and another MMA coach from Chicago, Jack L, came to the visitation."

Steve: "Yes, Jack L was one of the top guys Dion was putting Renee with to be sure she was ready to compete. Renee was showing me things she was picking up from Chicago... 'Hey Guinn, look at this....'

"Dion and I are pastors. Those are our people. Dion took her under his wing. We lost someone who was part of our flock. As good shepherds, we have to go and give honor to her friends and family."

Karyl: "Tell me a little more about Chicago and this 'Dion.'"

Steve: "I was raised in a Baptist Church. In my early teens, I was saved but got bored. I did not turn away from God. I turned away from the church. When I listened to inspiring speakers in the charismatic movement, I got excited again. It's the Holy Spirit that gives us power. I was back into the Word. It was fresh.

"My MMA instructor in California suggested that I see Dion in Chicago. His Academy was Bruce Lee mixed martial arts (Eastern philosophy) but when Dion was saved, he converted the name to Victory Martial Arts Academy. He used 1 Corinthians 15:57: 'But thanks be to God! He gives us the victory through our Lord Jesus Christ.' His logo was victory with the cross for the 'T' in victory. Dion had five schools and sold several to his top students who wanted their own business.

"When I saw Dion, I said, 'Wow, that's it.' That became my greatest passion – to teach, train and develop others to find their purpose on earth, 'Why did God create you?'

"Dion was a spiritual father for me. He amazes me with how in tune with God he is. He is the most Godly human being I know.

"When I sent Renee to my teacher Dion, he said, 'Wow, your student is really on fire with this stuff.' He really believed in her and wanted her to succeed."

Karyl: "How did Dion make time for Renee and Angie S?"

Steve: "He made time for them because of me. They were my fruit. He knew they were representing me. He wanted to see my success. He put his best people training them in three-hour training sessions. He really pushed them. He said, 'If you guys are going to represent the Kingdom and Guinn, you have to be your best.'"

Karyl: "Angie S said you have T-shirts with scriptures."

Steve: "I was blessed to have a student who worked at a T-shirt shop.

The most famous one that everyone liked was Psalm 144:1-2

> [1] *Praise be to the LORD my Rock,*
> *who trains my hands for war,*
> *my fingers for battle.*
> [2] *He is my loving God and my fortress,*
> *my stronghold and my deliverer,*
> *my shield, in whom I take refuge,*
> *who subdues peoples under me."*

Karyl: "I understand you had conversations with Renee about Christians fighting."

Steve: "In my work as security at a nightclub or bar, where I was a bouncer, I was a protector ... keeping people safe, taking people home, calling an Uber. Now, as a sheriff's deputy for the Marion County Jail, I also am a protector.

"Renee had that same spirit. She was fighting injustice, a crime fighter, dealing with things the public cannot handle. We talked about being a sheep dog.

"Police are called sheep dogs. The wolf is always out there and then you have the sheep. The wolf is cunning, always attacking. Renee came to realize that it is a divine purpose to be a 'protector.' God puts the protector between the sheep and wolf. Her role was to protect the sheep from the wolf. She has to be able to defend herself first and then she can protect others.

"Everyone's purpose is different. Like the Bible talks about the hand and the foot...the eye says, 'I see everything' but the foot says, 'Yes, but I take you everywhere.'

"I told Renee, 'Look, you are a beacon of hope for someone who cannot protect themselves.'"

Karyl: Yes, Renee was a crime fighter, committed to fighting injustice. When she went to the Air Force Academy, it was to protect people, to protect our country and do the Lord's work in the midst. Our prayer was that she was in the Lord's will. My colleague and I prayed and prayed and prayed for her, not knowing that she was a part of a *Kingdom* mixed martial arts.

God is good, *all the time*. I got a glimpse into another area of Renee's life, her values and that she was about the Lord's mission. The Lord let me know that He *was* with Renee, all along, guiding, protecting and using her to fulfill His work at the Kingdom Academy. Steve, through his Academy ministry, answered one of my biggest prayers and concerns regarding Renee's participation in "fighting," usually linked to "warriors." Hmmm ... maybe, Renee was a "warrior for the Lord."

Chapter 32

Encourager for Young Children

I will not leave you as orphans; I will come to you. Before long, the world will not see me anymore, but you will see me. Because I live, you also will live. On that day you will realize that I am in my Father, and you are in me, and I am in you.
(John 14:18-20)
There is something dear to the heart of God when our kindness is extended to others. Renee was clear what the right thing to do was when she saw a need and did it with such love and kindness that it left the thumbprint of God.

Three young children came to the Mixed Martial Arts Academy with their father who regularly "worked out." Angie S, a friend of Renee at Mixed Martial Arts, shared, "Renee befriended two elementary school-age boys and their younger sister. At first, the boys (as typical boys) seemed bored and disruptive while waiting on their dad. Their dad was a single dad.

"Renee went over and talked to them at the edge of the mat, showed them her motorcycle and began to do things with them. Renee visited these children, played catch, soccer and even went to some of their baseball games. From Renee's South American trip to Peru, she brought back pearl-handled knives for the boys.

"One day, when the father needed additional assistance in caring for them, Renee took them to bumper cars. With great glee and laughter, Renee played 'crash' and raced the boys with the bumper cars. The boys loved this – true blue, young boys.

"Another whole day, Renee and the two boys with their younger sister went to the water park, totally laughing and enjoying all the water activities. The younger sister was much more timid and in some ways seemed to cling to Renee for love, attention, and support."

According to Angie S, "The boys behaved better and were transformed when Renee began to pay attention to them. It felt great that someone cared."

Renee said, "If I ever have kids, I would want some like these two boys. They are polite, have lots of fun, and are open to encouragement with their studies."

Renee encouraged all the children to do well in school so they would be eligible for military academy or perhaps college scholarships. For the younger son, Renee even recommended finding a tutor for a subject he was not doing so well in school.

She told him, "For a short time, I had a writing tutor in the third grade. It made all the difference in the world. I learned to say what I wanted to say easily in writing." As a young adult, Renee excelled in communication, both in writing and verbally.

Renee's perspective was "This dad just does not know how to have fun with his children!"

This family came to the visitation. Tears rolled down the cheeks of the young boys (ten and twelve years old). Following the funeral, the father and three children visited us. In memory of Renee, with their dad's permission, we gave each of the boys one of Renee's coveted police knives. We gave their seven-year-old sister one of Renee's favorite stuffed animals, an albino tiger.

As they were leaving, the father said, "Renee taught *me* how to have fun and enjoy the journey of life." Amazing. Awesome. God is good, all the time.

In a follow-up letter, the father shared that his children were well. The older son, Jade, is in the Indiana National Guard and trying to make a decision between going active-duty army or going to school to apply for an Indiana State Police or a Deputy Sheriff's position. The younger son is on active duty in the army, based at Fort Lee in Virginia. His daughter is in high school at Greenfield Central High School, loves dance and has not stated her plans for the future except to be a flight attendant. She loves to travel.

The dad wrote, "She (Renee) will always be with me. I use a picture of her to mark my place in my Bible during my reads. Renee once asked me if the kids and I would like to go to Tincup with her and her parents for a week. I hesitated because I had not met the two of you and wasn't sure how my kids would act. I look back and wish I had taken the trip with her and her family. She impacted my life in more ways than anyone will ever know."

Chapter 33

Renee and Guys

This is what the LORD says, your Redeemer,
the Holy One of Israel:
"I am the LORD your God, who teaches you what is best for you,
who directs you in the way you should go." (Isaiah 48:17)
God does whisper to us through His promises and
even though I did not see Renee married, I saw Renee
fulfilled and full of joy as a young woman.

Renee was definitely a charismatic and attractive young lady to the fellows around her. They really enjoyed her sense of humor, laid-back acceptance of almost everyone, although she may not have agreed with them. Most of all, she just was witty, quick and 'with it' in everything she did.

The Lord protected her from unhealthy relationships in her schooling, for the most part. Except for one she met as a young adult, while riding her motorcycle. According to Renee, "He sleeps most of the day and works as an insurance agent during the evenings and nights. I am not sure how he financially survives with his work in insurance."

Finally, Renee realized, "He is selfish, unloving, and demanding of his mother. He does not treat me with love and respect, either." She did not continue to date him.

Whew. Thank goodness that did not work out. Yes, the Lord protected Renee, who in many ways, was a bit naïve about dating relationships.

One of the training leaders in her Basic Training at the Academy also was very interested in dating Renee. Her policy was never to date friends or professional colleagues. After he completed the Academy, he asked her for several dates. As he went into pilot training, it became clear that he, too, had some personality weaknesses.

Renee began to be very careful about dating some of her military friends. Bryan, a friend from the AFA Preparatory School, was one of the best 'true blue' friends. Prior to the AFA Preparatory School, he was a helicopter mechanic in the army. Renee never dated him but since he was a straight arrow and knowledgeable about military life, she trusted him. They had a solid friendship with respect for one another.

We came to know Bryan relatively well since, when we went to the Academy, Renee and some of her friends were given a pass to go "off base" for dinner with us. Bryan often was a part of that group. Bryan clearly knew the ins and outs of military life and gave great wisdom to Renee regarding political and military correctness at the Academy: "Follow the rules and regulations and be wise about what one says."

Then, there was the young soccer coach and Safety Trainer/ Inspector for magnet trains who Renee met. After her passing, he called and said, "I am so saddened to hear about Renee's passing. You had an amazing daughter. She was kind and generous. The world is hurting without her. Renee was the Light. Knowing Renee, she's up there in heaven making it easier for us."

Another young man, Cade, knew Renee in preschool and reconnected with Renee a year before her passing. He graduated from Purdue University in Graphic Design and continued in his profession in Lafayette, Indiana. He texted Renee perhaps six times the afternoon she passed away. Finally, I asked Jacqueline to call him. She was the one who reconnected Renee to him.

Chapter 34

Unimaginable – State Capitol Recognition

Wisdom's instruction is to fear the LORD,
and humility comes before honor. (Proverbs 15:33)
Humility is a prerequisite for honor and blessings.
I am speechless at the way God brings honor to His children.

A former Indiana State Capitol Police Officer, Aaron, contacted Connie Lawson, the Indiana Senate Majority Leader and Senator from Brownsburg where Aaron lived. He requested that Renee be honored for protecting the Senate and House chambers and keeping the Capitol safe.

In an interview, Aaron said, "When I heard that Renee had suddenly passed, I was in shock because she was so young, so vibrant, so alive and so committed to what she did. I wanted her to be honored for doing her job so well – protecting the legislators, the senate and the house.

"One of the things I noticed about Renee was the way she was navigating the police world, dominated by men. We were on the same night shift. Everyone on our shift respected everyone. If Renee was made fun of, it was no different than anyone else on the shift. If I did something stupid, I got flack for it. It's the way we burned off stress.

"Yes, Renee carried herself well and I respected her. That's the best compliment I can give. She was really committed to doing well. She was doing the MMA (Mixed Martial Arts) on her own time, practiced as a sharp-shooter and practiced speaking Spanish with me because I was a pretty good Spanish speaker. You just don't see that dedication usually."

As we entered the Capitol building, the magnificent Italian Renaissance style dome was captivating, the sun shining through the multicolored blue glass. On February 14, 2011, it was awesome and humbling to stand in front of the Senate and the House during the reading of the Indiana Senate Concurrent Resolution 24 Memorializing Officer Renee Rickard. Gene and I, Ruth, Renee's adopted grandmother, and Anjie G, a representative of the State Capitol Police and a friend of Renee, were ushered into the front of the Senate and the House as the resolution was read. The Indiana Senators and Congressmen were in attendance. This was a sweet blessing on Valentine's Day. We were deeply touched.

The small gathering and refreshments afterwards with the Indiana State Capitol Police Officers and friends was another way of acknowledging Renee. Just nice.

Here is the resolution:

First Regular Session 117th General Assembly (2011)

SENATE CONCURRENT RESOLUTION No. 24

A CONCURRENT RESOLUTION Memorializing Officer Renee Rickard.

Whereas, State Capitol Police Officer Renee Rickard, of Indianapolis, passed away unexpectedly on September 19, 2010;

Whereas, Renee Rickard served as a State Capitol Police Officer since October 2008;

Whereas, After graduating from Pike High School in 2001, Renee Rickard attended the United States Air Force Academy and Purdue University;

Whereas, During Renee Rickard's service as a Cadet in the United States Air Force Academy, she received numerous awards, including a National Defense Service Medal;

Whereas, Those who knew Renee Rickard describe her as a caring person, dedicated to serving others with excellence, dignity, and respect;

Whereas, Renee Rickard exemplified these qualities as an Indiana State Capitol Police Officer, a career she was passionate about and greatly enjoyed;

Whereas, Renee Rickard always looked for ways to improve herself as a police officer. She studied mixed martial arts, practiced her proficiency with her sidearm, and could speak Spanish, all of which helped her become a better police officer;

Whereas, Off-duty, Renee Rickard enjoyed spending time with her two dogs, riding her motorcycle, snow boarding, and hiking in Colorado; and

Whereas, State Capitol Police Officer Renee Rickard will be remembered for her dedicated service to her country and the State of Indiana: Therefore,

Be it resolved by the Senate of the General Assembly of the State of Indiana, the House of Representatives concurring:

SECTION 1. The Indiana General Assembly memorializes Officer Renee Rickard.

SECTION 2. The Secretary of the Senate is hereby directed to transmit a copy of this Resolution to Eugene and Karyl Rickard, and the Indiana State Police.

Chapter 35

Renee's Continuing Influence - Out of this world into the Beyond (Heaven)

Love never fails. (1 Corinthians 13:8)
And now these three remain: faith, hope, and love.
But the greatest of these is love. (1 Corinthians 13:13)
But [if I] do not have love, I am nothing. (1 Corinthians 13:2b)
Renee left a legacy of love to all whom
God brought across her path.
None were too beneath her to take a moment to love and
none were too great a sinner to cast judgment upon.
She knew humanity was vulnerable and there
was always a choice to love or not,
but in those decisions it seemed she learned to love and be loved.

This book shares memoirs of Renee and her life and the whispers from the Lord that allowed her to grow in character and faith and protected her. Ultimately, through the Lord's love and guidance, she was able to bloom into a young adult who made a difference in the world.

Perhaps the most noteworthy aspect of Renee was her contribution to the police in defending our capitol and country, making a safe place for us to live. Remarkably, however, through all of Renee's life, she contributed significantly to those around her.

Through the Lord's whispers, gentle nudging, perfectly timed "God incidences," the Lord kindly showed me how He answers prayers – my prayer for a little girl, one that almost perfectly met the description I wanted and then some. Yes. He, too, answered more than a bucket-full of prayers for Renee's safety, divine guidance and for fulfillment of her life purpose. Little did I know the adventure that I was about to begin with Renee.

In a nutshell, Renee's life was marked with: richness (adventure), vibrancy (aliveness), energy, compassion and caring, and a passion for justice and righteousness (doing what's right). She had a zeal to have fun while making a difference in her work and in the lives of others as well as an incredible ability to problem-solve and manage stressful situations.

We realized more fully after Renee's passing the legacy she left: the richness and aliveness of the Lord in the lives of her colleagues, friends and us.

A Peek into Heaven

Irene, Jacqueline's Grandmother

Through the grief journey the Lord gave me a peek into heaven – a richer, fresher, more alive reality of heaven and as a special gift, a sense of what Renee may be doing there. Too, I know and preciously keep in my heart so much more that I learned about my dear Renee after her passing.

Maria and I visited Irene, the 80-year-old grandmother of Jacqueline at her northern Indiana home shortly after Renee's passing. Trips with Maria to her mother Irene's home were routinely a part of more than eighteen years of our lives. These were the years that Jacqueline and Renee were growing up; so many times we shared prayer requests with Irene. She was a devout Christian and a person of prayer. She prayed for Renee's safety and well-being every morning and night for years, through Renee's teen and young-adult years. After Renee passed, she said "I talked to the Lord and Renee, with folded arms on my dresser, looking at Renee's picture of her smiling."

I asked, "What do you say?"

"Renee, you are soooo pretty. We miss you so much."

Irene continued, "Pretty soon the picture seemed to move back and forth. In my mind, I saw Renee laughing."

Now, to Renee, that would be funny coming from Irene. Renee never thought of herself as pretty although she was very attractive in real life.

I asked Irene, "So what do you see?"

"Little angels flying around her."

I turned to Maria and asked, "Little Angels?'

"Yes, you know the little cherubim who guard the Ark of the Covenant in the Old Testament."

"Irene, do you mean to tell me that Renee is in charge of the cherubim, the little angels who guard the Ark of the Covenant?" The Ark of the Covenant, described in the Old Testament, held the Ten Commandments for the Israelites. The cherubim hovered over the "Testimony Seat" on top guarding the Ark of the Covenant.

Irene's response, "You had better believe it!"

Maria, Irene, and I laughed. I can imagine the little angels flying around her, Renee laughing and helping the angels stay committed to whatever the Lord has for them to do. Indeed, Renee may be in charge of something very important to the Lord – little angels, perhaps the cherubim. Wow. I was awed at this peek into heaven and comforted. Now, this *is* a mystery but when we join Renee in heaven, we will know!

The Holy Land

I sensed Renee's presence (spirit) at special times – funerals and celebrations. I cannot imagine how the Lord does this. Very humbling. In our hearts and prayers, Renee is still with us!

In a sense, she continues to "appear" as the Lord shares messages from beyond. Brilliant, mind expanding, totally unexpected visions and messages related to Renee came several times: one right after Renee passed (described in Chapter 3), several during an Israel trip at the Wailing Wall and the Lord's tomb site in Jerusalem and one at Dr. Robert W's death. Dr. Robert W was a professional colleague, neighbor and father of a daughter, Beth W, who babysat Renee. Beth W began Renee's soccer journey. All the visions came during or after precious prayer times, as an answer to concerns shared with the Lord. Never did I seek to talk to the dead.

My dear Renee (in a vision), generally not a hugger and kisser, gave me a great big hug and kiss on the cheek at the Wailing Wall and then later at the Garden Tomb of Jesus burial site in Jerusalem, while I was praying. Stunned. Surprised. Smile.

The Lord reminded me, "Renee loves you. So do I." The Lord knew exactly what I needed, since I was oh-so-much missing Renee.

Dr. Robert W's Passing

Renee appeared again after Dr. Robert W passed. When I learned he died, I was bummed that I had not thanked him enough for all he and his colleagues did in supporting my doctoral research.

As a MD, he supervised the medical care of children with cancer and participated in clinical nutrition trials, ones that evaluated the significance of nutrition in the care of children with cancer. Dr. Robert W had a major role in making possible extraordinarily demanding research, ultimately important for the patient's quality of life, ability to tolerate treatment and fight infections. Through clinical trials, we advanced the nutritional care of children with cancer. This was not a walk in the park, to say the least.

After retirement, Dr. Robert W was diagnosed with a brain tumor and became quite ill within a year. The week before he died, he came by our home with Barbara W, his wife, to say hello. Only Gene was there to encourage him. I was devastated to learn that I missed him at our home. He died from a complication that Friday. As I was leaving for Philadelphia to present at FNCE (Food and Nutrition Conference and Exposition, Academy of Nutrition and

Dietetics), Susan, his daughter, called and let me know the funeral would be the next Tuesday.

Upon a quick return from Philadelphia, I prepared a pot of old-fashioned chicken soup for their family and friends. I felt the loss deeply. It was so unexpected.

One of the ways I work through my deep sadness is to exercise at the Fitness Center. Often during jogging on the elliptical machines, I pray and talk to the Lord. Indeed, I did that, deeply seeking the Lord and his forgiveness for not saying thank you for all the years of collaboration.

Suddenly, in my mind, I saw a light – a divine bright light – in something like a movie with Dr. Robert W, a halo around his head in the middle of several people. On one side was Renee with Sumi, their black Shepherd dog who died during Renee's elementary years, and Granny Mary. On the other side were my mother and father who passed away when I was just beginning to work at Riley Hospital for Children some forty years earlier.

Renee was telling Dr. Robert W, "Thank you for all your family did for us."

I was stunned. This was totally unexpected — out of the box. Two dear, precious people in heaven — Renee and Granny Mary, former Director of Child Life Services at Riley Hospital, thanking Dr. Robert W for me and sharing my work with my mother and father. Mary was an incredible support and advocate for all the children at Riley, especially those with cancer. She walked with me closely through the first years of our clinical research so she knew well the trials and triumphs of the journey.

At Dr. Robert W's funeral, I realized more fully the depth of his faith and love for the Lord. He not only provided the best, up-to-date medical care for the children with cancer and spent much time with parents, but also, after retirement, called upon the "sick" regularly, encouraging the living and dying with his unique experience and expertise.

Deep Reflections Related to Heaven

For those who believe in the Lord and Jesus' death and resurrection, life does not end on earth but continues in heaven. Through the forgiveness of our sins, we have eternal life. I wonder, "When life ends on earth, are those in heaven really gone, out of touch with us?"

Such are the mysteries in the Word. Some we will not understand until we are in heaven. I certainly do not know how this works but the Lord does. I just know that Renee showed up in my mind, something like a movie scene several times in the most startling and reassuring ways, always during prayer times and in response to a deep concern. I could not have made up these scenes in my mind.

Inner City Youth Ministry Fund Honoring Renee

In honor of Renee, Mark and Rorie gave a substantial contribution to the Inner City Ministry led by Rick H. According to Rick H, "The ministry house garage became the perfect teaching center with a fireplace that provided warmth. Renee's picture and obituary were placed atop the fireplace ledge. This opened the door to conversations with many in the inner city who were a part of the inner city ministry.

"Renee has a story but it is the Lord's story. Without the Lord's Hand, Renee's life and death would be meaningless. Renee engaged the Lord's story with different people in a different way. She didn't fit in the box. She chased the lion."

Rick H observed, "You can see God's glory in Renee's story and his miraculous works."

As already mentioned, the fund assisted with the remodel of Ruth's kitchen and bathroom, an awesome answer to her prayers. Even in Renee's passing, she made a difference for Ruth, a dear "grandmother" for Renee and Mark. Ruth was thrilled to tears. So were we.

Celebration of Life, One Year Later

Renee is continuing to live on in other ways.

Several stories come to mind, ones shared at the one-year celebration. Maria, my dear friend, was the moderator for this celebration. "Renee was our surrogate daughter, she got reprimanded just like our daughters. That was not her favorite part, but she took it well.

"We are here to commemorate Renee's life and what has been going on since her passing. At the visitation before the funeral, we had an open sharing. You now have an opportunity to share again, one year later. You may share whatever you like, what you learned in the past year and how this touched you."

Erin

Erin was Renee's friend for a little more than ten years, from elementary through high school.

"I shared last year that when I was younger I felt like an outcast. I was used to not being a part of the group. At recess, I used to sit under the playground equipment and cry while the other kids played. Even before I knew Renee, I saw her with other kids. Something about her stood out to me. When she and I were in class together, she brought me out of my shell. She invited me to be part of the activities. I was no longer crying under the equipment.

"Renee was interested in so many activities. She didn't just decide what she was going to do and make it happen. She made it happen for other people, too. We went to the Boundary Waters together and since we had such a wonderful time, we decided to do it again. I just would have talked about it the rest of my life and never would have done it. Since Renee was with me, we were back there again. I will never forget those two trips. Pictures of the trips, some with Renee, are now in my daughter's bathroom. I will never take them down because Renee meant so much *(crying)*.

"I think it is important to talk about Renee's compassion. She had so much compassion for others and for her animals. She and I were talking about opening a veterinary clinic together. That didn't happen. She said, 'I will only open a veterinary clinic if you agree to open it in Colorado.' I was not a fan of Colorado but she was. She made going to Colorado happen.

"Renee's life was not long but it was worth it. She used every minute of it. Her twenty-eight years were incredibly full, well-lived and well-loved.

"Last year, I also talked about the hardest thing to ever forget was her sense of humor. Whenever I think of her, I think of her laughing. She laughed so hard. She would laugh from the gut. She would topple over. I just remember all of my time with her just filled with joy. When I think of her now, I think of her looking down and laughing with us, cracking up at everything. That brings me joy too.

"At the viewing something amazing happened. I had lost touch with almost every single person except my husband. At her viewing, I saw so many people we had grown up with. It was like our class reunion. It brought me back in touch with Jacqueline and so many other people. I was updated on their lives. I realized that a lot of the people that I did not think I needed any more are important to me and will still be a part of my life.

"Even in Renee's passing, she changed my life and the lives of others. I will never forget her. I will never forget her laughing."

Jessica H

Jessica H met Renee during the summer before her eighth-grade year. At the graveside service, she shared, "When I was in a new school and a gym class without any of my friends, I was feeling very alone. When the teacher told us to run a mile around the track, I was sure I couldn't do any more than the first lap.

"After the first lap, I was sooooo exhausted.

"Renee said, "Hop on my back and we will make it around the track together." Renee and I jogged almost all the way around the track when I said, "Okay, I have to get off or I will get in trouble.

"That was when the gym teacher saw us and said, 'No, you can't do that.'

"We laughed at that because we already had done it!"

At the one-year celebration of Renee's life, Jessica H shared this:

"Renee would always give me strength to go forward. Renee's courage inspired me to apply for the Assistant Manager's position at Michael's, an arts and craft store. After Renee's funeral, I applied and actually got it!

"At first, I thought, 'I am not going to apply.'

"Then I thought of Renee who would be saying, 'Go, girl. Just go for it. You have to apply. If you don't get it, oh well.'

"So far, it's going really well. I would not have been this strong if Renee had not been part of my life, encouraging me to do things and be better."

Two years later, Jessica H was promoted to the position of Manager for another Michael's store in Carmel, Indiana. Again, she attributed her continued confidence to Renee.

Humbled, yes I am humbled to realize that every small act of kindness and act of encouragement can make a lifelong difference in another person's life and that Renee lived a life that made a difference for others and the Lord. The Lord is good, all the time.

Dr. Joan L

Dr. Joan L was Renee's professor in a class she was taking at IUPUI (Indiana University-Purdue University at Indianapolis). She shared at the one-year celebration:

"Renee had such a broad range to her personality. I would like to underscore that. I did have the honor of spending a little time with Renee at the Air Force Academy. It is amazing to know someone who can show the extremes of fitting into the strict and regimented Academy and subsequently the police force, which also is very strict, and yet have that totally opposite free way about her.

"You heard about her sense of humor. I have to underscore that. When she saw the ridiculousness of something, she could let go and laugh. And yet, when it was important for her to be vulnerable and compassionate, she was. Her compassion came from her ability to be vulnerable and open. In some ways, I think it is her vulnerability that we treasure in her. In her death, she showed us the importance of life."

Rick H

Rick H was a neighbor and a youth pastor who baptized Renee. He said, "A little over twenty-four years ago, in the spring of 1987, we dug a hole in the ground to build a home across from the Rickard's. Renee was five and Mark was seven years old.

"We have a cat named Simba, fifteen years old, an old cat now. Renee was in middle school when we got the gift (from Renee), a visual reminder of Renee. I am not a real big cat lover, but Simba has a special place because the gift came from Renee.

"Also, Mark and Rorie, unbeknownst to Gene and Karyl, this fall sent a gift in honor of Renee for the inner-city ministry to help with some local needs.

"Ruth, a 'grandmother' to Mark and Renee over the years, needed some new windows. So, we put them in. Then, while doing that we saw that she also needed a kitchen and some fix-up in the bathroom. That was a part of what the Lord did this year in our ministry. We went into Miss Ruth's house and put in a new kitchen. We also did some bathroom fix-up and fixed up the yard. More importantly, through a divine intersection of love, we had over a dozen young men who heard Miss Ruth's story and also Renee's story.

"The stories are about loving enough to give and to keep giving. Miss Ruth's a giver, too. Every time our guys would come to her home, she would say, 'In the refrigerator is a Coke and on this table are some candy bars. Now don't eat Rick H's caramels – they are for him!'

"Now, we take care of her yard.

"When I was in Iowa, a young man called and asked, 'Does Miss Ruth's yard need mowing? It's been a month since we have seen her.'

"No, we just got it the other day."

"Aw. I was just checkin.'

"That's how the seeds are planted, the giving from one to another. You can't out-give God. God so loved us, he gave."

Jack G

"We don't live too far from the grave site – 1.72 miles. The reason I know is that Jacqueline has run to the gravesite a number of times. One time, she and I ran to the gravesite. This goes back to Renee and her sense of humor. We would always say, "I can hear Renee now saying, 'You weenies. Get back out there and do another three miles. That's not far enough.'

"Again, Erin shared about the gusto of Renee's laugh. I shared at the visitation about my misfortune of getting into the wrong car. Renee was literally falling out of my car laughing about it. A number of times over the past year, Jacqueline and I have said, 'Wouldn't Renee have enjoyed that.'

"It's been so nice that 'In her death, she's bringing joy to people.'"

Veronica

As Maria started to read an email sent (February 2011) from Veronica, her daughter, tears began rolling down Maria's cheeks. She shared, "Renee's love keeps on touching. The reason I am so touched is because we know how Jacqueline felt about Renee. But what's really neat was that Veronica felt the same way, too.

"Of course, for Veronica it was more for survival because when Jacqueline and Veronica were not getting along, Renee was always the person coming to Veronica's defense, 'Come on, give her a break.' Veronica and Jacqueline have tried to keep a reminder to the Rickards that even though Renee's not here, her friends are."

Veronica shared, "I never got a chance to tell you, but shortly after her funeral I ran a marathon in California. My right knee started to give out half-way through. I finished, of course, but I was in a lot of pain and didn't make my goal time.

"For most of the race, I literally pictured Renee and Jacqueline cheering me on. I figured they'd be on their bikes chatting and every time I would look over Renee would punch (gently) Jacqueline's shoulder to get her attention to look at me and say something like 'Whoa! GO V!' I can imagine just how she'd say it and then they'd ride along with me the entire race.

"I think that if I had not pictured that, I would not have made it across the finish line. Also, Jacqueline had given me some of Renee's energy gels and I used them during the marathon. I love incorporating part of her life into mine in ways like this.

"I think about Renee every day. I've always looked up to Renee and she's always been my other sister (trust me, only family can see the sides of me that she saw!). I talk about her with my friends and they are getting to know about her as if they really knew her."

Jacqueline

"So I know most of you listened to me for a long time at the funeral. I will let you know what's happening in the year since the funeral. All my good friends, everyone knows about Renee. It's just like they all know about Veronica, my sister.

"'Oh, how is she doing?'

"My friends know that we are just coming upon a year since Renee's passing. So, they asked, 'How are you doing?'

"I have stopped and thought about 'How am I doing? My mojo is typically, 'Let's not think about it. Let's just think about the positive things. I wouldn't want to think about how I feel; then, I would cry and Renee would just make fun of me. I wouldn't want that!

"So, just like Veronica, not a day goes by that I don't think about Renee, that I don't miss Renee. Three hundred sixty-four days have gone by and there are still times when I can't remember she is gone. I have to call Renee and tell her about this. Dang, I can't do that. She probably already knows, so that's a good thing.

"I can't wait to plan this event and who will come – of course Renee will come. Well, perhaps not physically. It has given me great comfort to know that in some ways Renee is with me and with all of us more now than she was able to be in person. It's like everyone is talking about.

"It's Renee's sense of humor that helps me get through the times I want to cry; it's the thought that she would not only laugh at me, but also say, 'Jacqueline, come on, it's been a whole year, let's get on with it.'

"The fact is Renee is up there in heaven. I imagine her – when I have rough times – interceding with God. I feel like I have another ally up there talking to God. Just as Gene said, with the insistence of making things happen, she would be up there saying, 'Come on, come on, God.'

"I miss her incredibly every day. I am comforted that in some ways, she is never gone."

Renee is continuing to live on in other ways through her friends, colleagues and our family.

Cousin and Friends Weddings

Renee was acknowledged at the beginning of three different weddings. Julia, her cousin, had a destination wedding on Vancouver Island, British Columbia. During the time for acknowledging the bride, Richie, Julia's brother, started with, "It is with regret that not everyone can be here...."

Tears started rolling down both cheeks. I couldn't stop them. Richie's remarks were an answer to a prayer: "Lord, please help me know Renee in spirit is here at the wedding with one of her favorite cousins, Julia."

I was so embarrassed, sitting next to the bride's aunt from Germany, that I left the ballroom for the bathroom. Franziska, the bride's sister, was sobbing, too. I asked her, "Was Richie referring to Renee?"

"Yes," she said and gave me a big hug. We both sobbed together.

Veronica, the sister of Jacqueline, also had a destination wedding in Mexico on the fourth of July. Veronica, four years younger than Jacqueline, adored Renee. In many ways, they were so similar. They both laughed a lot, were very creative, very social, and loved adventure. Jack G, her father, acknowledged Renee in his prayer at the beginning of Veronica's wedding.

As mentioned earlier, Matt W and Ashley W, a fellow police officer and friend, also took a moment to remember Renee at the beginning of their wedding.

It is just humbling to learn that her close friends and cousin continued to remember Renee.

Babies Named after Renee

Several years after Renee's passing, Mark and Rorie had a dear little girl, our first grandchild, "Rachel Renee Rickard." They asked Jacqueline to be her godmother. Not surprisingly, Jacqueline said, "I am delighted to be her 'godmother!'" Then, as she was leaving our home, tears began to roll down her cheeks.

Renee's cousin, Jenica, a high-school science teacher in Oklahoma, also had a sweet little girl, "Lauren Renee Long." Jenica was one of the pallbearers who carried Renee's casket. So was Jacqueline. This would have pleased Renee!

Jenica, several years younger than Renee, lived in Indianapolis three years during her grade-school years so we were able to share special times with my brother and his family. In a tribute to Renee, Jenica said, "Of all the things I remember, what I remember the most was that Renee always made sure I was a part of everything when I came to visit. I never felt left out. Thanks! Love you Renee!"

Renee Named as Godmother

Anjie G was a fellow police officer with Renee, one who was planning to be a roommate with Renee before she married another police officer. She posted on the Memorial Tribute site for Renee:

"I finally found the courage to write a note here. I have been delaying because it is so final and it means I have to finally accept that I will receive no more texts or phone calls from Renee and see her no more. I miss her dearly. She has done so much for Joe G, the kids and me. I wouldn't be where I am now if it wasn't for her. Renee will always be a part of our family and missed forever. All the good times and memories we had together will never be forgotten."

"The Officers G – Fellow Law Enforcement and friends."

A year later, Anjie G posted, "Hey, lady! I was not able to make it yesterday to your memorial service due to training. But I wanted to stop by and say it's been a long year without you! You are named as baby Kendyl's godmother and she is getting big. I wish you could see her. Anyway, just wanted to say you are still missed more than ever and will always be!"

Near Kendyl's one-year birthday, Anjie G posted, "Hey, woman! We are missing you more than ever. Kendyl just turned one and is walking everywhere! We are taking her to come see you soon! Miss you lots!!!"

Two years from Renee's passing, Anjie G posted, "Well, it's officially been two years now and it doesn't get any easier! We still think of you and miss you all the time! Your God daughter is getting bigger and is a pain. She makes me think of you all the time because she is a major tomboy and loves being outside and getting dirty. She is as adventurous as you were. We miss you lots and always will!!!"

Renee's Prison Trip with Deb

Deb, my dear friend and colleague, relocated to Florida and became involved in prison ministry through her local church. She was inspired by Renee's love and acceptance of all people. Renee's ability to seek justice while having empathy and compassion opened Deb's awareness to the power of helping people through difficult circumstances. During a prison service, Deb became aware that the prisoners had no process for acknowledging and grieving loved ones who passed away.

Deb asked the Chaplain and Warden in charge of the prison, "Can we have a Memorial Service for the men in prison?" This was an 'out of the box' request, one never done before in Florida prisons. The Chaplain agreed to hold the service.

For the men who attended, the chaplain requested, "Please bring pictures of your loved ones who passed away."

He put the pictures into a power point presentation that ran continuously throughout the service. Some of the pictures were of loved ones in a casket because that's what the inmate had. Others had pictures of loved ones who were alive at different ages. The pictures were very personal.

Sixty-three men attended, some with as many as three life sentences.

Deb began the Memorial Service by honoring Renee. Deb shared, "I told the men about Renee, her life, untimely death, and my very deep level of grief with the loss of Renee." Renee, in spirit, went with Deb into a Florida prison.

Deb felt the presence of the Lord and Renee with her during this transformational time for the prisoners. These prisoners, unable to attend funerals of close family, needed the grace and comfort that came from being able to share about their losses, grief, and pain. This was the beginning of healing and their walk through the grief journey.

Deb further shared with the inmates, "You have permission to cry as a symbol of your friendship and love for your loved ones who passed away. Jesus cried at the gravesite of Lazarus. Through tears, he shared his deep love for his friend Lazarus."

She continued, "Each inmate, in turn, stood up and expressed love or appreciation for his loved one. As they talked about their loved ones, some cried pretty hard. They did not realize that they would break down and cry. For most, this was the first time they had permission to express the pain from the loss. Usually, in prisons, no emotions are expressed. So, it was surprising to the other inmates that so many had deep sorrow about their loved ones. They all thought they were pretty tough."

Jenny M

Renee is continuing to live on in other ways.

One of Renee's friends in junior high, Jenny M, came to the funeral and afterward wrote this letter.

"Dear Karyl,

"Hello! I am not sure if you will remember me or not but this is Jenny M, one of Renee's friends from the fifth grade through high school. I confess that I delayed writing this email, for I have no wish for it to be painful in any way. Instead, the goal is to share how much of a gift Renee has been and continues to be in my life.

"When Jacqueline called with the news of Renee's passing, I was shocked first for the obvious reason and second to learn that Renee had been living in Indy for some time."

"I, too, have been in Indy working for the University. In fact, I have seen you from a distance a few times, walking near campus and at the Indy Monday night BSF (Bible Study Fellowship) class.

"The few times I saw you, I told myself I should run up to say, 'Hello,' see how you were and see how Renee was. Now I really wish that I had! Please forgive me for not doing so.

"What I remember most about Renee is her smile, her laugh, and her fun-filled attitude. Also, as a friend, she was an incredible support. I remember sleepovers and band concerts and class projects we did together.

"Many of my best school-time memories have Renee in them! The funeral service was one of the most beautiful services I have attended. I have to tell you, something that happened at that service kicked off a major change in my own life.

"When we walked through the doors of the sanctuary, we were handed a memorial button with Renee's picture and it really struck a chord in me. Renee was one who went after life. She had fun. It's beyond tragedy that she was taken from us so soon, but for the time she was here, she really lived. At that moment, I realized that for quite some time I had been letting life live me instead of me living my life. And being handed that button sent the truth – time has no guarantee – echoing around in my head.

"From that moment forward, that button and Renee's spirit and memory have been with me, encouraging me to be more proactive. Renee is still the supportive friend.

"Consequently, I summoned up the guts to apply for a promotion that I never would have considered before. I got the promotion and moved my house and job to the Bloomington campus. Basically, my entire life has turned upside down and instead of caving in to my fears (like I would have done before), I have stepped forward, trusting in God and thanking Him for friends like Renee who leave a lasting impact even when they are no longer with us.

"I would like to thank you and Gene, as well, for bringing up such a wonderful lady and allowing me to share in her growing-up years. What a joy she was and is!

"Here's wishing you most well. Take care and God bless.

"Jen"

Renee's Life – Final Reflections

I have seen answered prayers (the Lord's influences), unfolding miracles, deep love and joy in Renee's life through the interviews and sharing of her colleagues, teachers, family, and friends. In almost every chapter, especially those related to her school years and young adult life, I was truly blessed, as I heard old stories and new stories.

Renee's life reminds me in some ways of George Baily (actor Jimmy Stewart) in the movie, *It's a Wonderful Life*. George had no idea the difference he made in the lives of others. Indeed, Renee could never have imagined the impact or influence she had on persons in her life. She was sooooo humble. She never thought she made a difference.

In many ways, Renee was an ordinary person ... no fame, wealth, power, nor authority of position. But, her influence was extraordinary.

Tammy Jo Schultz in her book, *Nerves of Steel: How I Followed My Dreams, Earned My Wings, and Faced My Greatest*

Challenge (1919) wrote, "Heroes do not require a title. They don't need to land a crippled plane (as Tammy did). A hero is someone who takes the time to see and makes the effort to act on behalf of someone else. In a word, they care."

I am quite sure that Renee would *NEVER* consider herself a hero or extraordinary; rather she would humbly walk through her day (with the Lord), seeing the humor and joy in the circumstances and caring for those with whom she worked and loved – her colleagues, family, friends, and pups.

Chapter 36

The Big Why Question

The Lord is close to the brokenhearted;
He rescues those whose spirits are crushed.
(Psalms 34:18, NLT)
God whispers even in the season of death.

T he "Why" question consumed us immediately after the funeral. Why did Renee die when she seemed so healthy and so fit? My sister who is a physician and I with medical experience as a clinical dietitian were deeply concerned about what happened. Although the MD in the Emergency Room said, "Most apparently healthy young adults similar in age to Renee die from an embolism," this was not the case for Renee.

Renee had a viral infection about a month and half earlier. At the time, Renee said, "This viral infection is the same that the other police officers had. There is nothing I can do except ride it out."

Shortly after the viral infection, she successfully completed a sprint triathlon – swam 500 meters in the Indy canal, bicycled thirteen miles and ran five kilometers (3.1 miles). At the end of the marathon, she said, "I am really, really tired. I don't understand why."

Also, during that time, Renee did the RAIN – Ride Across Indiana – with her friend, Jacqueline. She stopped in Plainfield half way across Indiana and said at least five times, "Jacqueline, we are going to complete this ride next year." Actually, Renee did quite well, considering she only prepared for the bicycle ride two weeks before the RAIN.

We were unable to get the Indiana state pathologist's reports for several weeks. We finally reached the physician who completed an autopsy, routine for deaths of young adults. She reported, "Renee died of pneumonia, not an embolism."

We asked, "How could Renee die so suddenly from pneumonia without obvious symptoms, be so active, and appear to be so healthy?"

Her response, "There is no doubt about the cause. As you know, the screens for drugs were negative. We did not do other laboratory tests, such as for H1N1 or other virulent infections."

This was hard to believe. In conversations with several other physicians, including an Emergency Room physician, we learned it is not uncommon for someone with a newly diagnosed virulent form of pneumonia to rapidly progress to death, even within eight to ten hours. Possibly, the earlier viral illness with symptoms of a cough, runny nose, fatigue, and fever along with her strenuous exercise weakened her immune system.

We will never know. Renee is in God's hands now. In retrospect, both my sister and I wondered why we missed this and if there was something else we should have done. Renee was a strong, courageous young lady, not likely to complain about pain or other physical problems. Even when she was young, she rarely was ill. One time when our son, Mark, had severe strep throat and all the symptoms, Renee had none. We insisted that she have a strep test. Sure enough, she was positive for a strep infection.

We will never know why we did not have a warning. We just have to trust God that we did all we knew to do and that the Lord's timing for her to leave this earth was in His Hands.

As I was waiting in an ER side room to see Renee, I prayed fervently for Renee and searched the gospels for all the times when Jesus healed. The prayer of *Thy Healing Angels carried from God by Archangel Michael*, shared by Lorna Byrne (http://lornaby-rne.com/prayer-of-thy-healing-angels/) was in the middle of my Bible. The Holy Spirit prompted me to pray this prayer for Renee and turn her over to the Lord, reminding me that He knows what's best for her. The Lord heals in many ways, including in heaven.

Prayer of Thy Healing Angels

Pour out, Thy Healing Angels,
Thy Heavenly Host upon Renee,
And upon those that I love,
Let her feel the beam of Thy
Healing Angels upon her,
The light of Your Healing Hands.
I will let Thy Healing begin
Whatever way God grants it,
Amen

Index of Many Who
Shared Our Lives

Renee

Renee: a vibrant young lady who showed us what is really important – loving others and living a courageous, adventurous life with a sense of humor. Simply, we enjoy life more!

Family

Barbara F R: aunt, mother of Franziska, Julia and Richie (cousins), Richard's wife

Ben, Pastor Ben: uncle, a pastor who participated in Renee's funeral and gravesite service, Karyl's brother, Jenica's father

Chris: uncle, Mary Bess's husband (deceased), shared many holidays

Franziska: cousin, shared many adventures on Grampa Rickard's farm, Richard's daughter

Gene: beloved father

Jay B R: older cousin loved by the younger cousins, Roger's son

Jenica: cousin, very close during elementary years, pallbearer, Ben's daughter

Julia: cousin who had many adventures on the farm, Richard's daughter

Karyl: beloved mother

Mark: brother, two years older than Renee

Mary Bess: aunt who lived in Indy, frequent participant in family gatherings, Karyl's sister

Peter: nephew, son of Mark and Rorie

Rachel Renee: niece, Renee's namesake, daughter of Mark and Rorie

Richard: uncle, father of Franziska, Julia and Richie (cousins), Gene's younger brother

Richie: younger cousin, son of Richard

Roger: uncle, father of Jay B R, Gene's older brother

Rorie: sister-in-law, Mark's wife

Ruth: beloved grandmother figure for Mark and Renee throughout their lives, babysitter

Family Friends and Bible Study Members

Ann: close family friend, prayer warrior, came to the emergency room and assisted during the week of the funeral, wife of Rog

Anne SF: parent's friend who came to the emergency room and coordinated food for the week of the funeral

Barb B: Karyl's friend and prayer warrior, one of the first to come to the Emergency Room

Duane: came to Emergency Room, husband of Eileen

Eileen: good friend, came to Emergency Room, wife of Duane

Glenda S: wife of Jim S, good family friend who spends summers in the Colorado Rockies

Irene: close friend, prayer warrior, Maria's mother and Jacqueline's grandmother

Jack G: father of Jacqueline and Veronica, husband of Maria

Jane: Karyl's dear friend from Bible Study Fellowship

James S: son of Jim S and Glenda S, pallbearer for funeral

Jim S: Gene's long-term friend who spends summers in Colorado Rockies near us, pallbearer for funeral

Louise: a retired nutrition faculty member at the University of Delaware, Karyl's housemate during graduate school years at the University of Wisconsin, Madison

Maria: dear family friend, loved Renee as a daughter, prayer warrior; assisted with funeral planning and moderator for funeral visitation and one year celebration, Jack's wife

Roger (Rog): close family friend, Ann's husband

Friends of Renee: K through 12

Andy: friend and classmate, second grade through high school

Ashley J: Boundary Waters Canoe Area wilderness trip in Minnesota

Erin: childhood friend, Boundary Waters Canoe Area wilderness trip in Minnesota (nickname "Moonshine"), spoke at visitation and one year celebration

Jacqueline: classmate, close lifelong friend and fellow adventurer, gave the eulogy at the funeral, daughter of Maria and Jack

Jeff: friend and classmate, second grade through high school

Jenny M: good friend and classmate who shared a poignant letter after Renee went to heaven

Joy: close friend and classmate, fellow musician in symphony, sojourner on Boundary Waters Canoe Area Wilderness trip in Minnesota

Jessie B: Boundary Waters Canoe Area Wilderness trip in Minnesota (nickname, "Nippy")

Jessica H: good friend inspired by Renee

Kelly: close friend, participated in Youth Ministry and mission trips, played soccer

Laura: classmate in third grade, comforted by Renee when she lost her canine friend

Mandy: close friend, participated in Youth Ministry and mission trips, played soccer

Marlene: good friend and classmate

Mary F: Boundary Waters Canoe Area Wilderness trip in Minnesota

Melissa: good friend and classmate

Michael: elementary school classmate

Veronica: Jacqueline's younger sister and good friend, daughter of Maria and Jack

Yves: athlete and close friend through high school and several years beyond

Friends of Renee: Young Adults

Angie S: close friend and competition partner in Kingdom Mixed Martial Arts

Brooke: close friend who Renee met while at Purdue University

Bryan: good friend, fellow cadet, and classmate at the Air Force Academy

Cade: knew in preschool and reconnected as a young adult, last person to text Renee

Karyl's Coworkers and Friends

Granny Mary: former Director of Child Life Services at Riley Hospital for Children, master teacher and colleague who worked with Karyl in developing *Healthy Eating, Active Play* programs for young children, now in heaven playing with Renee

Deb: dear friend and colleague who was with Karyl when Renee collapsed; prayer warrior, came to the emergency room, liaison for Bible study friends and colleagues

Judith (Judy) Ernst: friend and colleague who was a significant part of Renee's first five years, vocal soloist for funeral

Mixed Martial Arts (MMA)

Dion: top mixed martial arts coach from Chicago, worked with the Kingdom MMA competition team

Jack L: one of the best coaches in mixed martial arts from Chicago, worked with Kingdom MMA competition team

Steve: Director of the Kingdom MMA Academy, made available coaching for the competition team by Dion, owner of five studios in Chicago

Neighborhood friends

Beth W: Dr. Robert and Barbara W's daughter, babysitter who started Renee's soccer career!

Cathy H: mother of Scott and Gabe, who played with Mark and Renee; often assisted with after-school care

Barbara W: wife of Dr. Robert W, long-time neighbor, shared a garden plot with our family, willing cat sitter and generous host during the funeral

Dr. Robert W: research colleague with Karyl; pediatrician who supervised cancer care at Riley Hospital for Children in the Indiana University Medical Center, Indianapolis

Gabe: after-school playmate, son of Rick H and Cathy H

Rick H: former youth pastor for Trader's Point Christian Church who baptized Renee; father of Scott and Gabe

Sonya: owner of Duber, a dog who adored and protected Renee

Scott: after-school playmate, son of Rick H and Cathy H

Police Officers and Indiana Law Enforcement Academy Friends

Aaron: former Indiana State Capitol Police Officer, nominated Renee for Indiana State Senate Resolution memorial honoring Renee

Anjie G: police representative who joined us for the reading of the Indiana State Senate Resolution memorial, wrote several yearly tributes to Renee after the funeral

Ashley W: friend and wife of Matt W, police officer on the same night shift as Renee

Chaplain C, Chaplain Coffey: capitol police chaplain who knew Renee, participated in funeral service

Jarett: Indiana State Capitol Police Officer and loyal friend

Joe G: police officer and Anjie G's husband

Matt W: Indiana State Capitol Police Officer and friend on same night shift as Renee, Ashley W's husband

Sergeant B: sergeant for the Indiana State Capitol police and shift supervisor

Sergeant C: one of Renee's shift supervisors, a veteran police officer for more than thirty years

Teachers

Mr. Cody S: middle school social studies teacher, sponsor for Washington DC trip

Mr. David P: band teacher for middle school and junior high jazz band

Mrs. Donna C: English and debate teacher for high school extended learning program

Dr. Dorothy P: Karyl's retired professor at the University of Wisconsin, Madison who helped Mark find housing

Mr. Ed S: Renee's symphony teacher, coordinator of Boundary Waters Canoe Area wilderness trips

Dr. Joan L: dear family friend and fellow faculty with Karyl; Renee's professor at Indiana University Purdue University

Mr. John M: Renee's band teacher in high school, musical inspiration for Renee

Ms. Julie G: second grade extended learning teacher

Mrs. Karen A: third grade extended learning teacher

Mrs. Kris M: fourth grade extended learning teacher at College Park Elementary School

Mrs. Linda C: middle school Spanish teacher, Reverend Jim C's wife

Mrs. Mary Beth D: high school English teacher for extended learning program

Mrs. Melanie R: middle school math teacher and swimming coach, sponsor for Washington DC trip

Mrs. Connie R: teacher of the teachers for the preschool cooperative program, Mark's preschool teacher

Rick R: high school women's soccer coach

Ron: spring indoor soccer coach for the "Fish" team, high-school years

Trader's Point Christian Church (1986 to 2001)

Brenda: youth leader and mentor for a small group of girls and for Mission trips

Don: youth pastor responsible for the youth ministries

Reverend Jim C, Reverend Jim Craig: pastor at Traders Point Christian Church and longtime family friend; gave the homily and accompanied vocal soloist at the funeral

Marty: youth leader and mission trip leader

Rick H: neighbor and youth pastor for the youth ministries

Renee's Animals

Cats: Million Dollar Princess rescued from horse barn; her kittens (Simba, Mufasa, Scar) named after lions in the Lion King movie

Comet I and Comet II: Renee's guinea pigs during elementary years

Duber: neighbor dog who adopted five-year-old Renee, even played soccer with her

Lily: Renee's Chihuahua, mourned Renee's passing, friendly sweetheart

Stokley: Renee's Chihuahua, now Gene's best friend

Other Friends or Participants in Funeral

Jay R: Funeral Director for the Flanner Buchanan Funeral Home, Indianapolis

Joe Z: Mark's policy debate partner

Luke: Mark's friend

Maggie: Granny Mary's daughter-in-law

Mrs. Barb M: Andy's mother who organized and orchestrated the second-grade play "Cinderella," in which Renee was a stepsister

A Special Word of Thanks

To the Lord

First and foremost, to the Lord for his faithfulness, boundless love, grace, and mercy. It is Your whispers from heaven that provided the light for Renee's amazing life and ours through the dark valley following Renee's passing. You carried me through the writing of this book. I now know You answered years of prayers in ways far beyond my imagination. You showed me the value of seeking You with patience and persistence and ultimately the willingness to surrender to You and Your will.

To the Lord for His presence in trials and tribulations. The biggest one was losing our beloved daughter unexpectedly, suddenly. You were there. Not only during the years after but certainly beforehand. You showed us that You were with Renee and with us all along. Through more than fifty interviews, letters, and tributes, You showed us how you answered what seemed like millions of prayers.

Thank you for showing us Your Hand consistently through many, many whispers from heaven, ones that provided clear direction and divine guidance through Renee's life and afterwards when she is in heaven. This has been an awesome and humbling journey. Simply, thank You Lord. Amazing Love!

To Renee

To Renee for coming into this world, a vibrant young lady who showed us what is really important – loving others and living a courageous and adventurous life with a sense of humor. You brought richness to our lives and expanded our love to include even cats and dogs! Now, we enjoy the freshness of new adventures. Simply, we enjoy life more!

To Gene

To my husband, Gene, for being a partner in prayer, seeking the Lord's will and desiring to honor Him in our daily lives. Thank you for your encouragement behind the scenes, for your impeccable formatting and all the other things that you did to support me while writing the book.

To Renee's friends

To Renee's closest friend from the second-grade on, Jacqueline, faithful to the end with so many precious, shared experiences with Renee. They shared nearly every activity in school and out. You knew Renee so well. I value your touching eulogy at the funeral. Thank you.

To all of Renee's friends, who provided extraordinarily wonderful friendships. Thank you for being with Renee in life, in her passing, and in sharing our grief journey. You so richly blessed our lives.

To Maria

To my dear Maria, my prayer partner and mother of Renee's close, lifelong friend Jacqueline. You loved Renee as your own daughter. Maria, with the Lord's presence, you graciously walked us through the funeral arrangements, moderated the memory-sharing at the visitation and the yearly celebrations of life for Renee. Thank you.

To Traders Point Christian Church Youth Leaders

To the Traders Point Christian Church youth ministries, especially youth leaders Rick H, Don, Brenda, and Marty, for their transformational youth ministry. Renee was privileged to participate in the mission trips to Mexico, Brooklyn, NY, and Florida. Thank you for your inspiration and wisdom in dealing with our young people.

To Police officers and colleagues

To the police officers and colleagues in the Indiana State Capitol Police, the Indiana Law Enforcement Academy and the Indiana Police Honor Guard who brought honor and respect to Renee as a police officer in both her life and afterward. Thank you for including her in your police family and sharing your memories.

To Steve Guinn and Mixed Martial Arts friends, especially Angie

To Steve Guinn, the director of the Kingdom Mixed Martial Arts (MMA) and all those who were a part of the MMA family, especially Angie, who trained with Renee. Steve, a gifted MMA teacher, taught Renee new skills for self-defense and the defense of others; ones useful in her police work. Thank you Steve, for generously arranging the times that Renee and the competition team worked with Dion Riccardo and Jack Lombardi, some of the best in the MMA field.

To Sisters and brothers in Christ

To my dear sisters in the Lord and prayer warriors, Deb, Maria, Ann, Jane, Barb B, Eileen, and Louise who are the "salt of the earth." They each have transformational lives, filled with the Lord and His whispers. Thank you for your generous spirit, powerful prayers and love. Thank you, especially, Deb, Ann, Maria, and Louise, for your support and assistance in editing this book.

To other dear sisters and brothers in Christ, ones in our Bible Studies and Bible Study Fellowship, who were prayer warriors during Renee's life, through the grief journey and now the sharing of the Lord's precious Hand in Renee's life. It is your prayers that moved mountains over many years and most recently undergirded the writing of Renee's and the Lord's book.

To Tom Bird and his staff

To Tom Bird and all his staff for their continuous efforts to bring forth books that transform lives, both the authors' and others in the world, using a writing method with the "divine author within" that I call the Holy Spirit. It was Tom's course "Write Your Book in a Weekend" that began this journey of writing with the Lord's spirit.

To Denise Cassino

To Denise Cassino, my book coach, who has a brilliant ability to successfully bring books to final publication with ease and joy. Her assistance in bringing Renee's book to market exceeded my expectations.

About the Author

Karyl Rickard balanced her professional career with family by working part-time during the early years of her children, Mark and Renee. Throughout her career, she viewed her dual roles of motherhood and career as the Lord's missions.

During her life-long career as a leader in pediatric nutrition, she was a trailblazer who helped bridge clinical practice and academic scholarship to advance the field of pediatric nutrition. Her leadership advanced the nutritional care of critically ill children at Riley Hospital for Children and nationally.

Renee died suddenly at age 28. Initially, participation in the Grief Share* program assisted Karyl and Gene in dealing with the overwhelming loss of their daughter. As Karyl became more aware of the many ways that God cared for Renee in her short life, she wanted to share Renee's extraordinary story in this book, *Whispers from Heaven...Then she was gone.* The journey was not only difficult but also encouraging as she experienced more fully the grace and goodness of God.

Now, Karyl and her husband, Gene, a chemist, enjoy active time at their cabin in the Rockies with family and friends. Both have a facilitating leadership role in small group Bible Studies and continue active involvement in church activities.

Karyl Rickard, PhD, RDN, FADA, FAND, Professor Emerita of Nutrition and Dietetics, Indiana University School of Health and Human Sciences, Indianapolis

*Grief Share is a national, thirteen-week program sponsored by local churches for those who have lost a loved one. Karyl continues to volunteer as a Grief Share facilitator for this program. https://www.griefshare.org/

CPSIA information can be obtained
at www.ICGtesting.com
Printed in the USA
LVHW081007030221
678122LV00033BC/721